Bog Bodies Uncovered

Miranda Aldhouse-Green

Bog Bodies Uncovered

Solving Europe's Ancient Mystery

foreword by
Val McDermid

To Merleen, Paul and Grace

Frontispiece: The preserved body of a man, strangled with a rope, still visible around his neck, and placed in a bog at Borremose, Denmark, in the 8th century BC.

First published in 2015 in hardcover in the United States of America by Thames & Hudson Inc., 500 Fifth Avenue, New York, New York 10110

thamesandhudsonusa.com

Library of Congress Catalog Card Number 2015932410

ISBN 978-0-500-05182-5

Printed and bound in India by Replika Press Pvt. Ltd.

CONTENTS

Val McDermid

We all carry our history under our skin. Where we've been, what we've done, how we lived. But for thousands of years that history, which our ancestors took to the grave, remained secret. Now, thanks to the giant leaps science has made in recent years, we can read those messages from the past. And finally, we can begin to peel back the layers and reveal the answers to mysteries that have confounded us for generations.

Among the most puzzling of those mysteries was that of the ancient bog bodies of Northern Europe. Buried in peat marshes and bogs, the unique environment meant their remains were preserved to a remarkable extent. That was exciting enough in itself for archaeologists and anthropologists. But what gradually became clear was that many of the bodies discovered – generally by chance, by farmers and peat cutters – had met violent deaths at the hands of others.

What crime writer wouldn't be fascinated by this phenomenon?

My own interest in the subject was piqued by an idea I had for a book that had its roots in the relatively recent past, a mere couple of hundred years ago. *The Grave Tattoo* was inspired by one fact and one rumour. The fact: the poet William Wordsworth and the *Bounty* mutineer Fletcher Christian went to school together in the Lake District. The rumour: Fletcher Christian didn't die on Pitcairn Island in the South Seas – he returned to England, where he was sheltered from the forces of law and order by his friends and family. I began to build a present-day thriller round these historic events, but I needed something dramatic to kick-start the story.

I remembered seeing the recovered bog body known as Lindow Man on display in Manchester Museum in the late 1980s. I'd been astonished at the degree of preservation it displayed, and the amount of information scientists had been able to garner from it. I wondered if a body that had only been in a bog for two hundred years could reveal even more.

I soon discovered how forensic techniques had evolved – and are still evolving – to provide data on everything from the diet these people consumed to the places where they lived and travelled while they were alive. Analysis of teeth and bones gives us an astonishingly detailed timeline of their movements. Thanks to mass spectrometry, now we can even tell where their mothers were living when they were pregnant. Facial reconstruction experts reveal what these people looked like in life. And we can uncover the violence with which they met their deaths. All perfect grist to the mill for my fiction. Because I get to make up the bits between the science, the pieces of the puzzle we can't quite grasp.

What we can't know are the underlying reasons behind the facts. But by learning all we can, it's possible to come up with coherent theories that make sense of what we see. And that's where Miranda Aldhouse-Green has come to our aid. In this fascinating exploration of the phenomenon of bog bodies, she whets our appetite with the big picture of where, when and how these bodies began to turn up.

Then she examines the detail of a selection of the bodies, revealing how they gave up their secrets to us over the years and exposing the violence and apparent ritual that mark so many of their deaths.

Finally she delves under the shroud of mystery that surrounds them, exploring theories and suggesting histories for their lives that make sense of their deaths.

Human beings are curious by nature. We like answers. That's one of the reasons I believe crime fiction is so popular. We can never know for certain how these bodies ended up with this very particular form of burial. The reasons are lost in a past that left no written records. All we can do is interrogate what is left. And that is what this book does so satisfyingly.

Unveiling the Dead:
Introducing the Bog Bodies
of Ancient Europe

Prince or priest, reared for this moment
your life a preparation for this death,
an honour to appease the thirsty Gods –
for Tarainis, the shattering head-blows,
for Esus, the garrotte and slit throat,
for Teutates, the face-down drowning.

GLADYS MARY COLES, *LINDOW MAN*[1]

In 1969 Professor P.V. Glob, of the Museum of Prehistory at Århus in northern Denmark, published his now famous and seminal book *The Bog People.*[2] In it he drew people's attention to a dramatic archaeological phenomenon, the preservation of whole bodies from the remote past. Ancient human remains almost always survive only as skeletons. Mummified bodies from the arid deserts of Egypt, and frozen bodies, such as occur in the ice of Inuit lands of the far north, are exceptions. What Professor Glob did in his book was to make accessible an incredible archive of ancient human bodies from Europe. They were preserved because of the peculiar properties of the raised bogs in which they had been deposited after death.

Most of the ancient bog bodies belong to the Iron Age and Roman periods, between the 8th century BC and AD 400, although some Neolithic

The peat bog at Haraldskaer in central Jutland, where the
body of a middle-aged woman was pinned down with hurdles,
after she was hanged, in the early 5th century BC.

bog bodies have also been discovered (see Chapter 2). They occur, naturally
enough, in regions with large areas of raised bogland: Ireland, mainland
Britain, the Netherlands, Denmark and northern Germany. During this
time and in these regions, most dead people were disposed of by burning
or by inhumation in dry graves. But occasionally, for some reason, communities chose instead to place their dead in marshes, often in voids left
by the extraction of peat or iron ore. What is more, there is forensic evidence that these bog people met untimely, often violent deaths involving a
third party. In other words, they were done to death by others: murdered,
executed or even ritually killed.

Bogs were and are special places, miasmic and fearsome. They hover
in the 'tween space between land and water: they are both and they are
neither. They cannot be cultivated like normal land and they support vegetation peculiar to themselves. They may look innocent but can trap the
unwary into a horrific and lingering death by slow, inevitable immersion.
Such is the climax of Sir Arthur Conan Doyle's Sherlock Holmes tale set
on Dartmoor in southwest England, *The Hound of the Baskervilles*, where
the murdering villain meets his end in the grip of the Great Grimpen Mire.
Bogs form from shallow lakes and ponds where the dying plants surrounding them fall into the water. Because of a lack of oxygen in these
lakes, the vegetation does not fully decay but stays in a half-decomposed

The beautifully mummified body of 'Queen Gunhild', the Iron Age
woman found staked to the bed of a peat bog at Haraldskaer in 1835.

state. The layers of plants build up over time, the lakes become bogs and
peat is formed. If other organic matter, whether it is food, wood, animals
or human bodies, is put into these bogs, it does not decay either. It used to
be thought that bog bodies were preserved by a combination of anaerobic
(airless) conditions and bog acids, but another factor is equally important.
A particular bog moss called *Sphagnum* has unique and tanning properties that act as a powerful preservative. This is why the skin of bog bodies
is a deep brown and their hair is often reddish in colour.

Bog bodies are an archaeologist's dream. Although they will inevitably
have sustained a degree of damage as a result of resting under a weight of
boggy material over several millennia, they can survive as actual bodies,
complete with soft tissue, skin, hair, finger- and toenails and with their
internal organs intact too. The seemingly magical preservative properties
of the bogs, together with the wealth of forensic tools now available, allow

scholars to come face to face with the ancient dead, enabling them to tell not only the age and gender of the bodies but also the kind of life they led, their social status, the cause of their deaths, what kinds of food they ate and what sorts of diseases they may have suffered from. These uniquely freeze-framed bodies can be interrogated in so much more detail than is true for skeletal remains that it can seem as though possible to talk to the ancient dead.

In the autumn of 1835, Danish peat cutters came across a human body in the Juthe Fen, near Haraldskaer in central Jutland.[3] The dead person was a middle-aged woman who had been placed naked in the bog, her body secured in position by stout branches that skewered her elbows and knees and lay across her chest and abdomen. She was immediately identified as the early medieval Norwegian Queen Gunhild. The story goes that in about AD 1000, the Viking King Harald Bluetooth persuaded Gunhild to come to Denmark to be his wife. Instead, once she arrived, he murdered her and sank her body in the bog. When the woman's body was discovered 900 years later, the then king of Denmark, convinced that she was indeed Gunhild, had an ornate oaken coffin made and honoured her with a Christian burial fit for a queen. She was laid to rest in the little 12th-century church of Set. Nicolai at Vejle, close to where she had been found, where she still had pride of place, greatly treasured by the pastor, until very recently. But despite local opposition, the lady from Haraldskaer has been removed to the National Museum of Denmark in Copenhagen, so that her remains can better be preserved for the future.[4]

At the time of her discovery, the corpse was subjected to an autopsy, the pathologists reaching the conclusion that she had met the dreadful end of being pinned down alive in the bog so that she would slowly drown. The swelling of the knee-joint, where one of the hurdles had been driven in, suggested to the scientists examining her that she had still been alive when the injury occurred. A second post-mortem, conducted in the winter of 2000, confirmed that the Haraldskaer Woman was not in fact a medieval queen but a well-nourished early Iron Age woman, about 40 years old, who died in the early 5th century BC. The swollen knee-joint has been reinterpreted as a post-mortem injury, the oedema the result of bog acids. The modern forensic examination also detected the line of a narrow ligature around her neck, indicating that she met her death not by drowning but by strangulation, probably with a garrotte. In life, she probably enjoyed high status. She had none of the degenerative diseases that afflicted so many Iron Age people as the result of heavy and sustained manual labour. She was well fed, and had beautifully kept hands.

I had the privilege of visiting 'Queen Gunhild' in 2000, as the guest of the archaeologist Lone Hvass and the Department of Archaeology at the University of Århus. As I looked down at her in her coffin, in her quiet dark corner of the church, I almost felt that I knew her. Her face, with its delicate and clean-cut features, narrow high-bridged nose and high cheekbones, could have belonged to any number of women I had encountered during my stay in Jutland. Her preserved body, like that of her Iron Age fellow bog people, allows those who see her to engage intimately with individuals who belonged to the 'foreign country' that is the remote past.

Hundreds of bog bodies and parts of bodies have been found. The great majority are of medieval and more recent dates. Many were found during the 19th and early 20th centuries or earlier, when it was not known how to conserve them. Many have disintegrated, have become skeletonized or have disappeared altogether, leaving their ghostly shadow as 'paper bodies', preserved only in literature. The written records are often unreliable and tend to overestimate the numbers. In this book, I discuss about 25 bodies,[5] a fraction of those that once existed. Because of the fragmentary and sometimes questionable nature of recording and the disappearance or destruction of evidence, it is very difficult to make an accurate estimate of the ancient bog body population, as currently known. I suspect that the total figure is near a hundred.[6] More are being found all the time. In December 2012 a new Irish bog body, known as Moydrum Man, was discovered in County Westmeath.[7] Badly mauled by the peat harvester that revealed him, and represented only by his trunk and a hand, he has been dated to 700 BC. The fruit stones in his stomach suggest that he died in the autumn, but it is not known how he perished or whether he joins the ranks of the untimely killed.

This book is a quest, a journey towards an understanding of an ancient people, their lives, deaths, their hopes fears and beliefs. Who were the bog people? What kind of lives did they lead? How and why were they violently killed, and who murdered them? How were they chosen to be hanged, bludgeoned to death, beheaded or stabbed? What did these people look like when they were alive? And why did those who disposed of their bodies decide that they should be placed in bogs that would preserve them undecayed forever? Attempts to resolve such puzzles can only be made with the help of forensic science, and the application of that science is only possible because of the way that bogs preserve not just ancient bones but soft tissue, skin and internal organs. This freak of bog preservation allows us to approach the bog bodies as though we are crime scene investigators and pathologists. Answers to the mystery of the bog people and much more are contained in the following pages.

Chapter 1 discusses the manner of discovery of bog people, almost all of whom have been found by accident during peat cutting, between the 19th century and the early 2000s. The study is confined to northwest Europe and, naturally, the distribution of the bodies coincides with the position of large tracts of raised bog: in Ireland, northwest England, the northern Netherlands, Lower Saxony and Schleswig-Holstein in North Germany, and Denmark. The date of the bodies considered here ranges from the earliest Iron Age (8th century BC) to the later Roman period (4th century AD).

Chapter 2 puts the bog people into their later prehistoric and Roman context, examining the evidence for the way they lived and the kind of society to which they belonged. In Chapter 3, the mysterious nature of bogs themselves is explored and their remarkable facility for preserving organic material, including human flesh, is considered. Chapters 4 to 7 focus on the forensic evidence, asking the same questions as would a modern police investigative team dealing with a crime scene. Chapter 4 is concerned with the scientific methods currently employed to establish age, gender, date and time of death and internal and external details of the bodies. Chapter 5 examines the injuries sustained by bog people and attempts to establish whether individuals died of natural causes, met with accidents, were deliberately killed as punishment for crimes or were murdered. Chapter 6 investigates the modus operandi (MO), establishing the precise methods used in the deliberate killing of bog people, and Chapter 7 highlights the high level of violence inflicted on many of the bodies.

Chapters 8 and 9 discuss the possible reasons for these people's untimely killing and investigate the killers and the tools they used on their victims. Chapter 10 poses the million-dollar question: whether human sacrifice was behind some or all of the Iron Age and Roman-period bog deaths. The Epilogue is a personal reflection on the bodies, so intimately revealed in their preserved state. Of all the ancient dead, they are the most immediate and so demand our particular respect as fellow humans.

CHAPTER 1

Discoveries
& Discoverers

The axe-men came on an ancient and sacred grove.
Its interlacing branches enclosed a cool central space into
which the sun never shone, but where an abundance
of water spouted from dark springs

LUCAN, *PHARSALIA* III, 399–400[1]

Even today, the exact spot where, in the early 5th century BC, the middle-aged Haraldskaer Woman was strangled and fastened down beneath the cold dark water is a remote and desolate place. This is particularly so in the sombre Nordic winter months, when the sun struggles to light the sky and the surface of the water gleams icy and grey even at midday. Small trees flank the bog and a tangle of vegetation litters its surface. The watery grave of this woman is full of atmosphere, and the horror of her death and immersion still seems to cling to the place, as though an unquiet spirit continues to have a restless presence.

A lonely 19th-century peat cutter, digging up turves and unearthing a well-preserved but leathery body, might easily have thought it was a bog sprite whose dwelling place he had inadvertently disturbed. Today's peat harvesters use huge mechanical diggers rather than spades but, even so, to come across a human body lying in the peat is not something to forget in a hurry. The same feeling of shock and disbelief is experienced. But

Early 20th-century peat cutters, working with traditional
horizontal-bladed spades, in southeast Drenthe, Netherlands.

the modern industrial methods used in cutting peat mean that ancient
bog bodies are more likely to sustain catastrophic damage, and body
parts may be dragged for considerable distances by the machinery before
they are recognized for what they are. So, although our knowledge of bog
bodies is vastly superior now compared with that of more than a hundred
years ago, paradoxically those early discoveries are often more complete
than the bodies that still turn up in the peat.

'MAIDENS OF THE MIST':
EARLY PEAT CUTTERS AND THEIR FINDS

The 16th century saw the first major exploitation of bogs. Marshes were
drained by digging channels through them, and the peat harvested and
cut into turves, to be taken to cities and sold for fuel. Driven by the increas-
ing demand for peat-fuel, new settlements grew up amidst the bogs and
a new profession, that of the peat cutter, was born.[2]

It was a 17th-century Dutch clergyman, the Reverend Picardt, who
coined the phrase 'maidens of the mist' to describe the mythical creatures
presumed – by the people of Drenthe in the Netherlands – to inhabit the
ancient burial mounds in the vicinity of raised bogs. The notion that bog
spirits could emerge from the vapours lying on the surface of peat bogs

An 18th-century pharmacist's 'mummy pot', from the
Netherlands, used to store ground-up bog body parts for
medicinal purposes. Dutch people still ingested these
powders until the early 20th century.

is as old as the tradition of bog drainage for cultivation and peat cutting
for fuel. The presence of human remains in European bogs was noted at
least as early as the mid-17th century, along with clothing, leather, coins
and jewelry. Most of these early human finds were discarded but some
were ground up into a powder, put into jars labelled 'MUMIA (Mummy)'
and sold as a medicine.[3] By the middle of the 19th century, people with
civic authority were becoming aware of a need to conserve the past, and
the growth of town and city museums provided a focus for the storage
and display of ancestral relics. Museums offered to pay for finds and so
peat cutters began to look for ancient objects to augment their meagre
income. Of course, when human bodies were found, they were immediately suspected of being the victims of contemporary crime and were the
subject of police investigations. But usually the bog bodies were even-
tually dismissed as those of poor travellers who had wandered off the
paths and drowned in the treacherous marshes.

FINDING THE YDE GIRL

Last Wednesday, men working for Mr. L. Popken in Yde
discovered a complete human skeleton in a boggy area between Vries
and Yde. The hair, which was over 18 inches long, still covered the skull.
There were also some remains of clothing. Since things decay very slowly
or not at all in bogs, the corpse could have been lying there
for at least a dozen years.

FROM A DRENTHE NEWSPAPER ARTICLE, MAY 1897[4]

On a balmy day in May 1897, two peat cutters were working just outside the village of Yde in Drenthe, when they came across something that chilled their blood. Uttering the curse 'I hope the Devil gets the guy that dug this hole', they flung their spades aside and ran away to their homes, scared to death. Tongue-tied with fright at first, they gradually recovered sufficiently to tell what they had seen, and the local newspaper carried the story of the bog body the two workers had found. It was a strange sight: the mummified remains had been placed in the bog wearing a long robe, half the long hair torn out, the neck still bearing the strip of fabric that had strangled the victim, wound tightly round the throat. The remains were taken to the Provincial Museum of History and Antiquities at Assen. The mayor and the museum committee realized that the body was valuable and, based on its location deep in the uncharted bog, they considered that it must be at least 600 years old, and almost certainly that of a female. The only sceptic was the museum's president, who was convinced that it was not a human being but an ape!

Dating the body was a problem. In 1955, the original estimate of 600 years was revised: peat fragments adhering to the feet contained pollen, and its analysis showed the body to be far more ancient. A date of between AD 200 and 500 was estimated. The remains were redated in 1988, using the radiocarbon method, and the date of death now accepted is between 54 BC and AD 128. Recent scientific tests indicate that the body was indeed female, but she was a teenager, 16 years old at most, and was buried wearing a threadbare woollen coat that might suggest low status in life. The Yde Girl is one of very few ancient bog bodies to have been interred fully clothed. As well as the garrotte that finally killed her, she was found to have sustained a knife wound close to her collarbone. Her life was not only short but painful and difficult, for she had acute curvature of the spine,

The body of a teenage girl, strangled and knifed in the 1st century AD,
and found in a peat bog at Yde in the Netherlands in 1897.

which would have severely compromised both her growth and her mobility.[5] A sad end to a sad life, but perhaps her long coat demonstrated that someone cared enough about her to ensure that she kept warm in her final hours. In his poem *Punishment*, about a fellow bog victim, the adolescent from Windeby in Germany, Seamus Heaney affectionately refers to a 'little adulteress', citing sexual misconduct as a reason for the killing. That is a possible reason for the Yde Girl's fate, but – as argued later – her strangulation and immersion may have been more complicated than that.

GRAUBALLE, TOLLUND AND ELLING: THREE DANISH
BODIES UNCOVERED

He was a handsome and stately figure and is very heavily built
and any presumptions of a certain crudeness in our Germanic ancestors
in the Iron Age is upset by the fact that he has beautiful hands and
almond-shaped nails.[6]

It was just an ordinary morning in Tage Busk Sørensen's daily life, in April
1952. He had set out as usual with fellow Danish workers to cut peat in
the Nebelgaard Mose. But his life was changed forever when his spade
struck something odd, softer than the branches of bog oak he was accus-
tomed to encounter during his work. Tage had found Grauballe Man. Like
something out of a children's story, the village postman arrived, he told
the local doctor, who in turn contacted Professor P.V. Glob of the Museum
of Prehistory at Århus.[7] Glob's primary and immediate concerns were the
preservation of the body once it had been extracted from the protecting
bog, and its context and chronology. Detailed analyses of the stratigraphy,
the associated pollen and the body itself revealed that the Grauballe body,
that of an adult man, died in the early Iron Age (from having his throat
cut from ear to ear), and that he had been stripped naked then deliberately placed in an ancient flooded peat cutting (PL. V). In 1952, the liver
was taken from the body for radiocarbon dating, a technique then in its
infancy. The initial analysis was carried out four years later, giving a date
between the 1st and 5th centuries AD. Problems arose because of the plant
tissue that had grown up through the body, meaning that it was difficult
to determine what was actually being dated. After many subsequent
attempts to refine the chronology, in 2002 came the most accurate date:
Grauballe Man died in the early Iron Age, perhaps as early as 390 BC.[8]

The ethical debate that surrounded the find gives an interesting insight
into 1950s Denmark. There was a sensitivity about the public display of
human remains that is less evident today. This being so, cosmetic considerations came to the forefront, and it was deemed particularly important that
the ancient body should look as good as possible before he met his public.
Furthermore, permission had to be granted by the local bishop before
Grauballe Man could be seen outside the scientific community. Huge interest surrounded his discovery and subsequent display in the museum and
18,000 people visited the 10-day exhibition. After it was over, it was time

The face of Tollund Man, killed by hanging in the 4th century BC. After his death, he was placed carefully in a Danish peat bog, naked but for a cap and belt.

to address the urgent issue of preservation. The story of this battle to keep Grauballe Man from turning to dust from exposure to the air is told in Chapters 3 and 4.

The circumstances surrounding the discovery of the body from Tollund, further south in central Jutland, show marked similarities with the Grauballe Man. Found on 11 May 1950, just two years before Grauballe, Tollund Man's dead body had also been deliberately placed in a peat cutting within a bog. He may have met his death at around the same time: radiocarbon dating has established that he died in the 4th century BC. He was an adult male, a little older than Grauballe and, like him, he was interred naked, although a leather belt encircled his waist and he wore a pointed sheepskin hat. His killers hanged him with a plaited leather cord. The body was found by two farmers who had just completed spring sowing, and were now engaged in cutting peat for fuel. As Professor Glob later wrote: 'As they worked, they suddenly saw in the peat layer a face so fresh that they could only suppose they had stumbled on a recent murder.'[9] The two shocked men immediately told the police at nearby Silkeborg of their gruesome discovery. Going to the site to investigate, the police took with them local museum officials, in case the body turned out to be ancient. Professor Glob was called to see the find. The thing that struck him was the peaceful way in which the man lay on his side in his boggy grave, eyes closed as if he had fallen asleep (PL. I). Somebody, either

The Elling Woman, who died by hanging in 200 BC, and was placed
in a bog close to Tollund Man. Her hair was dressed in an elaborate
French plait, and her body was covered in two skin cloaks.

his killers or, perhaps, one of his relatives, had gone into the peat cutting
and arranged the body with respect. All signs of his violent, agonized
death had been deliberately erased. None of the savagery that seemed
to surround the body from Grauballe was present on the Tollund body.
Glob and his team placed the body and its surrounding block of peat in
a hastily constructed crate, to be transferred to the National Museum of
Denmark at Copenhagen. In a spooky piece of drama, one of the men who
helped lift the heavy box onto the cart that was to take it to the nearest
railway station collapsed and died of a heart attack. It was difficult not to
think that the Tollund Man's re-entry into the modern world was being
balanced by a new death, claimed by the old gods in recompense for the
loss of their ancient gift.

Some 12 years before the discovery of Tollund Man, the body of a female
known as the Elling Woman was found close by in the same bog. The farmer
who discovered her body thought at first it was the carcass of a drowned
animal, but then he spotted the woven woollen belt around what could only
have been a human body.[10] She was about 25–30 years old when she was

killed. The mode of killing was similar to Tollund Man: she was apparently hanged but, unlike him, her remains were covered with two cloaks, one of sheepskin, the other cowhide. Before or after death, her hair had been elaborately dressed in a 'French plait' that extended from the crown of her head and down her neck to her shoulders. The presence of two bodies in relatively close proximity to one another suggests that certain marshy places were deemed so special that they warranted multiple burial. If so, the specialness of this particular marsh must have remained in the folk memory of the local community over a long period, for the Elling Woman died at least a century later than Tollund Man, probably in about 200 BC. If the dressing of her hair took place after her death, such an act shows signs of reverent treatment by her killer or by a witness to her killing; and the two cloaks, surely valuable garments, were certainly laid carefully on the corpse and left to cover her forever. Why did she have two cloaks? Was one placed there for her and the other for her spirit self? Bearing in mind the deposition of some bodies – such as those from Hunteburg and Weerdinge – in pairs (see Chapter 3), could the Elling Woman's two cloaks represent both her and a surrogate companion?

SEX AND SUEBIAN KNOTS:
THE BOGMEN AND BOGWOMEN FROM NORTH GERMANY

> It is the special characteristic of this nation to comb the hair
> sideways and fasten it below with a knot. This distinguishes the
> Suebi from the rest of the Germans; this, among the Suebi,
> distinguishes the freeman from the slave...All this elaborate
> make-up is to impress the foe they will meet in battle.
>
> TACITUS, *GERMANIA* 38[11]

In about AD 100, at Osterby in North Germany, a man in his 50s died and was decapitated. His head was then carefully wrapped in a deerskin and placed in a bog, pinned down by wooden stakes. When the head was discovered in 1948 (the rest of his body has never been found), the soft tissue of the face had gone, but adhering to the skull was a full head of hair, dyed bright red by the bog acids but probably originally light-coloured: blond or grey. At the right side of the head, the hair had been twisted into an elaborate form, fashioned by twining two braids together into a looped knot, remarkably similar to Tacitus's description of the free Suebian

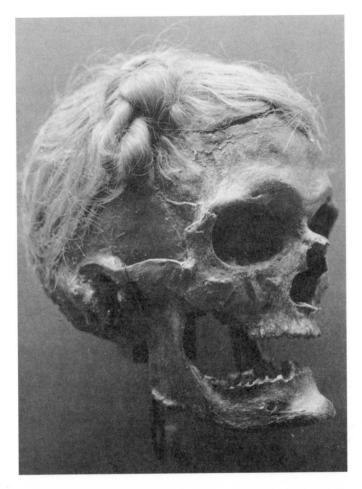

The severed head of an elderly man found at Osterby in Schleswig-Holstein. His hair
was worn long, twisted into a Suebian knot, and the head was placed in a deerskin pouch
before being pegged down in the bog with wooden stakes in about AD 100.

male hairstyle worn by warriors.[12] Another male body – this time complete – from the region, found in 1959 at Dätgen, also wore the Suebian
knot. He was about 20 years younger than the Osterby Man, and had been
stabbed in the chest before being decapitated. Like the Osterby find, his
remains were securely skewered down into an exact position in the bog.
Radiocarbon gives a date for Dätgen Man of about 150 BC. The practice
of growing, plaiting and knotting scalp hair was thus tenacious, lasting
at least 250 years. Michael Gebühr illustrates very graphically the complicated procedure involved in achieving the perfect Suebian knot (see

The body of a teenage boy with a malformed hip found in a peat bog
at Kayhausen in Lower Saxony in 1922. He died in the 2nd or 1st century BC
from a slit throat but his body was hog-tied before its deposition.

p.120).[13] Tacitus was clearly fascinated by the custom and, interestingly,
the same knot was depicted on images of Dacian barbarians from the
Danube on Trajan's Column.[14] So perhaps the Suebian knot was a form of
ancient body art adopted widely in northern and eastern Europe.

In contrast to the mature bogmen from Osterby and Dätgen, the
'Windeby Girl' was an adolescent, about 12 or 13 years old when killed
and placed in a bog at Windeby in Schleswig-Holstein (in the far north of
Germany) in the 1st century AD. The body, discovered during peat exploitation in May 1952, is small and slight, the hair shorn close to the scalp.
A peat cutter spotted what he thought was a stag bone, but it was one of
the child's legs.[15] Like Tollund Man, the Windeby Child had been carefully
arranged in an ancient peat cutting within the marsh, naked but with a
cowhide cloak over one shoulder and a staff of birch placed by the corpse's
right elbow. There was a woven woollen band originally worn round the
head but mistakenly thought to have been a blindfold. Always accepted

as that of a girl, new forensic analysis has cast doubt upon the body's gender, as we shall see. There are no signs of injury on the body but tell-tale so-called Harris Lines (horizontal striations) on the leg bones indicate periods of arrested development through malnutrition. This person might have died naturally, or may have been drowned. However, in the same year and only a few metres away, the body of a middle-aged man was also discovered. Once again, he had been placed naked in a peat cutting but, unlike the child, he was garrotted with a twisted hazel withy, found *in situ* around his neck.

Like the adolescents from Windeby in Schleswig-Holstein and Yde in Drenthe, the Kayhausen Boy, found in 1922 in Lower Saxony, was on the cusp of adulthood when he died, probably from a slit throat. His body was hog-tied, perhaps after death, so that his neck and hands were lashed with the same piece of cloth, and his legs were also bound. Like the similarly aged Yde Girl, this boy's mobility was compromised: his problem in walking was caused by a diseased and malformed hip joint.[16] One of the most recent finds from Lower Saxony is that of a girl from Uchter Moor, found in 2000.[17] She died early in the Iron Age, between the 8th and 6th centuries BC. At 19 years of age, she would have been at the height of her reproductive capacity. Could there have been some aspect of her sexual behaviour that brought opprobrium upon her head and led to her death and interment in a North German marsh? Or was she chosen to die because she was left-handed?

THE LINDOW STORY

> Young man, we know your features
> recreated from the bogland skull.
> Your unblemished body was well-fed,
> not scarred either by work or by harp-strings.
>
> GLADYS MARY COLES, *LINDOW MAN*[18]

The remains of more than one ancient bog body were discovered in the same area of peat bog at Lindow Moss in Cheshire in the 1980s. Two were youngish adult men, one of whom had been decapitated; both had been placed naked in the marsh. The first find was a disembodied head (Lindow I). It was the discovery of this first body part that led to the confession of a local man for his wife's murder.

Modern peat workings at Lindow Moss in Cheshire, findspot
of at least two ancient bog bodies, Lindow II and Lindow III.

The peat workings at Lindow Moss cover an extensive area of low, flat land that stretches desolate and featureless as far as the eye can see. Sticking up out of the ground are the remains of ancient trees and shrubs, a truly Shakespearean 'blasted heath'. On 13 May 1983, two peat workers found an odd spherical object on the elevator that fed peat into a shredding mill. 'It was soft and pliable and, jokingly, it was called a dinosaur's egg. The manager thought that it might have been a burst football...'[9] But once the peat-ball had been cleaned, a human head emerged, and was taken to the police. A Home Office pathologist identified the head as that of a mature female who had died recently (that is, between the 1960s and 1980s). Meanwhile, in Macclesfield, the police were engaged in a long-standing investigation into an unsolved murder. They had in custody for another crime two men whose former cell-mate, Peter Reyn-Bardt, had apparently bragged to them about the murder and dismemberment of his wife that he claimed to have carried out 20 years earlier, telling them that he had partially buried her remains in his back garden at Lindow Moss. The police found nothing in January 1983 when they searched Reyn-Bardt's garden and the suspect flatly denied the crime. But when, in May, the finding of the woman's head, only 300 m (1,000 ft) away from the man's cottage, was reported, Reyn-Bardt confessed to his wife's murder.

But the Lindow Moss murderer had opened his mouth too soon. The police were not happy about the identity of the head and sent it for

Lindow Man (Lindow II), the body of a young man found during peat cutting
in 1984. He had suffered a 'triple' death; he was bludgeoned about the head,
garrotted and his throat cut. His gut contained traces of mistletoe.

further forensic tests at the Oxford University Research Laboratory for
Archaeology and the History of Art. It turned out that the woman had
died in the late Iron Age or early Roman period.[20] In November 1983,
Reyn-Bardt was convicted of his wife's murder on the basis of his confession, even though her remains were never found.

In February 1987, peat workers at Lindow Moss found a lump of human
skin, part of a human back. More body parts were then discovered but no
head. These remains belonged to a man (subsequently known as Lindow
III), about 35 years old and 1.75 m (5 ft 7 ins) tall. He had been decapitated
and his surviving right hand possessed a vestigial extra thumb. It is now
thought extremely likely that the disembodied head (Lindow I) found in
1983 (and then identified as that of a woman) and this headless corpse
belonged to the same male individual. The head and the body were found
some distance apart, possibly due to the action of the diggers used in the

peat harvesting operations but also, perhaps, a result of the deliberate separation of body parts to prevent the men's spirits from entering the world of their ancestors. I shall explore such issues later in the book.

Lindow II, the most famous and informative body from Lindow Moss, now known as 'Lindow Man' (and nicknamed by the press 'Pete Marsh') was discovered in August 1984. His remains were gradually released from the peat during harvesting: on 1 August, a foot was rescued from the works depot; the next day the torso was recovered *in situ* from the peat; finally in June and September 1988, the buttocks and the left leg were unearthed. His was the most complete body found at the site and the one on which the most scientific analyses were subsequently undertaken (PL. VIII). He was younger than Lindow III, at about 20 to 25 years old; his hair and beard were neatly trimmed using shears, and his fingernails so smooth that it is unlikely he undertook habitual manual labour. As far as we know, he was naked except for an armlet on his left arm. He was not beheaded like the older man but had sustained a range of life-threatening injuries just prior to being garrotted with a rope of sinew. His killers had rained blows upon his head and, at about the same time as he was strangled, his throat was cut. The presence of other injuries indicates persistent abuse. As a final act of violence, one of his killers pushed him hard in the small of the back with his knee, causing the kneeling man to topple face down into the water. It is just possible that he was kept hovering at the point of death until this last act, for he had ingested water containing the bog moss *Sphagnum* while still breathing.[21] Lindow Man has provided some of our most convincing evidence that the ancient victims of bog killings were the object of the 'overkill' violence that is explored in Chapters 6 and 7.

BOG DEATHS IN THE FAR WEST: THE BOG BODIES OF IRELAND

Besides some small islands round about Britain, there is also a large island, Ierne, which stretches parallel to Britain on the north, its breadth being greater than its length. Concerning this island I have nothing to tell, except that its inhabitants are more savage than the Britons since they are man-eaters as well as herb-eaters.

STRABO, *GEOGRAPHY*[22]

Strabo was an ancient Greek geographer and ethnographer, writing in the late 1st century BC and early 1st century AD. Like many of his Greek and

Gallagh Man, from Co. Galway, Ireland, was discovered in 1821. He wore
a deerskin tunic, and the woven hazel collar round his neck was used
to throttle him. He died in the 1st century BC.

Roman contemporary commentators, he painted a picture of the lands to
the north and west of the Roman Empire as essentially 'other', more or less
barbaric and 'not at all like us'. Britannia was different enough but Ireland,
scarcely visited by any traveller from the Mediterranean world, was a land
about which anything could be invented, however wild, because nobody
was sufficiently familiar at first hand with its customs to challenge it.

The bog body from Gallagh in County Galway is one of the earliest to
have been found and recorded. It was discovered in 1821, 3 m (nearly 10 ft)
below the surface of the bog.[23] It was treated as a freak show, first being
reburied and subsequently dug up time and again so that people could
gawp at it. A similar practice was recorded in the early 18th century in the
case of a man and a woman who died of cold on a Derbyshire moor at Hope
in 1674. The couple were found frozen in a snowdrift some months after
their deaths, and were buried in the peat bog where they had perished.
The extraordinary preservative properties of peat bogs were well known
to local people: nearly 30 years later, the pair were dug up to see how much
they had decayed, and onlookers 'found them no way altered...'.[24]

Unlike the Danish bodies from the 1950s, no attempt was made to
preserve the Gallagh Man's body. It was put on show at the Royal Dublin
Society and then presented to the Royal Irish Academy (now the National
Museum of Ireland in Dublin), having shrunk and withered through
neglect. But notes were made about the body at the time it was discovered, so at least some details are known. It was apparently that of a young,
bearded man with long dark hair, wearing a close-fitting knee-length

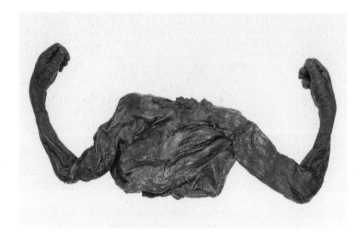

The mutilated torso of Oldcroghan Man, from Co. Offaly, Ireland, found in 2003. He was huge man and he had suffered massive trauma to his body before being placed, headless, in the bog in about 300 BC.

deerskin tunic. A band of woven hazel withies was found at his throat, and this might have been used to strangle him. His watery grave was marked by two wooden stakes driven firmly into the marsh, and it is thought that he probably died in the 1st century BC.[25]

Ireland continues to reveal its Iron Age bog treasures. In spring 2003, peat management operations revealed the presence of two individuals, both about 25 years old and both of whom died in about 300 BC. One was found during drain-digging along a parish boundary in County Offaly. This was Oldcroghan Man. He was a gigantic fellow, 1.91 m (6 ft 4 ins) tall, with an immense arm-span. His huge size puts me in mind of Grendel, the man-eating monster from the Dark Age epic poem *Beowulf*.[26] As soon as the body was reclaimed from the bog, it became clear that it had sustained multiple injuries, some pre- and some peri- or post-mortem. Death was caused by a stab wound penetrating his left lung, despite an attempt to parry the blow evident from defence wounds to one arm. He was then decapitated, his body chopped in half at the diaphragm and his nipples sliced through; his upper arms were pierced and twisted hazel withies were drawn through the holes.

There are some striking similarities between Oldcroghan Man and Lindow Man (Lindow II). The fingernails of the Oldcroghan body were neatly manicured and, like the Cheshire bog victim, the Irish giant died wearing nothing but an armlet on one upper arm; Lindow's was of fox-fur, Oldcroghan's was of plaited leather adorned with metal mounts bearing

One of Oldcroghan Man's hands, showing its remarkable
preservation and neatly manicured fingernails.

Celtic (so-called La Tène) motifs. This detail is important, for it corrobo-
rates the radiocarbon dates, and places this Irish bog body firmly in the
middle Iron Age.[27] The armlet, with its Celtic designs, was a valuable ornament, and its wearer's meat-rich diet and well-groomed appearance are in
accordance with his high status – until his violent death and the apparently humiliating treatment of his body.

A few months before, in February 2003, peat extraction workers at
Ballivor, County Meath, discovered the body of a man. Unlike Oldcroghan,
these remains were those of a much smaller, slighter individual. Ballivor
was not the original site of his deposition. A peat-digging machine had
dragged it from its prehistoric resting place in the deep Clonycavan bog
near the border with County Westmeath. He met his death at roughly
the same time as Oldcroghan, but Clonycavan Man's head was intact; it
had sustained several blows rained down upon it with an axe. His body
had also been disembowelled. Clonycavan's body was stripped before
he was placed in his bog grave but, again like Oldcroghan, he may have
once enjoyed high rank, for his long hair, piled up high on his head, had
been elaborately dressed with an expensive hair gel, made from a blend
of animal fat and aromatic pine-resin, imported from southern France or
Spain. This calls to mind a phrase written by Diodorus Siculus:

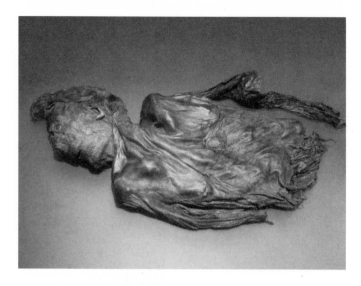

Clonycavan Man, found in Co. Meath, Ireland, in 2003. He died from savage blows to his head, and he had been disembowelled. His hair had been dressed with costly foreign hair gel.

...the [Gauls'] hair is so thickened with lime-wash that it differs in no way from a horse's mane.

There is evidence that the hair remained fixed in position for some time before death, without being washed, for it was infested with lice. Of course the high rank of this individual, implied by the costly hair gel, may have been part of a ritual associated with a death ceremony rather than reflective of status enjoyed in life but, if so, the presence of hair parasites implies that the preparations for such funerary rituals began months before he was killed.[29]

Both these Irish Iron Age bogmen had been subjected to extreme violence and abuse in the days leading up to their deaths and beyond. Yet another Irish bog body was discovered on an August afternoon in 2011 and this one, like the corpses of Oldcroghan and Clonycavan, also exhibited signs of extreme trauma. A worker operating a milling machine in Cashel Bog (County Laois) came across the body, but unfortunately his machine inflicted severe damage before discovery. Once it was realized what had been found, archaeologists and conservation experts from the National Museum of Ireland in Dublin began to investigate. The body from Cashel was a young adult male, like those from Gallagh, Oldcroghan and Clonycavan, and he had been carefully placed on the surface of the bog, perhaps in a natural pool. As had occurred at the grave of Gallagh Man, Cashel Man's resting place was marked by two hazel rods. The scientists working on the body had huge difficulties in trying to separate the original injuries from modern damage. Although it is suspected that he received multiple wounds before he died, it is impossible to be certain. What is particularly interesting, though, is the date of his death: radiocarbon analysis of the hazel rods and the peat on which the body was laid suggest that Cashel Man died in the earlier Bronze Age, between 2000 and 1600 BC,[30] and so well outside the Iron Age and Roman-period time frame of the main assemblage of bog people considered in this book. The discovery of Cashel Man indicates that the practice of violent killing and immersion in swamps preceded the Iron Age by at least 1000 years.

CHANCE FINDS AND PURPOSEFUL BURIALS

Virtually all ancient bog bodies have been discovered by accident, usually during the extraction and management of peat. Only a small sample of those originally found has been brought to the notice of archaeologists and conservationists. Many bodies, particularly those unearthed before the 19th century, were reinterred and given Christian burials; others were ground up to make medicines. And we know that even body parts found comparatively recently have been mistaken for branches, the bodies of animals and, in the case of Lindow I's head, an old football! So the process of discovery has been and still is a somewhat haphazard business. There is a stark contrast between the emergence of ancient bog people into the modern world and the manner of their original burial. Time and again, the evidence demonstrates that these ancient bodies were carefully put into specific places within peat bogs: pools and cuttings. The Haraldskaer Woman, mentioned in the Introduction, was deliberately positioned over a spring.[31] Bodies were pinned down in order to keep them in particular spots within the marsh, and care was often taken to mark the site of the grave with rods and stakes almost in the manner of tombstones. Perhaps it was important for the communities from which these bog people came to be able to remember where the corpses had been buried. These ancient dead were 'kept bodies', physically held and undecayed by the bogs and, at the same time, remaining in the memories of those who had shared their lives.

CHAPTER 2

The World of the Bog People: Space, Time and Society

One can launch an accusation before the Council or
bring a capital charge. The punishment varies to suit the crime.
The traitor and deserter are hanged on trees, the coward, the
shirker and the unnaturally vicious are drowned in miry
swamps under a cover of wattled hurdles.

TACITUS, GERMANIA 12[1]

The Roman author Publius Cornelius Tacitus wrote his treatise, the *Germania*, in AD 98. The term 'Germania' in this context is used to refer to the communities inhabiting northern and eastern Germany, the Netherlands and southern Denmark. For his information on these peoples, Tacitus drew on earlier sources, notably the writings of Julius Caesar, Livy, Strabo and the now lost books of Pliny. Tacitus had a distinct agenda in compiling the *Germania*. It was first and foremost a moralizing tract, designed to contrast the simplicity and integrity of the northern tribes with the complex degeneracy of Rome. The passage quoted here is a good illustration of Tacitus's moral tone. But at the same time, it is difficult to ignore the implication that one of the punishments he cites relates to bog bodies. Not only does he describe the immersion of miscreants in marshes, but he refers also to the archaeologically attested detail of pinning bodies down in bogs with branches.

BOG BODIES IN CONTEXT

Most ancient bog bodies date between the end of the Bronze Age and the end of the Roman Iron Age, with the majority falling into the period between 500 BC and AD 200. (But there is a distinct group of northern Neolithic bog bodies and, as we have seen, 2011 saw the discovery of an Irish body, Cashel Man, who was found to have died in the earlier Bronze Age.) The date range of deposition is thus quite wide, and so is the geographical scope (as discussed in the Introduction). It is becoming more and more apparent from archaeological study that there was enormous diversity in later prehistoric societies over time and space. But despite this, it is nonetheless possible to note some general points of common ground.

According to both archaeological evidence and the testimony of ancient authors from the classical world, the regions of northern and western Europe in which bog bodies have been found were inhabited by largely rural communities which, in the later Iron Age at least, combined farming with the manufacture, export and import of products such as metalwork, pottery and jewelry. In the middle and later Iron Age, towns, such as Manching on the river Danube, grew up as industrial and trading centres. Warfare was not uncommon, and ranged from small-scale inter- and intra-tribal skirmishes to the great battles with the Romans in the 1st centuries BC and AD. The most detailed information about these societies comes from the later Iron Age, the time when writers from the Mediterranean world began to take serious interest in the 'barbarian' communities that bordered the Roman Empire to the north and west.

> The customs of the Germans are very different from those
> of the Gauls. They have no Druids to supervise religious matters
> and they do not show much interest in sacrifices...Their whole life
> is centred around hunting and military pursuits: from childhood
> they devote themselves to toil and hardship.
>
> CAESAR, *DE BELLO GALLICO* 6.21[2]

Caesar's testimony serves as a warning against the denial of regional diversity between different cultural and ethnic groups that practised bog body burial. Ancient Irish society may have been quite different from that of Britain, and from that of Germany, the Netherlands and Denmark. The features that appear to have bound them together, including bog burial itself, have to be set against those that divided them. Caesar's testimony, particularly his ethnographical writing in Book 6 of *de Bello Gallico*, needs to be interpreted in the context of his own background as a high-ranking Roman military commander. It has to be remembered, too, that although Caesar had actively campaigned in Gaul for nearly 10 years, he possessed far less knowledge of the world east of the Rhine, except for his brush with the expansionist German ruler Ariovistus in 58 BC.[3] In any case, Caesar might well have emphasized the qualities of prowess in war and hunting, as noble practices among 'uncivilized' northern peoples living in vast forests, and with little familiarity with Rome.

BOG BODIES AND THE CELTS

In language, customs and laws, these three peoples are quite distinct.
The Celts are separated from the Aquitani by the river Garonne, and
from the Belgae by the Marne and the Seine.

CAESAR, *DE BELLO GALLICO* 1.1[4]

Most bog bodies have been found in areas of northern Europe never deemed to be Celtic, either culturally or linguistically. Happily, archaeo-logical scholarship seems largely to have moved on from its gratuitous denial of ancient Celticity that was so prominent in the 1990s and early 2000s.[5] But the good thing about the 'Celtic Debate' is that it challenged the rather cosy and facile assumption that all ancient Iron Age Britons, Gauls, Celtiberians and Germans west of the Rhine were Celts and were therefore the same. No ancient writer ever spoke of the Britons as anything other than Britanni. Caesar is one of the few authors who states that certain peoples in Gaul thought of themselves as Celts, and he makes it clear that only those communities occupying a very discrete area of central Gaul 'in their own language' called themselves Celts.[6]

Language is an important consideration in determining self-identity. The only areas where bog bodies have been found where Celtic languages were almost certainly spoken are Ireland and northwest England. The Danish, north German and Dutch bog bodies belonged to communities who spoke Teutonic tongues. So the great majority of bog bodies must be assumed to be Germanic rather than Celtic. Caesar was talking sense in making a clear distinction between the Gauls/Celts and the Germans.

KINGS AND COMMONERS, PRIESTS AND SLAVES

> They choose their kings for their noble birth, their leaders for their
> valour. The power of the kings is not absolute or arbitrary. As for
> the leaders, it is their example rather than their authority that wins them
> special admiration – for their energy, their distinction, or their
> presence in the van of fight. Capital punishment, imprisonment and
> even flogging are allowed to none but the priests, and are not
> inflicted merely as punishments or on the leaders' orders but in
> obedience to the god whom they believe to preside over battle.
>
> TACITUS, *GERMANIA* 7[7]

So wrote Tacitus in his description of Germanic societies living between
the Rhine and the Danube at the end of the 1st century AD. During the
period that communities were putting people into bogs, society appears
to have been highly stratified. Rich burials, such as those at Reinheim and
Waldalgesheim in the middle Iron Age Rhineland, indicate the presence
of high-ranking individuals, of whom many were women. At the other
end of the social scale were the slaves, those who were either born or
sold into servitude or became unfree because they were prisoners of war.

Reconstruction scene at La Tène on the shore of Lake Neuchâtel, Switzerland,
an Iron Age sacred lake. Here, over centuries, people deposited precious objects,
animals and possibly even people in the water to honour the gods.

They have left behind stark testimony of their bondage, in the form of iron gang-chains and shackles, such as the pair discovered at the remote votive watery site of Llyn Cerrig Bach on the island of Anglesey.[8] Tacitus, Caesar and other Roman writers are in agreement that among the highest-ranking individuals in Gallo-German society were the priests. Indeed, there is a striking similarity between Caesar's comment on the centrality of the Druidic priesthood in Gaul and Tacitus's emphasis on the importance of Germanic priests in all aspects of society, not only those concerned directly with religion.

An acknowledgment of the social structures in the world of the bog bodies is key to understanding the context in which certain individuals were killed and immersed in marshes and to any enquiry as to the identity of the victims. While the absence of the tell-tale signs of manual work on hands and in joints suggests high status, the lack of grave goods and the evidence of physical abuse and restraints might instead lead to a confirmation of the low rank that belonged to slaves and prisoners.

SETTLEMENT AND SOCIETY

By their very nature, people did not live in bogs and neither could they use them for arable farming or pasture. But despite the inimical environment, there is plenty of evidence that bogs and wetlands were exploited by people from the Bronze Age to the medieval period in northwest Europe. Crannogs were artificial islands created in watery places, partly for defence and partly in order to take economic advantage of the local fish and waterfowl. Such settlements have been recorded all over northern Europe, from Ireland to Poland. The shores of an Irish lake, Lough Gara in County Sligo, supported several crannogs. One of them, at Rathtinaun, was comprehensively excavated during the 1950s, and was found to have been occupied from the Late Bronze Age right through to medieval times, with temporary interruptions of use when the level of the lake rose too high. Timber roundhouses were constructed on the crannog, almost certainly thatched with reeds from the lake. There is evidence for a mixed economy that included farming, metalworking in bronze and iron, and the manufacture of pottery and wooden vessels.[9]

The most famous Iron Age lake dwelling in mainland Britain is the Glastonbury lake village in the Somerset Levels, excavated during the late 19th and early 20th centuries and reinvestigated in the 1990s.[10] The watery

A ball of Iron Age wool – the principal material used for clothing –
preserved in the peat at Roswinkel in Drenthe, Netherlands.

environment provided an incredible level of information about the villagers for, of course, organic materials, such as vessels made of wood and
basketry, were preserved. The Glastonbury lake-dwellers exploited the
natural resources of their marshy landscape. They had ready access to
salt water from local tidal estuaries, and fresh water from rivers, bogs and
natural pools, and to woods and fertile land. The artificial island was pro-
tected by a palisade and within this densely packed roundhouses were
built raised on clay platforms.

Similar communal wetland settlements are recorded right across
northern Europe. Away from Britain and Ireland, particularly in Germanic
regions (present-day Denmark, Germany and the Netherlands), the pre-
dominant form of dwelling was the wooden longhouse, thatched with
straw or reeds, and divided internally into sections, with cattle at one end
and people at the other. In the Drenthe area of the Netherlands, a region
where several bog bodies have been found, quite large Iron Age houses
were constructed along the shore of the North Sea. One, near Hijken, was
16 m (over 52 ft) long. Small storage buildings were erected nearby.[11] The
house was large enough for a 'village' community probably consisting of
an extended, multi-generational family, able to support itself by exploiting
both its maritime and terrestrial environments. In the 1970s and 1980s,
Dutch archaeologists were engaged in the Assendelver Polders Project,
in which investigations were carried out on a very well-preserved early
Iron Age house on the low-lying peat of the Polderland to the northwest of

Amsterdam.[12] The dwelling was a typical north European longhouse, again divided horizontally into living spaces for people and domestic animals (mainly cattle and sheep or goats). The house, built of wood, wattle and reed, was more than 18 m (59 ft) long and over 6 m (20 ft) wide. The builders exploited the oak, alder, willow, ash and birch trees that grew some distance away.

Certain features of the Assendelver house suggest that ritual and belief were never far away from the minds of those who built and lived in it. While willow was extensively employed for internal walls in the dwelling part, it was not used where the animals were kept: here the trees used for timber were alder, ash and birch. The excavators have suggested that the absence of willow in the animals' stalls was deliberate, citing medieval magical beliefs that contact between animals and willow should be avoided because this wood caused cows' milk to dry up. Conversely, other wood species might have been purposely included in certain parts of the structure for the positive magic they were deemed to possess. In the medieval Netherlands, purging buckthorn was believed to ward off sickness in both people and beasts. In the building at Assendelver, it was used to screen off both sleeping quarters and the area interpreted as a nursery for young livestock. There is evidence here, too, of other ritual activities. A complete pot had been placed on the floor by the first inhabitants, and was left carefully undisturbed when successive floors were built up over time. Another 'ritual' object was a wooden paddle, placed within the material used for heightening the floor in the third phase of its replacement. The investigation of the Assendelver house, with its remarkable preservation of organic material, indicates that the farmers who lived there were ritually aware, and had beliefs associated with the spirit world. Although no bog bodies have been found in the direct vicinity, the evidence for domestic occupation in the Polder peat fields perhaps allows us to imagine the kind of religious context in which the bog bodies of the Drenthe region, far to the north, might have been killed and immersed in the bog waters.

It is generally accepted that bogs were separate places, away from settlements, and clearly this was often so. But evidence for dwellings has been discovered close to bogs, even those in which bodies were immersed. One such is the Borremose bog, in the far north of Jutland. This region is famous not only for its multiple bog bodies but also because of its proximity to Gundestrup, the site where a great gilded silver cauldron, covered with images of gods and sacrificial ritual, was ritually dismantled and

The body of a woman who was killed and buried in a peat bog
in the 8th century BC at Borremose, Denmark.

reverently deposited on a tiny dry island in a bog in about 100 BC.[13] The
settlement at Borremose was constructed on a dry mound within the
bog itself but close to dry land, and occupied between *c*. 300 and 100 BC.[14]
At least 32 longhouses were built inside a protective rampart, and the
village was linked to the mainland by a robust causeway capable of taking
wagons as well as people to and from the settlement. The community
at Borremose kept cattle, and grew cereal crops in the fields nearby. The
surrounding bog has yielded three ancient bog bodies, a man and two
women, but these people were placed in the bog in the 8th century BC,
several hundred years earlier than the construction and occupation of
the village. However, the villagers dug an oval pond in one corner of the
settlement: it might simply have been used to water livestock, but it could
have been a sacred watery place, designed for prayer and the deposition

The 2nd-century BC trackway at Corlea, Co. Longford,
Ireland. Such ancient trackways are commonly found
in bogs all over northern Europe.

of offerings to the gods. If this is so, it suggests that the custom of placating the marsh spirits continued long after the three individuals were killed and laid in the bog to be preserved for ever. It is even possible that the later settlers knew the dead bodies were there and that they were deemed to act as bog-guardians to the living.

BOGS AND BELIEF

Mercurius Teutates is appeased in this manner among the Gauls:
A man is lowered head first into a full tub so that he drowns there.

9TH-CENTURY COMMENTARY ON LUCAN, *PHARSALIA* I, 444–46[15]

Sometime in the 2nd century BC, an individual or a group of people deposited a pair of wooden images, each larger than life-size, in a small remote bog at Braak in Schleswig-Holstein. They were each made from a single naturally forked branch, and represent a naked male and female human figure. Their faces have wide staring eyes and their mouths gape open as if

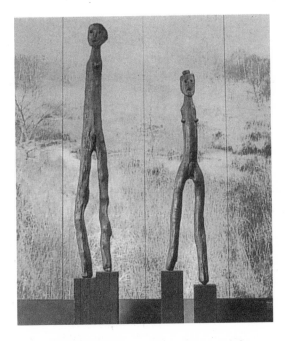

A pair of human images, one male, one female, made from
single timbers and erected in a small bog at Braak in North
Germany in the 2nd century BC.

chanting or screaming. When they were discovered in 1948, they were lying
flat beneath the bog surface, but they would have originally stood tall, presiding over their marsh and visible for miles in the flat landscape.[16] There
is evidence that fires were habitually lit close to their findspot, suggesting
ritual activities, even feasting. Who were they? Might they have been images
of dead bog people, memorials to their passing? Did they depict members of
the ruling elite? Could they have represented priests, who presided over ceremonial events? Or might they have embodied the spirits of the bog itself?
They may even have been images of gods like the Gallic Teutates mentioned
by Lucan in his *Pharsalia,* an epic poem written in the mid-1st century AD,
narrating the civil war between Pompey and Caesar that culminated in
Caesar's victory at Pharsalus in Thessaly in 48 BC. In the 9th century AD,
a Bernese scholar recorded a more elaborate version of Lucan's text, presumably because he had access to a lost archive. In the quotation above, he
commented that sacrificial victims to this god suffered watery deaths.

The title Teutates means 'the god of the tribe', or 'the people's god'. The
name implies that he was a kind of everyday deity whose primary concern

was the community's well-being. That being so, it is entirely appropriate that he presided over the *mores* of his people and was invoked at times of threat or crisis, whether in the form of external dangers, such as warfare, or internal instabilities, perhaps caused by an infringement of the proper rules of conduct, such as social deviancy, of the kind hinted at by Tacitus when he wrote of 'disreputable bodies'.

Teutates is not the only Germanic divinity possibly associated with bog deaths. Tacitus describes an earth-goddess, Nerthus, whose worship was held in common by most of the tribes east of the Rhine, including the powerful Langobardi who occupied territory to the northeast of Hanover.[17] Her shrine lay in a sacred grove on an island in the sea. Once a year, the people held a festival in her honour, and a cart draped with a cloth was driven round the fields in a fertility rite. This cart was so charged with sacred force that no one except her priest was permitted to touch it. The possible link with bog bodies is contained in Tacitus's description of the cleansing rituals that took place after the festival was over. Before Nerthus's cart and its shroud were returned to their grove, it was washed in a sacred lake by slaves. But they perforce had to touch the holy vehicle and therefore could not be allowed to live:

> This service is performed by slaves who are immediately afterwards drowned in the lake. Thus mystery begets terror and a pious reluctance to ask what sight can be which is allowed only to dying eyes.[18]

THE MAGIC OF THE MARSH

> I can see her drowned
> body in the bog,
> the weighting stone,
> the floating rods and boughs.
>
> SEAMUS HEANEY, *PUNISHMENT*[19]

Bog burials were not a normal Iron Age burial rite. In northern Europe, most people who were given formal interment rites were cremated or, less often, buried entire, in inhumation graves, sometimes with grave goods, such as personal possessions and the paraphernalia of funeral meals. The important thing to understand is that the remains of the vast majority of dead bodies in the Iron Age are invisible to us, having been either burnt or allowed to decompose naturally, in order for them to sink into the earth and replenish its nutrients and, more especially, to release the soul so that it could enter the Otherworld and join the ancestors. Bog bodies are different. The presence of strong preservative material in bogs, particularly the tanning agent within the *Sphagnum* mosses, interrupted the processes of decay, keeping the dead in the land of the living and preventing the freeing of their spirit. So, at one and the same time, the dead person was both preserved but denied resolution. Bog burials were the result of deliberate choice on the part of the disposal teams, mourners and those directing the funeral rites (PL. XI).

The persistent use of bogs as ancient fridges to preserve organic materials such as great wooden vats of butter,[20] indicates that prehistoric communities were fully aware of the special properties of bogs, and utilized them regularly. It would have been recognized that wooden objects, perhaps lost accidentally as people crossed the marshes, would remain unrotted. And so it was for the bog bodies. Some bogs were quite shallow and pale submerged corpses might sometimes have remained clearly visible, their places of interment perhaps regarded as a source of both reverence and fear for the living. Over time, the *Sphagnum* acted on the bog bodies, not simply preserving them but also transforming them, causing them to take on eerie, inhuman qualities: turning the skin to deep brown leather and dyeing the hair red, as if the spirits of the Otherworld were claiming the dead for their own. In early medieval Irish and Welsh mythology, red was the Otherworld's colour, and chthonic (underworld) deities frequently appeared to the living as sinister red figures in human or animal form.[21]

Bog bodies were deliberately interred in liminal territory, between land and water, between the living and the dead. Just as the natural processes of decay were interrupted, so were their lives, for they met untimely, violent deaths that abruptly severed their life force. In many cases they were hanged or strangled, literally stopping them in mid-breath. There is evidence, too, that – in a seeming paradox – those responsible for killing them knew how to manipulate the process of dying so as to keep the victims hovering on the brink of death,[22] as if the marginality of their burial places was echoed in the manner of their demise. Other things were done to these bodies that marked them out as special, as between worlds, denied access to transition to the world of the true dead. They were interred without grave goods: no pottery, no remnants of food, no weapons or obvious marks of their life status. It was clearly often deemed important, too, for them to go into the bog as naked as the moment of birth. Few of them have been discovered wearing the clothes that would have undoubtedly been preserved had they been on the body when immersed in the bog; weirdly, their garments were sometimes placed in the bog nearby. In addition, the scalp hair of certain bodies was shorn off or partially cropped and the lopped tresses placed beside them (PL. IV).

THE CAPRICE OF BOGS: BOUNTY AND DANGER

> No person had ever walked out on the bog but King Eochaid
> commanded his steward to watch the effort Midir and his followers
> put forth in making the causeway. It seemed to the steward that all the
> men in the world from sunrise to sunset had come into the bog. Into the
> bottom of the causeway they kept pouring a forest with its trunks and its
> roots, Midir standing and urging on the host on every side.[23]

This passage is taken from a medieval Irish mythic saga, 'The Wooing of Étain', which chronicles the love affair between the god Midir and the eponymous young girl, a liaison beset by calamities, set in train by Midir's jealous wife Fuamnach. The building of the causeway across a treacherous and impassable bog is one of several such tasks imposed by Étain's husband Eochaid upon his wife's suitor. The tale illustrates very clearly the fear with which bogland was regarded in early Ireland. It is easy to see how bogs encouraged awe, terror and wonder. Not only are they dangerous to the unwary but they emit vapours, curling from their surface like wraiths from the Otherworld, and little flames from bog gases can flicker into life, as if they are dancing spirits.

People chose to live in the vicinity of bogs because of the natural resources they provided and the protection they offered. But there was something else that attracted Iron Age communities to bogs: bog iron. In regions with extensive raised bogs, these wet places were one of the most lucrative sources of iron ore. Not only was it readily available, but the means to produce metal from the ore were also present, in the form of peat charcoal, a highly effective fuel for both smelting and forging iron, and far easier to acquire and use than making charcoal from trees.[24] There is evidence, in fact, that the ancient rituals associated with bogs and lakes were directly associated with the production of iron.

In 1911, workmen dredging a small lake, named Llyn Fawr, near Aberdare in the south Welsh valleys, for the construction of a reservoir, came upon a strange collection of bronze and iron objects that had been put into the water at the very beginning of the Iron Age, in about 700 BC.[25] Among these pieces were two beautifully made sheet-bronze cauldrons, at least a hundred years old when they entered the lake, and a group of metal items including personal grooming equipment, horse-gear and weapons. Some things, like a razor and an iron sword, were exotic, coming from far to the east in central Europe; and a group of Late Bronze Age socketed axes had been made in southeast England. But the most fascinating material consists of iron objects, including a socketed spear and sickle, that had clearly been made by smiths used to working with cast and sheet bronze but who were experimenting with the new technologies of iron. While it is comparatively easy for a skilled metalworker to cast an implement with a socket to hold a wooden handle, it is far more challenging to make the same object in iron, which could not be cast but had to be forged by hand from a red-hot, semi-solid lump of smelted metal.

The peaty layers in the ancient lake at Llyn Fawr were a rich source of bog iron, and local smiths were clearly exploiting the strange new metal, which must have seemed almost magical, with its robustness and its

One of two sheet copper-alloy cauldrons from the lake at Llyn Fawr, South Wales. The vessel dates to c. 800 BC and was at least 100 years old when it was deposited with other exotic Late Bronze Age objects dating to the earliest Iron Age, c. 700 BC.

capacity to hold a sharp edge which made it superior to bronze, although not as aesthetically pleasing (at least to modern taste). Iron's very novelty would have given it an exotic flavour and that in itself would endow it with great value and prestige. But what was going on at Llyn Fawr? The presence of so many valuable pieces, such as the cauldrons and the imported bronzework, indicates that this was not simply a quarry for bog iron. It was a highly sacred place to which communities and individuals came to offer gifts to the gods: perhaps a place of pilgrimage, venerated for providing the magical new metal. Cauldrons seem to have held a particular spiritual value. They were difficult and costly to produce, and they were used to cook large joints of meat for communal feasts that were often associated with ceremonial events. They are often found in marshes and other wet places in Britain, Ireland and northern Europe, where they were deposited right through the Iron Age. The most clearly sacred of such bog vessels was the late Iron Age Danish silver cauldron from Gundestrup, whose unquestionably religious character is declared by the sacred images decorating its inner and outer surfaces.

Even today, Llyn Fawr has a special atmosphere. Despite its location, in the middle of an industrial coal-valley landscape, it appears remote and mysterious, a dark sheet of water set against a backdrop of steep mountains;

Gilded silver cauldron from a dry island in a peat bog at Gundestrup, Denmark. The vessel is highly decorated, inside and outside, with images of gods and sacred scenes. It was made in the 1st century BC.

a lonely place, visited only by a few fishermen and the odd archaeologist. No human remains have been recorded at Llyn Fawr, but masses of hazelnuts were preserved in the peat, attesting – perhaps – to the ancient habit of offering foodstuffs as well as precious metal objects to the spirits of the lake.

RECIPROCAL OFFERINGS

The excavations at the Iron Age hillfort at Danebury in southern England conducted by Barry Cunliffe from 1969 to 1988 have provided remarkable evidence for a dynamic relationship between the people of Danebury and their gods.[26] Old underground grain silos were found to have had a use after the corn had been cleared away, as repositories for offerings that have been interpreted as gifts of thanks to the spirits for keeping the seed-corn safe over the winter. Such presents to the divine powers included meat and iron objects. But they also included the bodies or part-bodies of animals and, also, of people. The great majority of the animal remains were those of domestic beasts that included cattle, pigs and sheep but also horses and dogs, the latter two species sometimes associated. The exception was the persistent presence of ravens. The bones of at least 25 complete human bodies have been recovered from the silos and some were young adult men in the prime of their working (and fighting) lives. Why were humans and animals interred in these strange circumstances at Danebury? Their burial here could, perhaps, be interpreted as one element in a cyclical rhythm of activity that began with the digging and preparation of the pits for grain storage, their clearance and the deposition of goods, beasts and human bodies. The presence of ravens may have been a deliberate representation of chthonic or underworld symbols, and it is possible, too, that their feathers were used for ritual headdresses.

It *may* be admissible to see the finds from Danebury, and their interpretation, as broadly analogous to the bodies immersed in Iron Age peat bogs. Could these people have been placed in their watery graves as thank-offerings to the marshes that provided bog iron and allowed the preservation of food, such as butter? I suspect that the bog body phenomenon was far more complex than that. The violent deaths meted out to the victims have turned bogs into crime scenes, and the undercurrents of humiliation, violence and denial of identity present a kaleidoscope of possible interpretations that are the subject of the chapters that follow.

CHAPTER 3

The Magic of
Bog Preservation

> After eleven years, the brethren expected to find his flesh reduced to
> dust and the remains withered, as is usual in dead bodies...When they
> opened the grave, they found his body whole and uncorrupt as though
> still living,and the limbs flexible as though he were asleep, rather
> than dead. Furthermore, all the vestments in which he was clothed
> appeared not only spotless but wonderfully fresh and fair.
>
> BEDE, *A HISTORY OF THE ENGLISH CHURCH AND PEOPLE*, CHAPTER 30 [1]

The Venerable Bede was born in AD 673. He was a Northumbrian monk
and spent most of his adult life at Jarrow, serving under its abbot, Ceolfrid.
The work for which he is most renowned is his *History of the English Church
and People*, completed in AD 731. The undecayed body Bede describes here
was that of Saint Cuthbert, a Celtic monk who started his religious life
in the Scottish borderland monastery of Melrose and, in AD 661, became
prior of Holy Island (Lindisfarne) off the Northumbrian coast.[2] The mirac-
ulous preservation of Cuthbert's body was explained by the purity of his
life and the wisdom of his ministry.

Bede's description of Saint Cuthbert's exhumation serves to underline
one way in which the preservation of dead bodies was regarded in the past,
as a miracle, a gift from God, something that marked out the body's possessor
as someone deserving of veneration because of a special life. Apparently, no

mummification procedures had been carried out on Cuthbert's body. Divine forces had preserved his flesh and even his garments from the natural processes of dissolution. The preservation of ancient bog bodies likewise came about without their subjection to embalming procedures or other human intervention. But what did happen was their deliberate burial in a particular environment that effectively froze them in time and prevented their decay. Bogs were deliberately used by ancient Europeans to preserve their past, to create memory and to defy time itself.

MIASMIC MARSHES

A marshy neighbourhood should be avoided because the morning
breezes of the town, when mixed with the vapours arising from fens,
expose the bodies of the inhabitants to the poisoned breaths
of marsh animals, making the site pestilential.

VITRUVIUS, *ON ARCHITECTURE* 1.4.1 [3]

And neither should there be any marsh-land near the buildings...
for it throws off a baleful stench in hot weather and breeds insects
armed with annoying stings...then too it sends forth plagues of
swimming and crawling things deprived of their winter moisture
and infected with poison by the mud and decaying filth, from which
are often contracted mysterious diseases.

COLUMELLA, *DE RE RUSTICA* 1.5.6 [4]

It was widely believed in the Roman world that swamps and bogs harboured evil humours that spread disease, as well as being the haunt of noxious animal life. The Roman architect Vitruvius lived during the reign of the first Roman emperor Augustus. He thought marshes should be avoided because of their 'dangerous exhalations'.[5] Interestingly, Vitruvius seems to have been more worried about this aspect of bogland rather than its inherent instability for building. The same was true of Columella, who was writing in the AD 60s. Such attitudes, in a sense, go hand in hand with the Romans' belief that corpses were pollutants, and so all sorts of rituals and prohibitions were woven around their treatment and burial. Clearly at the heart of these was basic hygiene, the need to dispose of the body as safely as possible, but there was a spiritual element too. The Romans entertained an ambivalence towards their dead. Corpses could be treated with honour or contempt; they were the remains of human beings but also inanimate things that could be (and needed to be) controlled by the living. Miscreants or social outcasts were punished in life but abuse, including mutilation and mockery, could continue after death. The ultimate disgrace that could be meted out to an individual was denial of burial altogether. Even the memory of an especially despised person could be erased by an act called *damnatio memoriae*, which involved confiscation of property; mention of the shamed one's name was forbidden, and their entire identity denied.[6]

The Roman attitude to marshy places, on the one hand, and to certain of the dead, on the other, may inform our approach to the interment of Iron Age people in bogs in northern and western Europe. For the Romans, both marshes and corpses were unlucky, perilous things, sources of pollution and instability that threatened the well-being of the living, and had therefore to be avoided or treated with special protective ritual practices. The humiliation and disgrace of certain Roman dead strikes a chord with the way that particular bog victims appear to have been dealt with before and at the time of their deaths. One other aspect of Roman attitudes to the dead might also have relevance; it concerns those who handled the bodies, the morticians and the undertakers. They had an especially low place in urban society: they were unclean, and were tattooed in order to display their profession to the world. They were often segregated, forced to live in ghettos on the edges of towns. They were unholy, physically and morally dirty, and in some instances they were only allowed to enter populated areas if on official mortuary business.[7] Here we may raise the question of how far those involved in interring ancient bog victims were connected with the corpses they were handling. Were they, too, polluted people to be shunned by their communities for their intimacy with the dead? Or were they, instead, people of high rank, priests (sometimes even Druids, perhaps) who were responsible at least for overseeing the rituals associated with bog deaths, if not physically involved?

THE FORMATION OF BOGS

Bogs are primaeval nature at its most fascinating – vast treeless
and inaccessible landscapes. In Northwest Europe, the landscape
was characterised by bogs for millennia following the last Ice Age
as the climate gradually became warmer and wetter.

PAULA ASINGH, 'THE MAGICAL BOG'[8]

There are two kinds of bog: low-level marshes, whose water is provided by groundwater seeping up from beneath vegetation in wet hollows, and raised bogs, fed from rain in regions of high levels of precipitation. The ancient European bogs in which bog bodies were interred are raised bogs (PL. II). The absence of oxygen in watery environments means that dead plant matter does not decay fully but stagnates in a kind of limbo. As more plants die, so the wet layers of vegetation build up over millennia, to form peat bogs.[9]

Raised bogs are living things, composed of 95 per cent water. Trees (apart from bog oak) do not grow there: it is too wet, sour and lacking in nutrients for them to flourish. Conversely, particular and highly distinctive plant species, such as the great sundew and the red whortleberry,[10] flourish in bogs (PL. III). The absence of trees, coupled with the bright green of bog mosses and other plant matter – and, of course, their uncultivable nature – served to set ancient bogs apart and, perhaps, imbued them with sanctity or, at least, an air of difference that had to be respected and placated.

Bog plant species: (left) *Sphagnum acutifolium* (aka red bog moss);
(right) *Vaccinium vitas idaea* (aka lingonberry or cowberry).

AIRLESS AND BUGLESS: MOSSES AND MEMORIES

On either side and in front wide fens and mires now lay,
stretching away southward and eastward into the dim half-light.
Mists curled and smoked from dark and noisome pools.
The reek of them hung stifling in the still air.

J.R.R. TOLKIEN, *THE LORD OF THE RINGS*[11]

This quotation, taken from the second part of Tolkien's trilogy, describes the ghastly region through which Frodo and Sam had to travel on their way to Mordor, abode of the Dark Lord Sauron.

The phenomenal preservative properties of peat bogs allow organic matter, including human remains, to survive virtually intact until it is exposed to the air during excavation. The traditional view is that this unique quality is due to two factors: lack of oxygen, which inhibits bacteriological activity, and the presence of bog acids. It is now realized that the most powerful agent in organic preservation is *Sphagnum*, otherwise known as polysaccharides. This material is present in living bog mosses and, when the moss dies, it slowly releases its *Sphagnum*, which has the unique property of binding calcium and nitrogen. It is the absence of these elements that is the most powerful inhibitor of bacteria and, at the same time, the released *Sphagnum* causes the tanning of human skin and soft tissue, together with any other organic material present: wood, horn, fur, hair, textiles and so on. It is the tanning process that turns ancient human skin deep brown and dyes the hair red. The downside of calcium inhibition is that bones frequently suffer, becoming soft and deformed.[12]

One of the other tanning agents found in peat bogs is the bark of neighbouring bog oaks that has fallen into the marshes during their period of growth. When Grauballe Man was first discovered in the 1950s, his conservators constructed an 'artificial bog', whose active tanning agent was oak bark. In addition to other preservative agents, his body was packed with this material in water; after 18 months, Grauballe Man's skin had turned into effectively tanned leather. As an experiment in conservation, it was remarkably successful.[13]

The use of oak as a means of preserving human bodies can be traced in prehistoric Britain as early as the Bronze Age, when a high-ranking middle-aged man was buried in a scooped-out oak coffin at Gristhorpe in North Yorkshire. He was at least 1.8 m (6 ft) tall, his height attesting

Sphagnum, the raised bog vegetation with the most important properties for the preservation of organic matter. The presence of *Sphagnum* has allowed the unique survival of ancient bog bodies, including their skin, hair and innards.

to a good diet; he was wrapped in a skin cloak and accompanied by rich grave goods including a bronze dagger. He had also suffered from a brain tumour that may have caused him to have seizures.[14] Maybe this, or his probable prowess as a warrior, led him to be buried in such an unusual way, in a manner that would ensure his survival as an ancestor-protector to his community.

Stranger than the Gristhorpe burial was the small group of bodies found at the Bronze Age settlement of Cladh Hallan on South Uist in the Western Isles of Scotland, dating to around 1600–1300 BC. The bodies found here appear to have acted as foundation deposits for the round-houses the community inhabited, so the living literally lived on top of their dead. But the most astonishing thing about the human remains is that they belonged to individuals whose dead bodies had been kept for as long as 300–500 years before their interment under the houses. The excavators, from the University of Sheffield, argue that the only way in which these curated bodies could have retained their physical integrity over such a long time was if some connective tissue had been preserved during the time between death and final burial. The most likely explanation is that their bodies were artificially preserved by mummification. It is thought that the natural processes of dissolution were interrupted firstly by the removal of the innards and secondly by the deposition of the remains in an acidic environment (as evidenced by the demineralization of the bone surfaces): this acid is very likely to have been a peat bog. The Cladh Hallan bodies were immersed in a boggy pool, taken out as bog bodies, wrapped up and curated for centuries and then buried beneath the houses of their descendants.

But something was done to the two adult corpses before their final interment. One body was that of a woman, two of whose teeth were removed after she died, with one carefully placed in each hand. Stranger still was the other burial, where the 'body' was an amalgam of three individuals: the head and neck came from one man, the jaw from another and the rest of the body from a third person. Even the times of curation varied: while the head had been kept for about 300–400 years before its burial, the body belonged to someone who had died 500 years earlier. People at Cladh Hallan seem to have practised time-bending to an extreme degree. And central to this manipulation of time was the acid bath of the peat bog in which the bodies were immersed soon after death.[15] The bog was the means of creating and preserving memories that spanned nearly a thousand years. At Cladh Hallan, though, it was not just time that was being managed and manipulated but the very individuals that were buried. By mixing up their bodies, identities in life were challenged and altered after death by those who survived them.

Gristhorpe Man, the mummies of Cladh Hallan and the Iron Age bog bodies of northern and western Europe have one thing in common: deliberate preservation. While the scientific properties and processes of tanning, bacteria inhibition and denial of oxygen could not have been fully appreciated in antiquity, it was nonetheless understood that certain conditions lent themselves to the interruption of decay. It is becoming increasingly evident to archaeologists that memory and linkages with the past were important to ancient communities. This connection might be expressed by persistent use and reuse of Neolithic chambered tombs,[16] the way objects and monuments were produced that wove the past into the present (such as the reuse of Neolithic flint axes in Gallo-Roman temples or the Irish Celts' interpretation of Neolithic passage graves as homes for their gods),[17] or by the erecting of specific and permanent memorials to the dead, such as can be seen in every churchyard. The immersion of bodies in bogs needs to be seen within this wider context of connection between then and now and, indeed, between now and the future.

Karin Sanders, a professor of Scandinavian archaeology at Berkeley, California, has likened the bog body phenomenon to the sequential actions of a camera, calling the bogs 'nature's own darkroom'.[18] She describes the preservative action of the bog as akin to the first camera shot, where the body has been freeze-framed by its immersion; the second shot happens when the ancient body is recovered and conserved, the third occurs when this body has been presented to the modern public gaze. Sanders further argues for the presence of both natural preservation and what she terms 'prosthetic memories'. The bodies in the bog are preserved by means of particular but wholly natural processes but, when they are disinterred, they are both subject to artificial conservation and exhibited as if they are models from the past. A good example of this contradiction can be witnessed in the Tollund Man, apparently superbly preserved, with facial wrinkles, beard stubble and peacefully closed eyes. That is how he is presented in numerous book illustrations and in his display case at Silkeborg Museum. In fact, he survives as a very partial body: the side of his torso that lay uppermost in the peat and his limbs were badly damaged. In order to present Tollund Man as he was when he had first been put into the bog, much of his body had to be constructed anew, as a prosthesis.

CONDEMNED MEN AND HEARTY BREAKFASTS

Tollund man probably committed suicide to escape his wife's cooking.

SIR MORTIMER WHEELER[19]

The preservative properties of bog chemicals sometimes allow the revelation of a very particular detail of an ancient life: the final meal. Internal organs, including the alimentary canal, frequently survive sufficiently intact to enable study of the food still present in the stomach and gut of a bog victim. (What is more, intestinal parasites are often present and can be identified: Lindow Man suffered from round worm and whip worm.[20]) For the most part, the bog people's last suppers consisted of varied vegetable matter that was made either into a kind of gruel or a griddled flatbread. Tollund Man's last meal was reconstructed for a television programme made not long after his discovery in the 1950s. The flamboyant archaeologist Sir Mortimer Wheeler was detailed to taste it, and commented that it tasted so vile that the wretched man was probably glad to die! This

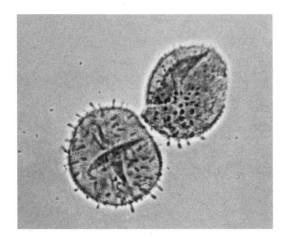

Pollen grains from Lindow Man's gut. Finds like this allow forensic
scientists to build a picture of the bogman's final meal.

unpalatable meal comprised a mushy porridge of barley, linseed and herbs,
together with sand grains and bog mosses. The absence of any fruit remains
suggests that he died in the dark and gloom of winter.[21]

The wide variety of seeds and cereals contained within some of these
meals suggests that trouble was taken to collect them, far in excess of
what was necessary for food production. It is almost as though those preparing the meal intended to include something from every part of the
landscape, so as to represent a range of environments. The contents of
Grauballe Man's gut revealed that more than 60 different types of plant
had been used in the preparation of his last meal of mash, a far bigger
final meal than Tollund Man's. The bulk of Grauballe's 'porridge' was
made up of cereals and the bitter-tasting weeds that grew among the
crops but more than 13 species of grass were represented. Meat was also
mixed up in the meal, for bits of bone were identified in the food remains.
All in all, the fare given to both these men was poor in both palatable and
nutritional terms.[22] The seemingly elaborate inclusion of so many plant
species might reflect a specially prepared 'ritual meal' but there is an
equal likelihood that the last food to pass the victim's lips was a kind of
'prison' fare, either because they died at a time of famine or because the
unpalatable food was fed to them deliberately in order to emphasize and
exacerbate their humiliation and degradation. The high levels of nitrogen
found through palaeodietary analysis of his fingernails indicate that the
Irish bog body known as Oldcroghan Man lived largely on a rich protein

and meat-based diet, as befitted his huge size. But the food remains in his gut consisted of buttermilk and cereal,[23] much cheaper fare, and this supports the idea of a deliberately 'low-key' final meal.

The bogmen of Lindow had very different diets from those found at Tollund and Grauballe. Lindow Man (Lindow II) had consumed what has been described as an 'upmarket' meal just before he was killed.[24] His dinner was composed largely of cereals, with few weeds, and the presence of charred grains indicates that he had eaten a form of griddled bread.[25] The state of Lindow II's body suggests that he was well-nourished, with finely kept hands, so his final relatively high-status meal might reflect his rank during his lifetime rather than a special death-supper. Lindow III's gut showed that he had eaten different fare, containing large amounts of hazelnuts. These were commonly available, and there is evidence that hazel grew in the vicinity of Lindow Moss.

The most remarkable thing about Lindow II's gut contents was the presence of mistletoe pollen, only four grains but sufficient for confidence that it was deliberately ingested. In her discussion of the possible significance of this, the Celtic scholar Anne Ross commented in her article 'Lindow Man and the Celtic Tradition'[26] that large quantities of mistletoe were also found in the covering of Gristhorpe Man's oak coffin. Ross believed that the presence of mistletoe in Lindow Man's food suggests a connection with the ancient Druids, citing in support of this theory the famous description by Pliny of the Gallic Druids' grove with its sacred rite of mistletoe gathering.[27] But it is not necessary to cite Druidic rituals to explain the presence of this parasitic plant in Lindow Man's stomach contents, for mistletoe has the reputation of possessing pharmacological properties, particularly for the control of nervous disorders.[28] So it may have been given to Lindow Man to calm him and to render him more amenable to his terrible death.

Other curious substances are occasionally found in the guts of bog bodies. The most potentially exciting of these is ergot (*Claviceps purpurea*), a fungus that grows on rotting rye and barley.[29] If ingested in sufficient quantities, ergot poisoning causes hallucinations and severe physical symptoms (known as St. Anthony's Fire), such as unbearable burning sensations, convulsions and catastrophic circulatory failure, causing the body to decay, and its extremities to turn black and fall off while still alive.[30] Grauballe Man was found to have the alkaloid toxins caused by ergot in his gut. The Dutch archaeologist Wijnand van der

Ergot, a fungus growing on ears of barley. It is highly toxic to humans, and has been found in the gut of ancient bog people such as Grauballe Man.

Sanden argues that 'Grauballe Man had ingested such large quantities of these substances that he must have been hallucinating and suffering convulsions and burning sensations in his mouth, hands and feet... The man was probably in a coma, or possibly even dead, when his throat was slit.'[31] But some scholars are sceptical about the levels of toxicity in Grauballe Man's innards, arguing that – according to current EU guidelines concerning acceptable amounts of ergot in human diets – the quantity found in the Danish bogman is on the upper limit of what is considered safe (500 mg), suggesting that it might not have had a markedly toxic effect.[32] But ergot is highly visible on cereals and this perhaps means that it *was* given to the bogmen deliberately, either to poison them and thus make their last moments even more horrifying than the violence they sustained, or to induce particular behaviour associated with ritual activity. These issues are explored further in later chapters.

POOLS OF SILENCE AND DANGEROUS BODIES

They lie in all the pools, pale faces, deep, deep under the dark water.
I saw them: grim faces and evil, and noble faces and sad. Many faces
proud and fair, and weeds in their silver hair.

J.R.R. TOLKIEN, *THE LORD OF THE RINGS*[33]

The climax of the second volume of Tolkien's *Lord of the Rings* trilogy is the end of the great ring's journey to Mount Doom in the land of Mordor, the Dark Lord Sauron's realm where the one ring had been forged. On their way there to destroy the ring (and thereby Sauron himself), Frodo and Sam are led by Gollum through the Dead Marshes. There, Sam and Frodo encounter huge numbers of the dead, slain in past battles, their bodies preserved in the bog, their pallid faces upturned as though sleeping.

Tolkien's vivid description of the horrors of the 'Dead Marshes' chimes with the cautious attitudes to boggy places displayed by such classical writers as Vitruvius and Columella (see p.51). This may throw light on the disposal of certain human bodies in such inimical places. In order to explore this idea more fully, it is interesting to take a sideways glance at a very different context from that of Iron Age Europe, namely Zorastrianism, the state religion of ancient Persia from the 6th century BC until the 7th century AD. Zoroastrianism is still followed by scattered minority groups, particularly Parsees, in parts of present-day Iran and India. Their attitude to the human dead has the central tenet that corpses are unstable and in a dangerously impure state. Bodies cannot be disposed of either in the earth or by fire because of the risk of pollution. The only safe way of dealing with the dead is by exposing their bodies in high places, the so-called 'Towers of Silence'. In this way, the flesh is quickly consumed by vultures and other creatures. The sun's rays gather the deceased's spirit towards the sky, and the fleshless bones can be collected and buried. It is the flesh rather than the bare skeleton that is perilous.[34]

Exploration of Zoroastrian attitudes to the deceased can serve as a way of understanding how people in European antiquity may have viewed some of their dead, causing them to act in a particular manner when disposing of them. It is possible to see the perception of ancient boggy burial places through the lens of the Parsees' 'Towers of Silence', and suggest that ancient bog burials might have been perceived as 'Pools of Silence', where the quiet, wet darkness somehow neutralized the dangerous dead (PL. II). The bog bodies might have been so placed either because of who they were in life or how and why they met their deaths. The bog victims all seem to have died violently and prematurely, and that – in itself – might have been sufficiently polluting to cause the living members of their communities to choose marshy graves for them. But we should not assume that the perception of ancient European bogs was the same as that indicated by Roman writers. The bogs may have been special places but not necessarily evil places. Unlike the Parsee 'Towers of Silence', whose purpose was to disperse flesh as fast as possible, the choice of burial in marshy locations seems to have been the opposite: to retain the integrity of the human body in perpetuity. An important factor in the preservation of human bodies in bogs is temperature. Ideally, it needs to be cold when the bodies are put into the water, and so we should expect the majority of the ancient bog victims to have died and been interred in winter.[35] However, this is by no means always so: the remains of fruit from the gut have revealed that several of the bodies from the Netherlands are likely to have died in the late summer or autumn.[36]

We cannot know exactly what was behind bog body burials, but we can be fairly certain that the perpetrators wished these bodies to be placed in spiritually charged, dangerous places, where they would never decay

JUST LIKE US: KEPT BODIES

The bog bodies were unwrapped on May 6...and it was revealed that
they were wrapped naked in a large cloth. Dr Schlabow [a textile expert]
moaned: 'No shirt, no pants!' And I grumbled: 'Not even the tiniest
buckle'. That is how the eagerly awaited opening of the block of peat
was recorded by Director K.H. Jacob-Friesen.

S. VEIL, 'TWO BODIES IN WOOLLEN CLOAKS'[37]

The context for this remark was the discovery of two ancient bog bodies found lying back to back in a peat bog at Hunteburg in Germany in April 1949. They were both men and they had been interred together and covered by woollen blankets. The comment about their nakedness was made by the Director of the Landesmuseum in Hanover, where they were taken for study, still in their block of peat. At first, it was suspected that the Hunteburg bogmen were victims of the Nazis, but it was quickly realized that they were ancient. Although the bog acids had dissolved away the men's bones, the skin was perfectly preserved as if it were tanned leather,

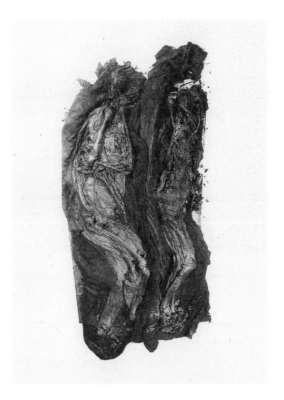

A pair of Iron Age bogmen found together, naked, beneath
two woollen cloaks at Hunteburg, Germany.

retaining the ghostly impression of where the bones had been. Even the
skin covering their genitals was intact and their manicured fingernails
suggest that they were of high rank. Moreover, the blankets in which they
were wrapped were of high-quality cloth, and each might have taken a
pair of skilled weavers a whole year to make.[38] They had originally had
blond hair and trimmed beards. One of them was about 20 years old,
the other nearer 30. The plant remains caught in the blankets revealed
that the two men had died in late summer. Each man had been carefully
buried in the bog, his blanket tucked neatly around his body. It was not
possible to establish the cause of death but they had died at the same time
as one another.

The duo from Hunteburg are not the only pair of young men to have
been entombed together in a bog. The same is true of a couple from
Weerdinge, Bourtangermoor, in the Netherlands, whose bodies were
interred actually touching one another (PL. VII). This intimacy at first

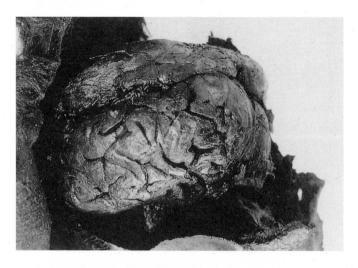

The beautifully preserved brain of the Windeby Child, an adolescent who died
and was placed in a peat bog in Schleswig-Holstein in the 1st century AD.

led to the assumption that they were the bodies of a man and a woman,
but it was later discovered that both were male.[39] When they were found
during peat cutting, in June 1904, one body was actually resting against
the extended right arm of the other. They were turned towards each other
as if in the act of embracing.[40] Sadly, attempts to study their DNA have
failed (immersion in bogs tends to make DNA analysis very difficult),
so it has not been possible to establish whether or not they were brothers or cousins. One of the men had sustained a huge wound in his upper
abdomen, exposing the small intestine, an injury that led to speculation
about the possible use of the individual for divinatory purposes. Both
Strabo and Tacitus allude to the practice of killing sacrificial victims –
among the Cimbri of North Germany and in north Wales – and consulting
their entrails to foretell the future and the will of the gods.[41]

Perhaps the most startling element in the preservation of bodies in
peat bogs is the recovery of the human brain, sometimes virtually intact.
The brain belonging to the adolescent who died at Windeby in Schleswig-
Holstein is remarkably preserved and, although the right hemisphere is
damaged, the convolutions of the left side are clearly visible.[42] It is not only
the brain that provides an intimacy between ancient individuals and those
who study them. I was touched by seeing the deformed ear of the disembodied male head from a bog at Worsley Moss in Lancashire, found in 1958.
And close scrutiny of the preserved portion of his neck revealed the marks

The body of Tollund Man, lying as though asleep. His fine-featured
face, with its high cheekbones and closed eyelids, has been perfectly
preserved by the *Sphagnum* growing in the bog.

of a cord showing that he had been strangled before he was beheaded. Is
that deformed ear the key to his life and his death? Had he been a professional fighter who suffered a 'cauliflower ear'? Or was he marked out for
death because of a congenital defect?[43]

But it is the face of Tollund Man that above all demonstrates the preservative power of the bog. To look at it, in a photograph or even as a personal
encounter, is to come literally face to face with a 2000-year-old person with
whom one can imagine holding a conversation or sharing a meal. Without
his leather cap, he looks even more real,[44] with his close-cropped hair,
heavily wrinkled forehead, level brows, aquiline nose and serenely pursed
lips, amid a light stubble of beard. His heavy-lidded eyes seem only just to
have shut in sleep, as if a touch on the hand or the cheek would cause them
to fly wide open to gaze at the one who had disturbed him.

CHAPTER 4

Crime Scene Investigation:
The Application of
Forensic Science

Forensic investigations of bodies found under circumstances
suggestive of a criminal act usually commence with an examination of
the scene of the crime carried out in collaboration with the police.

GREGERSEN, JURIK & LYNNERUP, 'FORENSIC INJURIES AND CAUSE OF DEATH
[OF GRAUBALLE MAN]'[1]

Between 2001 and 2004 new investigations were undertaken on the bodies
of both Tollund Man and Grauballe Man, by a forensic team led by Niels
Lynnerup of the Laboratory of Biological Anthropology at the Institute of
Forensic Medicine, University of Copenhagen. The aim of these studies
was to answer elusive questions about the manner of their lives and
deaths, using the latest techniques developed by forensic scientists primarily for modern crime scenes.

The discovery of bog bodies, whether in the 1950s (the case at Tollund
and Grauballe) or the present, necessitates two forms of crime investigation: real and virtual. At first, it is unclear if the body is ancient or modern.
Earlier chapters have explored the way in which, for instance, the head
from Lindow Moss and the two bodies from Hunteburg were initially considered to be modern victims of violence, the British remains supposedly
that of a woman killed by her husband (who confessed to the crime) and
those from Germany considered to have been the object of Nazi atrocities.

Given the well-preserved state of these bog bodies, it is easy to see how, when they were first discovered, they were taken for recent murder victims. It takes modern forensic science to tell us that these bodies were those of ancient individuals; the key scientific tool is radiocarbon dating. So one of the first and most essential aims is to establish the chronology of the death.

RADIOCARBON DATING

Research into atomic physics and radioactivity gathered momentum during the Second World War, and by chance it provided archaeologists with the most valuable chronological tool they will probably ever possess: radiocarbon (or C14) dating, first developed by W.F. Libby. Radiocarbon dating is independent of any other dating mechanism; one of its chief values is that it provides an absolute rather than relative chronology. The technique depends on a radioactive isotope, carbon 14 or C14, which is absorbed by all living organisms, whether human, animal or plant. When an organism dies, it ceases to take in this isotope and the C14 decays (like all radioactive isotopes) at a regular rate. Its half-life is 5730 years, meaning that half the carbon 14 atoms present decay in that period, then half again in the next 5730 years, and so on. The principle of radiocarbon dating is to measure the amount of C14 left in a sample of organic material. In practice, the process is much more complex and needs to take in all kinds of factors, including contamination and fluctuations in the amount of C14 in the atmosphere over time.[2] But the principle is sound and the method is still the key to dating once-living things, including bog bodies. It was radiocarbon dating that indicated the ancient status of all prehistoric and Roman-period bog bodies. This dating method will not give a date within months or even years, but it will provide a time bracket of perhaps 100–200 years either way. The study of the Grauballe Man, found in 1952, just when radiocarbon dating was being first developed, shows how the technique has been continually refined and sharpened to provide tighter dates. But even the most advanced methods still give a date for Grauballe Man's death no more precise than between 400 and 200 BC, although the likelihood is that he died in the early 4th century.[3]

The attempts to date Lindow Man using radiocarbon indicate very clearly how tricky the process can be, especially for bog bodies, for there is always the danger of contamination from the surrounding mosses and other plant matter present in the marshes, and sometimes bog plants can actually grow up through the bodies themselves. Several samples were taken from the body – bone, skin and hair – and some from the surrounding peat, and were sent off to the Isotope Measurements Laboratory at Harwell, near Oxford. Comparisons were then made between the analyses undertaken at Harwell and by the University of Oxford's AMS (Accelerator Mass Spectrometry) laboratory, and there were found to be significant discrepancies. After a great deal of testing and counter-testing, there is confidence that the Lindow Man dates to within a hundred years of the 1st century AD.[4]

AUTOPSY

When Tollund Man was discovered in Jutland in 1950, his body was subjected to the most advanced post-mortem techniques available at the time. He was X-rayed and autopsied, primarily in order to examine his digestive tract. His surviving right thumb was fingerprinted by the police, and was found to have 'a typical loop pattern, common also in fingerprints of today'.[5]

In October 2004, Tollund Man was removed from his bullet-proof display case in the Silkeborg Museum and transported, accompanied by a police escort, to the hospital at Århus for new and cutting-edge forensic analysis. A minute camera mounted on a probe, called an endoscope, was inserted into the bogman's head, permitting scientists to see his beautifully preserved brain. His head and neck were then put through a CT (computerized tomography) scanner, the results clearly showing a fracture of the hyoid bone in his neck, a sure sign that Tollund Man had been throttled (something already known because the noose was still around his neck when he was discovered). In order to determine the exact cause of death – whether by strangulation or hanging – an infrared camera was used to examine the back of the neck wound in precise detail. Niels Lynnerup found a significant V-shape left by the rope, indicating that the man had been strung up, hanged. For in this method of killing, the weight of the body pulls the noose up into a V at the back of the head. This is an important detail for interpretation of the manner and circumstances of Tollund Man's death. Hanging is a public, collective act, designed to present a spectacle for the community. The physicality of hanging, like

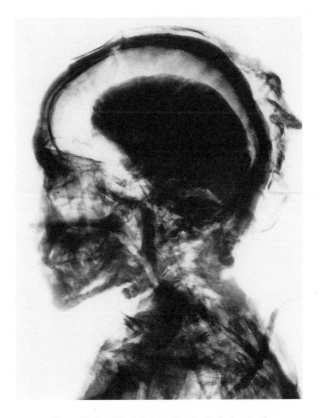

X-ray of Tollund Man's head and neck, clearly showing the
intact brain. This man was hanged and carefully positioned
in a Jutland bog in the 4th century BC.

crucifixion, displays the body for all to see – very different from a clandestine act of thuggery in which the killer creeps up behind a victim by
stealth and garrottes them.[6]

Similar forensic tests were done at Århus in 2000 on the female bog
body from Haraldskaer, found in 1835. Radiocarbon dating established
that she died in the early Iron Age, around 490 BC. The new autopsy
showed beyond doubt that she had died not from being pinned down in
the bog and drowned, as previously assumed, but by strangulation. A fine
red line around her throat was revealed by X-ray analysis. Sadly, because
she was found so early in the 19th century (when forensic science as we
know it did not exist), the Haraldskaer Woman's internal organs were not
kept, and so vital information about her life and her final moments was
thrown away. But the new autopsy did reveal that, although elderly by

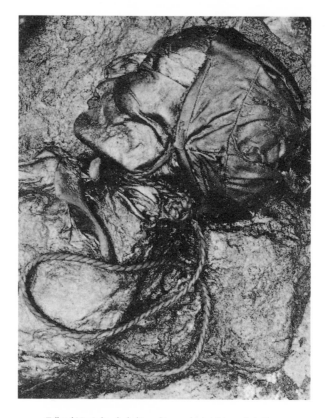

Tollund Man's head, clad in a skin cap; his neck is encircled by a
noose. The man's flesh and the rope that hanged him have been
preserved by the peat bog in which he lay.

Iron Age standards (45–50 years old), she was in extremely good physical
condition, her bones showing none of the arthritic signs of wear and tear
that might be expected from a woman of that age who had spent her life
doing repetitive manual tasks such as grinding corn. She was also sufficiently well-nourished to have been quite plump, so she certainly did not
live on famine food.[7]

GRAUBALLE MAN AND THE APPLIANCE OF SCIENCE

In 2001 and 2002 the Danish bog body known as Grauballe Man (PL. VI)
was subjected to a battery of scientific tests at the University Hospital
in Århus, using all the latest technology usually reserved for the treatment of living patients or for the newly dead. These fresh analyses had

two main purposes: to ensure and improve the long-term preservation of this 2000-year-old man's bones, his skin, hair, brain, innards and other soft tissue, and to find out as much as possible about his life, death and afterlife. Not only was the body subjected to radiocarbon dating, which indicated that he may have died as early as 390 BC,[8] but he was X-rayed, scanned using CT and MRI (Magnetic Resonance Imaging), and given endoscopies. His skin was examined with Infrared Reflectography (IRr) to ascertain its thickness, anomalies, the presence or absence of any body art, such as tattoos, and to establish changes that may have occurred since the body was originally 'tanned' during initial conservation in the 1950s. These tests were designed to answer questions about Grauballe Man's age, his state of health, his daily life and diet. All this information, of course, allows the construction not only of this individual's life and death experience but also a clearer picture of what it meant to live in northern Europe in the 4th century BC.

In order to address issues of conservation, it was necessary to under-stand exactly what preservation processes had taken place in the 1950s, and to correct and enhance the quality of the body's stability, so as to prevent further shrinkage and desiccation as far as possible. One of the first jobs for the new scientific team was to construct a new 'bed' for Grauballe Man, to enable him to be transported easily for examination, with the minimum of stress to the fragile remains. A new display case was made for him, to replace the one built in the 1950s. The old case had allowed the ingress of deleterious amounts of oxygen and, because the levels of knowledge available when he was first conserved were much lower than in the early 21st century, inevitable deterioration had occurred. The new case was climate-controlled, with a nitrogen atmosphere. Humidity and light-levels were carefully monitored in order to facilitate the optimum conservation of the bone and soft tissue. The skin surface was cleaned and analyzed,[9] and the teeth and gut examined, in order to see to what extent previous conservation treatments had acted negatively on the body. It was concluded that the 1950s team had done an extremely effective job in conserving Grauballe Man,[10] but that additional new treat-ments would enhance his preservation for posterity.

The raft of new scientific analyses carried out at Århus Hospital in 2001–2 examined the body in minute detail, from head to toe and from the surface of the skin to the deepest internal structures. The cause of death was obvious from the gaping wound in Grauballe Man's throat, but radiological and CT scans and an endoscopy indicated that his skull fracture – presumed in the 1950s to have been a pre-mortem injury – was in fact post-mortem. He had, however, sustained a leg fracture from a heavy blow to his shin before he died. DNA and blood-group analyses were not possible on this body.[11]

Grauballe Man's bones were subjected to microscopic analysis in order to determine his age and to identify any osteopathology. He was a mature adult over 30 years old and in reasonable health.[12] Dental examination endorsed the age indicated by the bone analyses. But scanning electron microscopy and micro-CT scans showed up Harris Lines on the teeth, indicating that Grauballe Man had suffered interruptions in his development during his childhood, probably due to poor nutrition. He had also suffered trauma to his jaw while alive, perhaps from a blow. Extensive toothwear shows that he had had a gritty diet (fine stone fragments from grinding stones would have found their way into his bread or porridge).[13]

Grauballe Man's gut was reanalyzed, using a variety of scientific techniques including MRI. The range of plants he had eaten, both wild and cultivated, was extensive; at least 60 species were represented in the intestinal remains. Plant roots had grown into the body while it reposed in the bog, and this discovery alerted the radiocarbon dating team to the possibility of cross-contamination and to the need to ensure that the samples from his tissue and the intrusive plant roots were compared.[14] Even samples of scalp-hair were sent for tests: isotopic analysis indicated a stable mixed diet of vegetable matter and meat. The bright red hair colour was found to be due to bog chemicals, and his original hair colour might have been quite different.[15]

THREE IRISH BOGMEN

The Iron Age bog body of a young man from Gallagh, near Castleblakeny in County Galway, was discovered in 1821, long before the development of the scientific techniques necessary to preserve his soft tissue after he was taken from his boggy burial ground. Contemporary records indicate that he had been interred wearing a knee-length deerskin cape, with a twisted hazel noose around his neck, his grave-site marked with wooden posts at his head and feet. He was left in the bog until 1829,[16] but during that period he was dug up several times in order to be displayed to the public. By the time he reached the National Museum in Dublin, his body had suffered from marked deterioration, and he survives today as a shrunken, dried-up mummy.[17] By contrast, the two bodies from central Ireland discovered in 2003, Oldcroghan Man and Clonycavan Man, have been given the 'voice' denied to Gallagh Man by the application of the same latest scientific techniques used to provide such a detailed picture of Grauballe Man, the bodies from Lindow Moss and other bog people found in the late 20th and early 21st centuries.

The finds from 2003, found within a few months of each other prompted intense interest both from the media and the international scientific community. In January 2006, the BBC's *Timewatch* programme focused worldwide attention on these strangely preserved bog victims, and attracted academic researchers from a wide range of disciplines. The Irish bodies' media exposure led to the setting up of a permanent exhibition, entitled 'Kingship and Sacrifice' at the National Museum in Dublin. There followed a multidisciplinary research programme that lasted 18 months, while the two bodies were subjected to careful scrutiny.[18] For the duration of the study, staff in the museum's conservation laboratories constructed an artificial bog environment that kept the bodies at a constant refrigerated temperature of 4°C and so replicated the conditions in which they had been buried.

The scientific investigative programme involved a number of phases, beginning with non-destructive, non-invasive techniques. The first stage involved physical examination: fingerprinting, the analysis of hairstyle (on the Clonycavan Man) and recording the bodies by drawing and photography. In the second stage, the 'imaging phase', the bodies were X-rayed and subjected to the 'virtual autopsies' provided by CT and MRI scanning, the former being particularly useful in giving 3D views of the bodies. Their skin was examined using infrared and ultraviolet techniques in the hope of discovering body art, though none was found. There followed a destructive phase, but one which involved taking only the tiniest samples from the bodies: of skin, hair and soft tissue. These were sampled in order to answer questions concerning the dates of the two men's deaths, their diet, the state of their health and to attempt to harvest DNA. Gut contents were sampled in order to glean details of their final meal. Perhaps the most interesting aspect of this research programme was the forward-thinking of the team, for extra samples from both men were taken to be stored for future analysis, as and when new technologies should be developed. Conservation was the final issue confronting the research team investigating the Clonycavan and Oldcroghan bodies. They were put into a bath of polyethylene glycol, a water-soluble wax preparation, for a month and then freeze-dried for a further six weeks.

So what were the results all of these scientific analyses? Radiocarbon dating indicates that both these men died in the middle Iron Age, around 300 BC, perhaps at the same time, or possibly Clonycavan Man died some decades earlier. Clonycavan Man was slightly built and about 1.79 m (5 ft 9 ins) tall. Analysis of his hair revealed that he had had a mainly vegetarian diet and certainly his last meal was plant-based. This may mean that vegetation was readily available and that therefore he died during the summer or early autumn. No DNA could be recovered. He was between 25 and 40 years old when he died, and his death was extremely violent: an axe was used to rain blows upon his head and upper body, killing him almost immediately, and he had been disembowelled. Perhaps the most interesting feature of Clonycavan Man was his hair. It had been treated with a gel made from a mixture of vegetable oils and the resin of a conifer (*Pinus pinaster*) that grows in the region of the French and Spanish Pyrenees.

Oldcroghan Man was a much bigger, heftier fellow than his fellow bogman, standing almost 2 m (6 ft 5 ins) tall and with a physique to match. Like Clonycavan Man, he was a mature adult when he died. Analysis of his finely trimmed fingernails revealed that he had enjoyed a protein-rich diet, leading to assumptions that he may have died in winter, when weaker animals would have been culled for meat. But his last meal was a vegetarian one, consisting of cereals washed down with buttermilk. Internal examinations showed scarring to his lungs, so he must have had pleurisy at some stage in his life. The powerful, well-nourished physique of Oldcroghan Man was not the only sign that he was a man of senior rank in his community. Like Lindow Man, he was placed naked in the marsh but for a single armlet made of leather, with fine decorative designs on a copper-alloy panel.

CASTING FORENSIC LIGHT ON THE LINDOW MEN

When Lindow Man (Lindow II) was discovered, piecemeal, during peat cutting between August 1984 and September 1988, the condition of the body, mangled though it was, made it immediately clear that he had been deliberately interred beneath the surface of the bog just after his death. Had he been left exposed even for a short time, his body would have been scavenged by foxes and other wildlife and insects would have laid their eggs on the surface of his skin: none of that had occurred.[19] These forensic details illuminate the immediate post-mortem actions of his killers or the witnesses to his death. He could have been left to rot on the bog surface, but it was clearly considered important to put him underneath, whether for fear of pollution, respect or the perceived need to preserve the body in perpetuity. He died in winter when the bog was freezing cold.[20]

Just as scrapings from the fingernails of modern murder victims are routinely taken for the analysis of skin or fabric debris that might identify the attacker, so peat from under the fingernails of Lindow II was tested. Scientists were particularly interested to find out whether these scrapings might contain evidence of minerals (woad or indigo, for instance) that could point to the presence of body paint.[21] Other peat samples from around the body were also taken for the same reason; the hope was that if such minerals were originally present on the skin, they might have leached out onto the surrounding soil. But the results from Lindow II were negative.

Analysis of Lindow III's skin, however, told a different story. 'Unusual concentrations of minerals found in his skin'[22] suggested to the forensic team that this individual had been adorned with a blue body paint made from copper minerals. There is tentative 'evidence' for the presence of tattoos on other prehistoric European bog bodies, but this suggestion is based on old documentation relating to bodies found in the 19th and early 20th centuries that is impossible to verify, for the bodies in question have not survived.[23] Yet there is evidence that people were tattooed in ancient Europe. One of the best examples is the Neolithic 'Iceman' (known as Ötzi) found in 1991, deep-frozen in the Austrian Ötztaler Alps. In his case, the skin was so well preserved by the ice that it was possible for the naked eye to discern a pattern of blue marks, made by puncturing the skin and rubbing in a charcoal-based compound. Some of the marks were concentrated around joints, leading to speculation as to whether these marks could have been intended to have a medical, healing, function.[24] If the body of Lindow III had been painted or tattooed, what was the purpose of such body art? In his discussion of the Iceman's tattoos, the archaeologist Konrad Spindler put forward a range of explanations: the enhancement of beauty, signatures of status (high or low), of belonging to (or exclusion from) certain groups, marks of valour in battle, signs of therapeutic 'acupuncture' or ritual markings.[25] John Speed's volume *The History of Great*

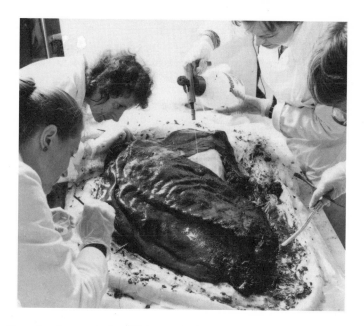

The post-mortem examination of Lindow Man by the British Museum. He was a young adult male, killed and placed in a peat bog in Cheshire, northwest England, in the 1st century AD.

Britaine, printed in 1611, contains a woodcut of an Iron Age Briton, a long curved (anachronistic) sword at his belt, a round shield in his left hand, a spear and a severed human head in his right. He is naked and covered in tattoos, signs of his prowess as a warrior.[26] Speed's illustration was clearly inspired by Julius Caesar's comment about the blue woad-painted people he encountered in wild Britannia.[27]

A crucially important element in the forensic analysis of Lindow Man concerned the nature of his injuries. Visual scrutiny, CT scanning and xeroradiography[28] revealed a constellation of wounds, including skull fractures and lacerations, injuries to the upper spine (commensurate with neck breakage during garrotting), a gash in the neck (consistent with throat-cutting) and the ligature on the neck that throttled the life out of him. The position of the head wounds indicates that Lindow Man was standing or kneeling when he was attacked (PL. IX). The unfortunate man had therefore been subjected to multiple injuries, of which at least three (the strangulation, throat and head wounds) were each individually fatal.[29] The plethora of serious injuries suggests that something was going on other than a straightforward dispatch. Whether or not it points to a ritual killing is considered in later chapters.

AN IMPIOUS GAZE?

Before you were clothed in sable and marten,
And decked with precious jewels,
Gems and pearls in your golden hair,
Wicked thoughts on your mind.

Now you lie naked, arid, foul,
With your bald head
Blacker far than the oak-stake
With which you were wed to the bog.

STEEN STEENSEN BLICHER, *QUEEN GUNHILD*[30]

In his 'Before' and 'After' poem, Blicher expresses the unease he felt about the exposure to modern eyes of an ancient person, the Iron Age woman from Haraldskaer known as 'Queen Gunhild', whose body had been intended to lie undisturbed in the bog forever. A chapter in Karin Sanders' book *Bodies in the Bog and the Archaeological Imagination*, is entitled 'Erotic Digging'.[31] One of the themes she explores is the ethical issue of the modern gaze, a scrutiny that not only concerns the outward appearance but the innermost recesses and orifices of the ancient bog body. Forensic science and the use of present-day autopsy techniques in order to milk the body of all its secrets may be perceived as a kind of violation, almost as a form of rape. In a way, the fate of ancient bodies exposed to detailed and invasive study is little different from that meted out to present-day victims of sudden death, whether through natural causes, accident or murder. The lifeless body is helpless, lying inert upon a slab while every part of it is probed, entered, analyzed and sampled. Forensic science provides wonderful opportunities to obtain information about past people, their society and culture, but it also raises ethical concerns about the way in which these ancient bodies are, in some senses, abused. The bodies of those hapless individuals who met their deaths in the remote bogs are objectified, they become artifacts and it is all too possible to forget their humanity and their right to human dignity. One method of scientific analysis provides the means of giving back to the bog bodies some of that robbed dignity, of de-objectifying them by returning their human identity. This is done by giving them faces and even voices.

FACING BOG BODIES

As poles to tents and walls to houses so are bones to living creatures,
for other features naturally take form from them and change with them.

GALEN, *DE ANATOMICIS ADMINISTRATIONIBUS*[32]

The principal purpose of all the foregoing scientific analyses is to construct a picture of Iron Age bog victims, how they lived and died. But one
cluster of techniques remains to be explored: those that would literally
bring ancient bog bodies face to face with their 21st-century public. The
most important of these is facial reconstruction. This was a technique
pioneered by Mikhail Gerasimov in the 1920s.[33] Another scientist in the
forefront of this field of research was Richard Neave of the Department
of Medical Illustration at the University of Manchester. In the 1980s, he
worked on the reconstruction of Lindow Man's face (PL. XII).[34] Neave's
skill has been used not only for bog body research; it has also been
invaluable in the identification of modern victims of violent death
where the soft tissue is absent. The double frontispiece of the British
Museum publication *Lindow Man*[35] shows the extent of Neave's skill
and that of his colleagues. On the left is the infrared photograph of
Lindow Man's head as it came out of the bog: grotesquely squashed
and distorted by the weight of the peat in which he was buried. On the
right is Richard Neave's suggested reconstruction: it shows the dignified
face of a young man with high cheekbones, well-defined brows, dark
up-springing hair, his chin and upper lip adorned by a neatly barbered
beard and moustache.

As the Roman imperial physician Galen of Pergamum (in Asia Minor)
wrote in the 2nd century AD, physiognomy is based to a large extent upon
the underlying bony structures of the skull. So by careful measurements
of key points on the facial bones, it should be possible to reconstruct
the soft tissue to a fair degree. But Lindow Man presented a particular
problem because the skull was too delicate and too crushed to use as scaffolding. Neave and his team overcame this obstacle by building a model of
Lindow Man's skull using photographs and radiographs. Once the model
skull had been created in clay, a plaster cast was taken, to be used as the
base upon which the soft tissue would be built up. This clay model had
to compensate for the distortion of his head and the result could only
be an approximation to the original shape of the skull. The first step in

constructing Lindow Man's face was the insertion of wooden pegs into the plaster cast at 24 precise points. The amount of projection for each peg was based on the average thickness of 20th-century male facial soft tissue. Glass eyes were placed in the eye sockets, the muscle groups, glands and the subcutaneous tissue of the face and neck built up. The whole process was designed to reconstruct the face from inside to outside, using the skull as the basic template. The final stages were key to presenting Lindow Man as a real individual, so care was taken over skin tone, the irises of the eyes and the hair.[36]

As technology advances in the early 21st century, it has become a basic tool in facial reconstruction, although many of Neave's techniques used on the Lindow face are still employed in the process. Neave himself utilized new and improved scientific methods when he worked on the Yde Girl's face in the 1990s, most importantly CT scanning of the skull for its initial reconstruction. One of the great benefits of computer technology is that even defects, such as distortion or missing fragments of the skull, can be corrected. The model of the Yde Girl's skull was made of a synthetic resin rather than clay and plaster, but clay was still used for making the muscles and other soft tissues. Then a model of the girl's head was created out of wax, a material which, when painted, lends itself to

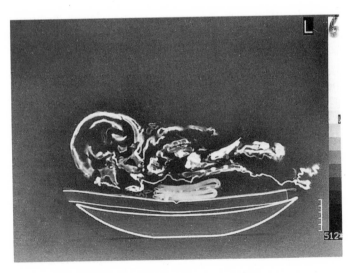

CT examination of the Yde Girl, at the Academic Hospital, Groningen in 1992. The body was re-scanned by Richard Neave at Manchester University prior to his reconstruction of her face.

the textured warmth of human skin. Finally genuine blonde human hair was inserted into the scalp. The result (shown in PL. XIII) was a portrait of a living girl, whose basic likeness can be seen on modern people walking the streets today.[37]

The reconstruction of Grauballe Man's face was undertaken in 2002 by Caroline Wilkinson at the University of Manchester. Her task presented particular challenges because the skull was so distorted (already misshapen because of the pressure of peat and further damaged by being trodden on soon after the body's discovery!). The skull was replicated in synthetic resin by means of stereolithography using CT information. The model was then cut into sections with a small saw and stuck together again using potter's clay. This allowed distortions in the original skull to be re-cast. The next stage was to produce a plaster cast of the skull from a mould made from alginic acid (a gelatinous carbohydrate found principally in seaweed). The skull itself provided a relatively poor scaffolding on which to build Grauballe Man's face, but the excellent quality of the original black-and-white photos taken when he was discovered in 1952 provided detail for the facial reconstruction. The replica skull was mounted on a pole and holes drilled into it at 32 anatomical points at a 90 degree angle to the face. Data from white European 40–49-year-old men were used for reference. Wooden pegs were driven into the holes and these provided guidelines for the application of replica soft tissue using layers of clay for the modelling of muscles, glands and cartilage. The skin was made from thinly rolled sheets of clay, and the eyeballs from plaster. The finished result showed the world a finely sculpted middle-aged male face complete with lambent eyes, frown lines between the eyebrows, nasal clefts and carefully delineated hair.[38]

Research by the University of Bradford on the well-preserved Bronze Age skeleton from Gristhorpe in Yorkshire provides a fitting coda to this chapter and its final section. Work carried out between 2006 and 2008 produced a wonderful new insight into this 4,000-year-old man. The scientific evidence indicated that he was tall, strong and well-nourished. Oxygen-strontium analysis of his teeth demonstrated that he was local and lived in the area for most of his life. He was in his sixties when he died, and had enjoyed a rich and varied diet. The preservation of Gristhorpe Man's skull was so good that the osteologist Alan Ogden was able to make a successful facial reconstruction. But what was especially thrilling was that his skills in dentistry led him to develop computer software that has allowed this prehistoric Yorkshireman to 'speak' for the first time since his death in

The reconstructed face of Gristhorpe Man, a 4000-year-old body of a man from Yorkshire, northern England, preserved in a waterlogged oak coffin. Scientists have even managed to give him back his voice.

the Bronze Age.[39] Despite the necessary use of computer-generated sound, Ogden managed to produce a lifelike 'voice'.

Forensic science has come such a long way since Grauballe Man's body was conserved in oak bark in the 1950s. But of all the information sophisticated scientific techniques has made possible, it is perhaps our ability, now, to see and even hear the ancient dead as they once were that – above all – captures our imagination and brings us as close to their world as it is possible to get.

CHAPTER 5

Accident, Execution or Murder?

One can launch an accusation before the Council or bring a
capital charge. The punishment varies to suit the crime. The traitor
and deserter are hanged on trees, the coward, the shirker and the
unnaturally vicious are drowned in miry swamps under a cover
of wattled hurdles. The distinction in the punishments
implies that deeds of violence should be paid for in the full glare
of publicity, but that deeds of shame should be suppressed.

TACITUS, *GERMANIA* 12[1]

Tacitus's text makes the unequivocal statement that, among the Germanic
peoples of the late 1st century AD, the favoured retribution for shamed
individuals was death by suffocation in bogs. He even adds the detail of
their concealment by wooden slats or withies. Such a description appears
to tally closely with the archaeological evidence for bog interments during
the Iron Age and Roman periods in northern Europe, with many of the
bodies tethered in the marsh by means of branches or hurdles. So according to a contemporary source, albeit someone who spent his life not in the
wilds of the barbarian north but at the Imperial court, ancient bog deaths
were the result of penitential execution.

The forensic analyses of bog bodies overwhelmingly suggests that
many of these people died by violence that involved a third party, or at

least that they met untimely deaths. But with the evidence available from the bodies themselves, how far is it possible to distinguish between accidental death, punitive killing or villainous murder?

WHY BOGS?

Does Tacitus provide at least part of an answer? Was marshland especially chosen for reasons of secrecy? Bogs were surely regarded as *terra inculta*, wild, ungovernable territory belonging to no one and beyond the bounds of order and control, places rarely visited and perhaps always feared. If bogs were thought to be the seat of disease and toxic vapours (see Chapter 3), it is easy to see how they might have been chosen as fitting places for the inexcusable dead (PL. II).

Previous chapters have explored the peculiar nature of marshes, not only as 'other' places, set apart from cultivated lands, but also as being endowed with special preservative properties. The spirit of a corpse perceived as tainted, by something in its living body or soul, might need to be prevented from joining the community's ancestors in the Otherworld for fear that they, too, would become contaminated and cause ill to the survivors. So, paradoxically, immersion in a stagnant, watery place could have served both to preserve the body and to prevent the drowned person's transition onward because the body's natural process of dissolution had been halted.

In his discussion of the rites associated with the frozen Iron Age Pazyryk burials of Scythia (southern Russia),[2] the archaeologist Tim Taylor talked about rites of transition being fraught with peril. His context was the killing of a dead nobleman's retainers to accompany him to the afterlife, as described in Herodotus's *Histories*.[3] If Taylor is right to emphasize the dangers associated with transition from one state of being to another, then the bog bodies – suspended in time and space – may have presented particular risks to the living. If so, those dangers were secondary to perceptions that these bodies must not cross over into the world of the ancestors. So we are left with a paradox: it seems that the liminality of bog bodies was both deliberate and dangerous. The bogs, then, were the freezers that halted time and, in a sense, denied the occurrence of death. The aura of danger already hanging over these treacherous swamps, ready to swallow the unwary in life, was perhaps reinforced by their use as repositories for the unsatisfactory dead.

STUMBLING INTO SWAMPS:
THE CASE FOR ACCIDENTAL DEATH

'That is the great Grimpen Mire,' said he. 'A false step yonder
means death to man or beast. Only yesterday I saw one of the moor
ponies wander into it. He never came out. I saw his head for quite
a long time craning out of the boghole but it sucked him down
at last. Even in dry seasons it is a danger to cross it, but after these
autumn rains it is an awful place.'

SIR ARTHUR CONAN DOYLE, *THE HOUND OF THE BASKERVILLES*[4]

Conan Doyle's chilling tale of a Sherlock Holmes murder mystery, whose
killer was alleged to be a huge, supernatural hound, is set on Dartmoor,
a wild, desolate and beautiful landscape but beset with perils in the form
of bogs, of which the most terrible was the Great Grimpen Mire, where
Holmes's evil protagonist met his end. To the uninitiated, these treacherous places looked inviting: they were bright-green and fertile, but to
venture into them without knowing the paths meant almost certain death.

The perils with which ancient Iron Age peoples associated marshes
and swampy ground were undoubtedly born both of real experience, the
result of getting lost and falling in, and of perceptions that malign forces
dwelt there. *Beowulf*'s Grendel – albeit an imagined creature of the Dark
Ages – is a prime example. He was monstrous, neither man nor beast, yet
both. He was a demon that belonged to the world of nightmare and of a
feared netherworld. As a liminal being, his home was the no-man's-land
of the fen, itself neither land nor water but possessing elements of each.
After Beowulf wrestled with Grendel and tore off his arm, the monster
was driven back whence he came, to the edges of the marsh, the 'fen-
banks', in Seamus Heaney's translation.[5] *Beowulf* illustrates very clearly
the link between miry places and hideous monsters, who emerged from
the evil swamps to have their wicked way with mortal men. It is almost as
if Grendel were a personification of the dangerous fens whence he came.

Conan Doyle's chilling novel reminds us how dangerous bogland could
be, both in imagination and reality. Daphne du Maurier's *Jamaica Inn*, set
on Bodmin Moor in Cornwall in 1821, is shot through with a menace that
comes both from the wreckers, who lit lamps to lure ships onto the false
security of the rocks, and from the desolate location of Jamaica Inn, surrounded, as it was, by treacherous bogs. When the heroine, Mary Yellen,

comes to the inn to stay with her aunt Patience and wrecker-uncle Joss Merlyn, after the death of her mother, she is warned not to stray from the paths when out walking because of the risk that she heedlessly wander into a bog. Mary hears from her uncle how his brother Matthew perished by drowning in the local mire.[6] This must frequently have occurred in the past, particularly in fog or darkness when it would be all too easy to lose one's way and perish. So, in theory, it is perfectly possible that some Iron Age bog bodies were the victims of accidental death.

One of the principal champions of accident as an explanation for ancient bog bodies is the archaeologist Stephen Briggs. According to him the majority of bog people can be accounted for in this way. The title of his paper, 'Did They Fall or Were They Pushed?'[7] demonstrates his scepticism of accepted arguments for punitive execution or ritual murder in relation to bog body deaths. Brigg's thesis has two main strands. The first concerns the formation of bogs themselves, where he raises questions about whether bogs would necessarily have been bogs as we know them when the people found in them died. In other words, were the conditions necessary for organic preservation in place when the bodies were placed there? To my mind, the actuality of these bodies' preservation speaks for itself. It is likely that many boggy places are now much drier than was the case in antiquity, when they might have contained stretches of open water, small pools surrounded by hummocky grassland. If an executioner wanted to drown a criminal in such a pool, he might well have put a noose around the victim's neck as a restraint and as a means of dragging the person to the water.

The second strand of Briggs's argument is concerned with the apparent evidence for deliberate killing. He first examined the forensic data which, in several bodies, seems to point unwaveringly towards systematic violence. (Of course, there is an intrinsic interpretative problem inasmuch as so many bog people were discovered in 19th- or early 20th-century circumstances that precluded detailed scientific analysis). An alternative to deliberate violence could be post-mortem damage. So at least some of the injuries sustained by these bodies might be explained in terms of pressures exerted by the weight of the marsh or by the peat cutter's spade. We know that soon after his discovery in 1952, Grauballe Man's carefully bagged-up head was squashed by the careless foot of one of his visitors (PL. VI).[8] Could Lindow Man's apparently cut throat have been the result of injury inflicted by the mechanical digger that disinterred him? The excavators soundly repudiate this theory, arguing that the side of the neck that received the throat-cut was the area least at risk from modern damage when the body was found.

The least convincing part of Stephen Briggs's contention of accidental death is his discussion of nooses and hurdles.[9] One of the strongest arguments for deliberate killing is the presence of the hangman's noose often still in place around the victim's neck (PL. I). Briggs explains these away by suggesting that, far from being instruments of death, these ropes were the result of desperate attempts to pull from the bog unwary travellers who had strayed into treacherous swamps by mistake. For me this simply does not work. The intricate knots around the necks of Lindow Man and Tollund Man, for instance, were carefully constructed to form running nooses designed to throttle rather than to rescue.[10] The noose around Elling Woman's neck had a running knot that would automatically tighten when pulled taut; Borremose Man's noose had a knot far too complex to have been hurriedly put together in an urgent rescue attempt; the rope that strangled the Yde Girl was made from a woollen girdle likely to have belonged to the child herself. Most complicated of all was the triple knot used to tighten the cord that strangled Lindow Man. It is tempting to link such a noose with the notion of the triple-fold killing advanced by Anne Ross, who connects Lindow Man's death with the trinitarian killings told in early medieval Irish texts describing the killing of kings.[11] Ross's interpretation may be too tenuous to accept, but threeness certainly contained a sacred dimension in the Iron Age and Roman-period traditions of Ireland, Britain and the near continent. It is a constant theme in La Tène art and religious stone imagery. The intricate triple knot at the back of Lindow Man's neck at least demonstrates special care and attention to detail at variance with the hasty knots one would expect in a mission of mercy.

Briggs's question 'Hurdles for Help or for Hindrance?'[12] challenges the notion that branches or hazel withies that pegged down corpses were part of death rituals, suggesting the alternative idea that the wood might have been hurled into the bog in the hope of providing the struggling victim something to grasp and haul themselves out with, or that the hurdles might represent a cage or similar construction also designed to be part of attempts at rescuing victims, by creating a stable platform from which a drowning person could be reached. These are attractive and feasible theories but they do not explain instances where the pieces

Wooden stakes used to peg down the body of a woman in a bog at Haraldskaer, Denmark, in the early 5th century BC. She was pinned down to ensure that her body would stay where she was placed.

of wood have actually penetrated the victim's flesh. The Haraldskaer Woman had a wooden peg driven through her knee-joint soon after her death; the Irish bog body, Oldcroghan Man, had his upper arms pierced through perhaps before he drew his final breath. So, in some cases at least, the pegging down of human bodies was not the result of a bungled attempt at saving drowning people but rather reflects either deliberate injury or the perceived need to keep the body in one particular spot in the mire.

VILE BODIES? HUMILIATION AND PUNISHMENT

So was Tacitus correct in his commentary on Germanic punitive practices to connect bog deaths with their shameful behaviour in life? Were degraded members of northern European Iron Age communities further humiliated by secret drowning in lonely marshes because of some hideous deed, of cowardice, or of sexual behaviour deemed to be unacceptable to society? In writing his poem *Punishment* about the adolescent interred in a peat bog in Schleswig-Holstein (PL. IV), Seamus Heaney picks up on the theme of punishment for a sexual crime as the reason for the Windeby Child's execution.[13] Tacitus's referral to *corpore infamis*, translated by the Latin scholar Mattingly as 'the unnaturally vicious',[14] has also been translated as 'notorious evil-doers'[15] or 'the disreputable of body',[16] among multifarious renditions.

Heaney's poem hinges upon the interpretation of the Windeby Child as female, although doubt has recently been cast on 'her' gender and Tacitus emphasizes the importance of female chastity among the Germanic tribes:

Marriage in Germany is austere, and there is no feature in their morality
that deserves higher praise. They are almost unique among barbarians
in being satisfied with one wife each.

TACITUS, *GERMANIA* 18[17]

Adultery in that populous nation is rare in the extreme, and punishment
is summary and left to the husband. He shaves off
his wife's hair, strips her in the presence of kinsmen, thrusts her
from his house and flogs her through the whole village...
It is still better with those states in which only virgins marry, and
the hopes and prayers of a wife are settled once and for all. They
take one husband, like the one body or life that they possess.
No thought or desire must stray beyond him.

TACITUS, *GERMANIA* 19[18]

But we have to be a little careful with Tacitus. As a member of the Imperial court in the late 1st century AD, he had become contemptuous of the corruption and excesses of the Roman aristocracy, and some of his writings reflect a yearning for the simple life of the early Roman Republic (for the

The head of the Windeby Child, showing the left side of the scalp which had been deliberately shaved. The 'blindfold' is the child's headband; its original position on the face is uncertain.

good old days that had probably never really existed, although emperors such as Nero and Domitian did take luxury and venality to a whole new level). So Tacitus's comments about German morality, monogamy and female virtue may have been salted with his weariness of his own meretricious society.

The left side of the Windeby Child's head had apparently been shaved shortly before death, although the German archaeologist Michael Gebühr[19] has queried whether this was deliberate or whether the hair was removed by accident by a spade (the shorn side was uppermost in the bog and therefore the most vulnerable to damage during discovery). But the same treatment is recorded on another coeval Germanic victim, also an adolescent and definitely female, at Yde in the Netherlands, one side of whose head was shorn, the cut hair left by her side (PL. XIII).[20] Were these shaven-headed bog bodies, young though they were, regarded in life as 'disreputable of body' and therefore condemned to secret suffocation? It is at least possible, and Tacitus's testimony is in accordance with such a theory. Yet if punishment was the reason for their deaths, many other social transgressions might have been responsible, including theft, the breaking of religious taboos or disobedience (such as refusing a chosen marriage partner).

In the classical world professional slave-hunters, called *fugitivarii* (literally 'fugitive-catchers') combed the streets and fields for runaway slaves. Persistent offenders could be shackled, but that impeded their capacity for work. More often, they were branded. But an alternative was *semitonsus*, the shaving of half the head.[21] This was a calculated way of demonstrating a slave's untrustworthy status, and the half-head-shaving distinguished the miscreant from those with fully-shaven heads, who might – for instance – have been priests or sufferers from head lice. Without seeking to forge direct links between Iron Age Germanic communities and the Mediterranean world, the Roman analogy serves as a broad lens through which to view a peculiarly distinctive way of marking someone out as being special, set apart and to be accorded singular treatment.

SHAME AND BONDAGE

No one may enter the sacred grove unless he is bound with a cord.
By this he acknowledges his own inferiority and the power of the deity.
Should he chance to fall, he must not get up on his feet again.
He must roll out over the ground.

TACITUS, *GERMANIA* 39[22]

A number of ancient bog bodies died with ropes around their necks, the nooses still in place. Apart from their presence being a powerful argument against accidental death, the cords around the necks of the Tollund, Elling, Lindow, Yde and other bodies may signify not only instruments of death but marks of restraint that symbolically reduced the victim to serfdom. (Indeed, the Kayhausen Boy was bound by the neck, hands and feet.) Such an interpretation chimes with Tacitus's comment above, inasmuch as he makes reference to the role of bondage as a symbol of subservience and, by definition, reflects dominance of others (whether sacred or secular). Michel Foucault's powerful analysis of the early 19th-century French penal system[23] argues convincingly that the gang-chains in which prisoners were transported served to humiliate and publicly disgrace. I have argued elsewhere that the Iron Age evidence for gang-chains, for example at Llyn Cerrig Bach on Anglesey, suggests similar degrading tactics, not least because modern experiments using these chains show that prisoners lose their identity, being forced to walk at exactly the same pace as each other, with tall members of the chain having to stoop and short ones to strain their necks, in an extreme form of humiliation and discomfort.[24]

Execution was a common and culturally embedded means of punishment in the classical world. Vestal Virgins, who tended the sacred fire in ancient Rome, were bound by oaths of chastity and celibacy for 30 years, until they retired. Those that fell from grace were buried alive. The Greek author Plutarch describes such horrific executions in gruesome detail in his biography of King Numa, who is alleged to have founded the College of Vestals.[25] This particular punishment was distinctive. The unchaste Vestal was carried to her subterranean cell by litter, accompanied by praying and lamenting priests. Before she was walled up, she was given a small quantity of food, drink and oil to burn in a little lamp. In this way, she was not actually killed by a violent human hand but was left to linger and be taken whenever the gods willed it. The provision of sustenance and light made the death all the more protracted and terrifying, as the food and water were expended and the lamp flickered lower and lower until it went out, leaving her in total, starving darkness, prey to hallucinations and nightmares as her life ebbed away.

In ancient Rome, executions were public spectacles, to which the people were summoned by trumpet calls in order that they might witness the violent and brutal deaths of condemned criminals. A variety of capital punishments were used: some miscreants were hurled from the Tarpeian Rock, others bludgeoned to death, beheaded, drowned in a sack thrown into the river Tiber, or devoured by wild beasts in the arena.[26]

So Roman executions were diverse and remarkably unpleasant. Some late Republican politicians and writers, like Sallust and Cicero, denounced the more barbaric practices, claiming that *humanitas* should be applied whenever possible. *Humanitas* allowed certain high-born miscreants to go into voluntary exile rather than be put to death. The most merciful executions involved beheading. Among the worst (the *summum supplicium*, or 'ultimate punishment') were the deaths meted out to virgins, who were raped by their executioners before being strangled. The Roman law that forbade the official killing of maidens was thus a nicely balanced piece of 'humanitarian' sophistry; it was fine to execute virgin women as long as they had been deflowered first. One of the important aspects of Roman capital punishment was its element of theatre, of public spectacle. Just as hanging, drawing and quartering in Tudor England was designed both to titillate and deter, so too was Roman execution.

Can we apply any of this digression into Roman capital punishment to the bog bodies? If we believe Tacitus, bog victims were guilty of shameful behaviour and so their demise had to be hushed up and carried out privately. Normal burial rites in the north European Iron Age involved cremation, a system of body disposal that is highly visible and, moreover, can be both heard and smelt a fair distance away. But to dispose of a person by throttling and immersion in a marsh could, by contrast, be a discreet affair, commensurate with the need for clandestine behaviour. What also makes sense in terms of the execution theory is the way that the bog-dead seem to have been shamed not only by the manner of their deaths but also their treatment prior to their dispatch. Many ancient bog bodies went into the marshes stripped naked; they were also denied grave goods. Even those people whose physicality suggests that they enjoyed high rank in life, such as Lindow Man and the Oldcroghan and Clonycavan men, were stripped of their status as part of the process leading up to their violent deaths.

SINS OF THE FATHERS

There is a potential problem in the notion of punitive killing as a universal reason for bog deaths: the presence of children and disabled people in significant numbers among the range of victims. If we discount the bizarre 2014 news story concerning the indictment of a nine-month-old baby, Mohammud Musa, together with his relatives on a capital charge of attempted murder in Pakistan (the charge against the baby was later dropped),[27] children do not generally figure as victims of punitive execution. An exception might be if the child were a hostage. It would be rare, too, for severely disabled people to be executed for criminal offences.

Robert Garland's study of the way disability and deformity were perceived and treated in the ancient world in his *The Eye of the Beholder* makes grim reading. It was certainly common practice in Greece to cause the death of malformed infants by exposure. 'The pressure to eliminate a congenitally deformed infant was fuelled not only by religious but also by practical considerations.'[28] Those children whose physical or mental problems did not manifest themselves until later on were often cast out of their homes and left to fend for themselves. Babies are rarely represented in bog body deaths but adolescents with obvious physical differences, particularly those whose mobility had been compromised, are over-represented. This is unlikely to have been the result of execution for miscreancy. So if execution is a valid explanation for certain bog killings, it is almost certainly not applicable to many others.

MURDER?

Now Grendel, with the wrath of God on his back, came out of the
moors and the mist-ridden fens with the intention of trapping
some man in Heorot.

BEOWULF[29]

In ancient Rome, homicide was a capital offence, as was treason.[30] According to Caesar, murder among the Gauls was dealt with at the highest level, by the Druids.[31] In considering murder in connection with the bog bodies, it is pertinent to ask two questions: could some of the people placed in bogs have been guilty of homicide, and punished accordingly? Or were they themselves victims of murder? This latter possibility is the subject of this section.

Murder could have been planned or the result of sudden anger. Clues may be sought in the manner of the bog deaths and the level of savagery directed at the victims. The hiding of bodies in lonely and dangerous places like marshes might favour a furtive killing, perhaps in the context of a robbery or revenge for a wrong. According to such a model, it is likely that the victim was waylaid as a lonely traveller going about his business; if that were so, he or she might have been mugged some distance away from the interment and then dragged or carried to the nearest wetland.

Local knowledge of the marshes and networks of trackways would have been needed, to avoid personal risk and to be able to select a good spot in which the body was likely to sink.[32] To move a fully grown adult man more than a few metres is a difficult task for a single individual, so if a bog body had been the victim of murder, perhaps more than one killer was involved. Some of the injuries sustained by the bog people are consistent with sudden, unplanned and violent murder: the stabbing of one of the Weerdinge pair from the Netherlands (PL. VII),[33] for instance, or the frenzied blows to the head suffered by Lindow Man (PLS. VIII, IX).[34] It is possible to argue, too, that strangling also carried the hallmark of murder: witness the methods of Thugs in 19th-century India, professional street-murderers who habitually crept up behind their victims and garrotted

The head of Lindow Man, displaying the catastrophic head injuries he sustained shortly before his death.

them at lightning speed with a square knotted cloth called a *ruhmal*.[35] This kind of murder is quick and quiet.

Could murder by bandits explain the nakedness of some of the bog bodies and the absence of personal possessions? For an Iron Age robber, a good woollen cloak and a pair of stout boots may well have been worth stealing, even if other booty was the primary target. Even in cases where bog bodies were clearly placed in the swamp with some care, as is true of Tollund Man, that does not, of itself, preclude a fatal mugging. Friends, relatives or even strangers might have come upon the body and arranged it decently, giving the dead dignity and respect, perhaps in the hope of negating the bad karma that must have attended an untimely and unnatural death.

NO ORDINARY MURDERS

Why 'kill' someone who was already dead? Was this a mark of honour or a gesture of fear? Whatever the motivation, the shafts of their spears would have stuck out of the resulting barrow mound, like bristles or spines. Taking years to decay, they would have become a long-lasting and dramatic reminder of the events that had taken place there.

MELANIE GILES, *A FORGED GLAMOUR*[36]

In her book on life and death in the British Iron Age, Melanie Giles explores the unique burials of East Yorkshire, the so-called 'Arras Culture' graves, some of which contain the bodies of warriors, some including chariots and even, occasionally, the horse-team that drew them. One, found near Garton Slack in September 1985, seems to provide evidence of a weird kind of funerary ritual, including 'ghost-killing', where the body of the dead man continued to be assaulted with spears after he was already dead. When the warrior had been laid in his tomb, at least four people 'took turns to cast their weapons into his body, as the grave was rapidly backfilled'.[37]

One of the most striking features of bog bodies is the evidence for 'over-kill', something not too dissimilar from the Yorkshire burial, though less visibly obvious. Those who interred the warrior at Garton Slack wanted his grave to become part of the visual landscape, arguably because remembrance was deemed particularly important. By contrast, the bog bodies which sustained multiple wounds took their secrets with them deep into their marshy pools. These several 'deaths' argue strongly against common murder for gain, revenge or some other mundane purpose. Multiple killing of a single individual suggests collective responsibility, on the one hand, and a certain ritualization of killing, on the other. I am reminded of the custom, in the classical world of, 'hobbling ghosts', by abusing the bodies of the untimely dead, especially murder victims, in order to weaken their spirits and thus render them incapable of revenge.[38] This idea is explored further in Chapter 7.

The original forensic analysis of Lindow Man (Lindow II) contains a formidable list of injuries, many of which would have been fatal on their own (PL. VIII). There were several severe lacerations to the head, involving fracture of the skull, a deep throat wound to the neck, injury to the cervical vertebrae, a deeply imbedded ligature around the neck, a stab wound to the upper chest, and bruises to the lower back, indicating that the *coup de grâce* was delivered by someone who viciously kneed him in the back while he was kneeling, causing his moribund body to topple into the bog; he was just possibly still just alive when he went into the water. In his remarkable book *The Buried Soul*,[39] Tim Taylor puts forward the notion that the violence inflicted on the Lindow body was the result of supremely controlled actions, designed to inflict maximum trauma on an individual but keeping him hovering in the no-man's-land between life and death, Heaven and Hell, as a 'vexed ghost', unable to move on to the Otherworld because of his disposal in the liminal realm of the bog where his body could not decay and his spirit be freed. The exquisite torture inflicted upon Lindow Man was thus very different from that perpetrated by an 'ordinary' murderer. This was planned to the last detail and, arguably, involved considerable anatomical expertise on the part of the practitioner.

Reference has already been made to 'last suppers' (see Chapters 3 and 4). But the identification of special final meals is important to the discussion of purpose. In Ireland, Britain, Denmark and the Netherlands, the gut contents of Iron Age bog bodies have been found to include peculiar mixtures of food, either in the form of bread or a thick gruel or porridge. Oldcroghan Man had enjoyed a protein-rich, meat-heavy diet appropriate to his enormous frame, but his last meal was a vegetarian one. Why? Some of the food was fairly unpalatable, containing a quantity of wild seeds and grasses; some was positively toxic (the ergot consumed by Grauballe Man and the mistletoe eaten by Lindow II). Surely it was more than coincidence that these bog victims all ate something odd just before they happened to be murdered.

I (previous page) The body of Tollund Man, partially reconstructed.
He was hanged and put into a Danish bog in the 4th century BC,
wearing only his skin cap and leather belt.

II (above) A bog pool near Henne Breach, West Jutland, Denmark,
a typical 'bog-scape' in which ancient bog bodies have been found.

III Plant species found in bogs. (Left) *Drosera longifolia*
(aka great sundew); (right) *Andromeda polifolia* (aka bog rosemary).

IV The Windeby Child. The naked, head-shaven body of an
adolescent, carefully placed in a north German peat bog in the
1st century AD. Over her shoulder was a cowhide cape.

V (above) The body of Grauballe Man. He bled to death
from a savagely cut throat and was placed in a Danish bog
in the early 4th century BC.

VI (overleaf) The well-preserved face and hair of Grauballe Man.
The bog-acids have dyed his hair red, but it may originally
have been fair or grey.

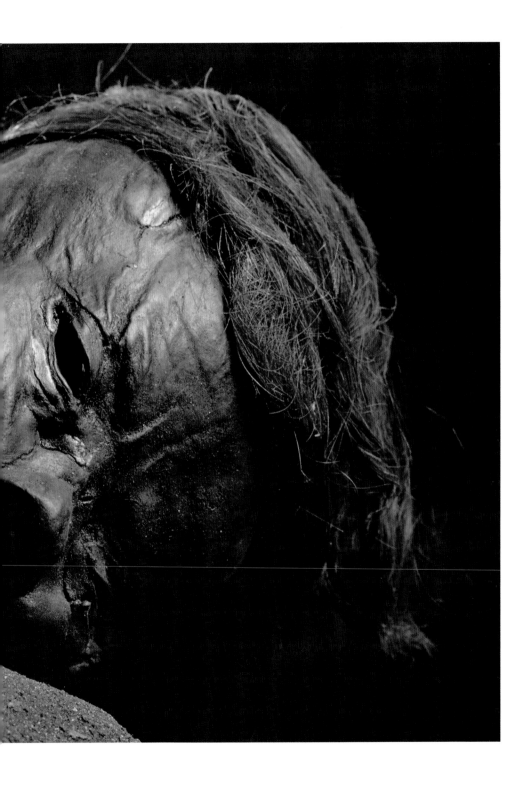

VII A pair of young men, possibly comrades-in-arms, who died
and were buried together in a bog, as if embracing one another.
They were discovered at Weerdinge in the Netherlands in 1904.

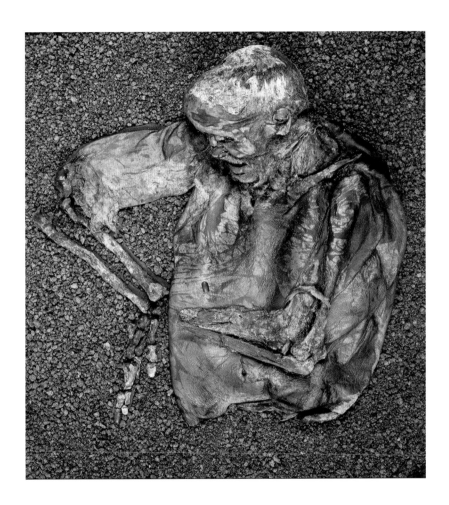

VIII (above) Lindow Man, a British Iron Age bog body from
Cheshire in northwest England. He had suffered a 'triple' death
before being consigned to the marsh. At least one other man
was interred in the same area after being decapitated.

IX (overleaf) The face of Lindow Man (his head had been
partially crushed by the weight of the peat in which he was buried).
His upper lip shows traces of a neatly clipped moustache.

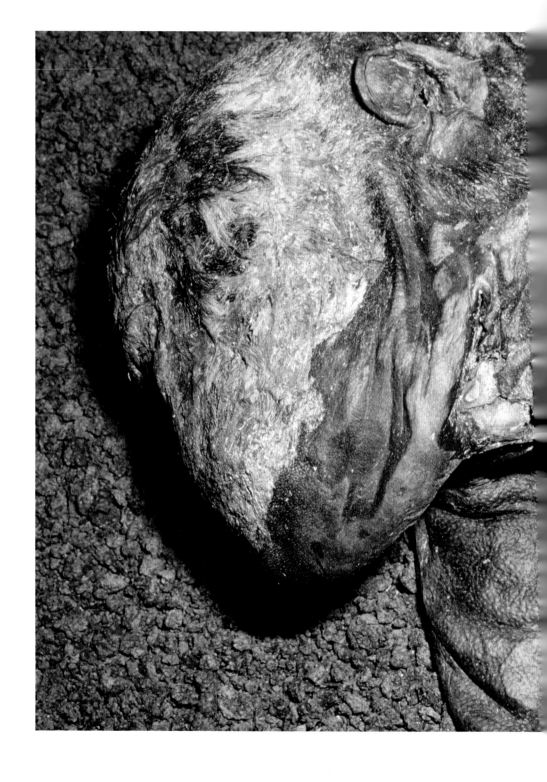

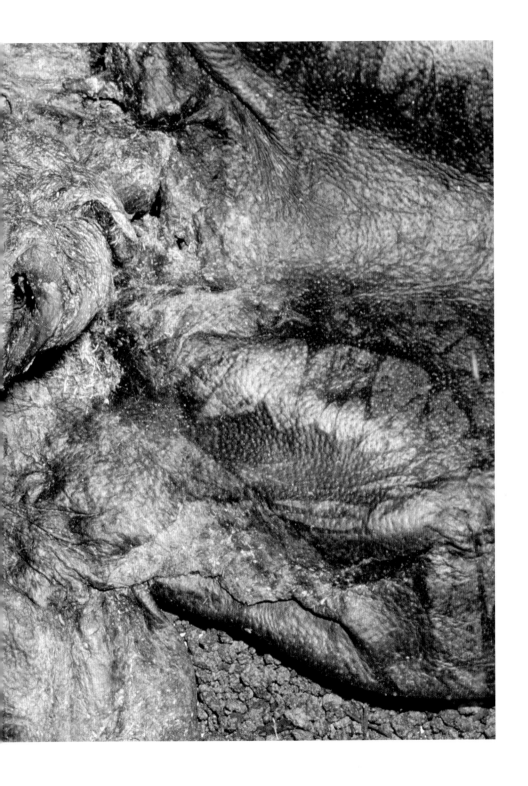

X The Huldremose Woman, who was killed and immersed in a Danish bog in *c.* AD 100. She had sustained several injuries including the severing of her right arm shortly before her death.

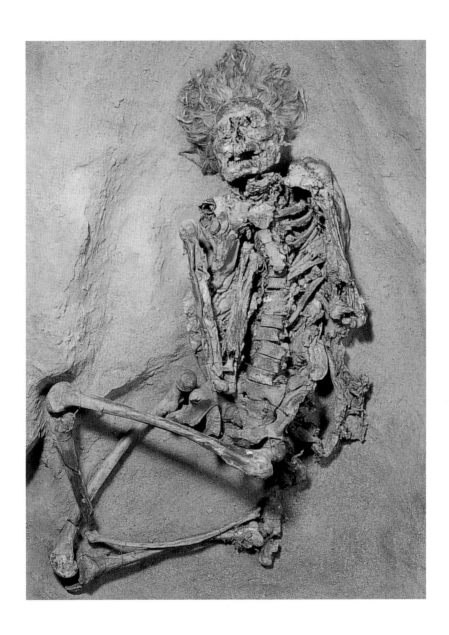

XI Red Franz, a man of about 30, his long hair dyed red by
bog acids, put naked into a bog in Lower Saxony in the late
3rd/early 4th century AD. It is not known precisely how he died
but his body had sustained a range of injuries.

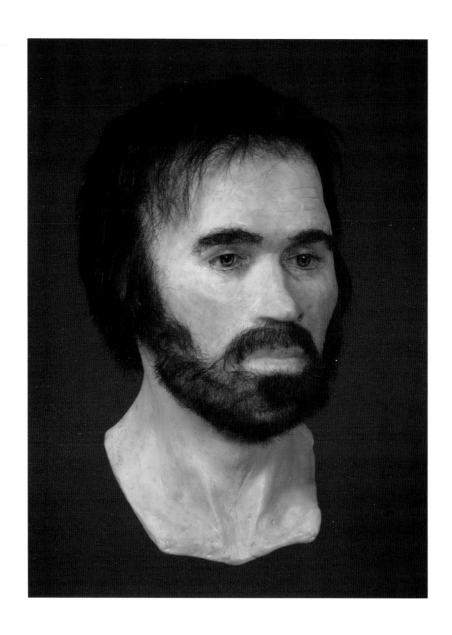

XII The face of Lindow Man, as reconstructed by Richard Neave
of Manchester University, from the skull and surviving soft tissue.

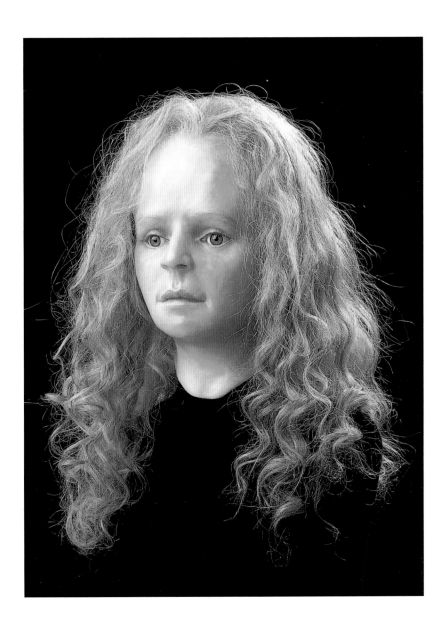

XIII Richard Neave's reconstruction of the face of the
Yde Girl, strangled and placed in a peat bog in Drenthe,
Netherlands, in the 1st century AD.

XIV The Wicker Man: a still taken from the iconic 1973 film of the same name. Caesar and Strabo both mention the ancient Gaulish custom of sacrificing people by burning them in giant wicker images.

WORKING OUT BOG BODIES

The evidence is mounting that Iron Age bog people did not die ordinary deaths. The presence of ritualization, of repetitive, formulaic action is inescapable and difficult to explain away in terms of either accident or murder. Execution, however, remains a viable explanation. In many ancient and early modern societies, punitive killings are hedged about with ceremony, with ritual that may have absolutely nothing to do with religion, though it may do so. The following chapters that tackle these issues, considering the modi operandi (the ways of killing), the level of violence, the selection of victims and their killers; all these things contribute to the discourse concerning purpose. The final chapter examines the evidence that these special deaths had a sacred dimension.

One more aspect to bog bodies remains to be explored in this chapter, and that is the nature of the bodies themselves and how they may have been used as objects both before and after their deaths. Karin Sanders[40] discusses the way in which bog bodies become artifacts, particularly after the centuries in the tanning *Sphagnum*-swamps turn human flesh into shiny dark leather, so that it can look almost sculpted. So is it perhaps valid to suggest that the way the bog people were treated peri- and post-mortem by their killers and those who witnessed their deaths played a part in what these bodies were and would become? Might it even be possible to think in terms of deliberate manipulation of live bodies in the playing out of identities and relationships?

The work of the social anthropologist Benjamin Alberti on body imagery in the ceramics of northwest Argentina in the 1st millennium AD explores the way in which, for him, the form and decoration on pottery of the La Candelaria people was concerned not with the completed pot but with the way it was made.[41] It is possible to use such an approach as a lens through which to view ancient European bog bodies (as well as Iron Age art). In such a model, the untimely deaths, the disposal of bodies in bogs and the ways of killing all may have had a role in investing these bodies with meaning that helped the living come to terms with the mystery of death, and enabled them to manipulate life and death in order both to understand and to control the connections between the worlds of the living and the dead.

CHAPTER 6

Modus Operandi:
Ways of Killing

The dead have no sense of time, no clear sense of place;
they are beyond geography and history.

HILARY MANTEL, *BEYOND BLACK*[1]

Mantel's novel *Beyond Black* explores the life of a modern English medium and her experience of the spirits whom she encounters. Her dead are intrusive, popping up and engaging her in conversation at the most inconvenient times and occasions because they no longer answer to earth-bound rules. Bog bodies share some of these features: they appear suddenly from their peaty graves; they are inappropriately whole, and their injuries present uncomfortable images of violence. Their preservation defies time, and the essential similarities of their treatment across time and space also chime with Mantel's observation. This chapter examines the processes by which ancient bog bodies came to die and be placed in swampy ground. Archaeologists studying these corpses are uniquely privileged because the preservation of soft tissue and innards allows them access to intimate detail that is lost if all they have are skeletons. There are so many ways of killing that do not leave a mark on bare bone.

If, as we suspect, the majority of Iron Age bog bodies ended their lives as the result of 'foul play', that in itself contains elements of risk, instability and disorder. The modern crime writer Rebecca Tope[2] speaks of murder as a destroyer of order and trust and thus in need of resolution and the re-establishment of control. There is a sense, then, that the murder of ancient individuals engendered a state that demanded particular expressions of redress. So, entwined within the killing process, we might expect to identify issues associated with the balance between order and disorder, what the ancient Greeks referred to as *nomos* and *physis*. Indeed, the bogs themselves represented *physis*, in contrast to the cultivable, ordered land around them, and so flouted human control.

WRITTEN IN BLOOD: THE STORY OF GRAUBALLE MAN

> He was a handsome and stately figure and is very heavily
> built and any presumptions of a certain crudeness in our Germanic
> ancestors in the Iron Age are upset by the fact that he has
> beautiful hands and almond-shaped nails.
>
> FROM THE DANISH DAILY NEWSPAPER *JYLLANDS-POSTEN*[3]

> What need we fear? Who knows it, when none can call our
> power to account: yet who would have thought the old man
> to have had so much blood in him.
>
> LADY MACBETH IN SHAKESPEARE'S *MACBETH*[4]

The hideously gaping wound in Grauballe Man's throat would have left a specialist in ancient pathology in no doubt about the cause of his death (PL. V). Someone yanked back his head by the hair, exposing his throat to a knife thrust of such savagery that it all but took his head off. It is useful to zoom in on this precise act, because hair-grabbing is classic shaming behaviour that is represented in imageries of humiliation widespread in the ancient world. Three examples from totally separate contexts serve to illustrate outwardly very similar acts. An early First Dynastic Egyptian stone palette or plaque (dating to about 3100 BC) depicts the Egyptian king Narmer standing above a kneeling naked Nubian prisoner whose hair he grips tightly, in an attitude of utter domination.[5] A painted Greek vase, dating to the 6th century BC, depicts the sacrifice of Polyxena at the tomb of Achilles: the scene shows the killer, Neoptolemus, grasping the girl's hair with one hand while with the other he plunges his sword into her throat.[6] Far away in Rome, on Trajan's column, erected in the 2nd

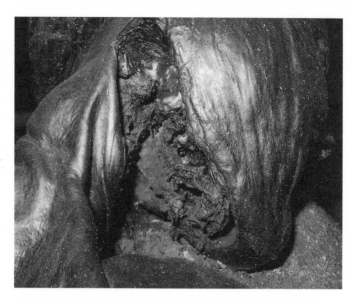

Close-up of Grauballe Man's neck, exhibiting the gaping throat-
wound from which he would have rapidly bled out.

century AD to celebrate the emperor Trajan's victories in Dacia, there are
scenes of Dacian prisoners being restrained by Roman soldiers who grasp
the shaggy hair of their subjugated enemies.[7] The Egyptian and Roman
images show hair restraint but not throat-cutting. In the case of Grauballe
Man, a single individual may have been involved in both acts, provided
that the victim was either bound or sedated. Otherwise, it would have
required at least two people, one to restrain and hold the victim still,
while the other slit his throat.

Lady Macbeth's tortured conversation with herself (quoted above)
graphically expresses the catastrophic and shocking blood loss resulting from fatal knife wounds. Both the victim and perpetrator would be
bathed in blood, and the spatter would splash onto onlookers as well.
Grauballe Man did not need a detailed post-mortem examination to tell
those who examined him how he died. He was subjected to two such
scrutinies, the first in 1952 shortly after he was found, and the second
in 2001. A major focus of the latter examination was the horrific injury
to Grauballe Man's throat. In fact, this wound resulted from one main
cut and some small subsidiary cuts with a smooth sharp-bladed instrument that struck the cervical vertebrae, severed the pharynx and made
a large hole in the mouth. It stretched virtually from ear to ear. Both

An ancient Egyptian carved stone palette depicting King Narmer
grasping a Nubian prisoner by the hair; *c.* 3100 BC.

carotid arteries and the jugular vein were severed. There is no way at
all that this could either have occurred accidentally after death or have
been self-inflicted.[8] The attack on Grauballe Man's throat was sustained,
excessively violent and designed to cause maximum harm. It was delivered with a sure hand by someone who knew exactly what he or she
was doing, with a controlled movement, not a frenzied slashing. The secondary cuts are likely to have occurred from jerking movements of the
knife blade within the wound, perhaps to wreak even greater havoc on
the man's throat.[9] The instrument used was large and very sharp: an Iron
Age sword, dagger or heavy-duty knife. The attacker pulled back the victim's head and stabbed him from behind. The victim would have become
unconscious very soon after the attack, and would have died within a
few minutes, partly from sudden, massive blood loss and partly through
suffocation caused by blood being breathed in and clogging the airways.

Grauballe Man was by no means the only Iron Age bog body to have
his throat savagely cut. For instance, the adolescent boy from Kayhausen
in North Germany is reported to have suffered three long cuts to his throat
and another wound in his upper arm. It is noteworthy that the garments
he was bound with were undamaged, leading to questions as to whether
the material was wrapped around his neck and limbs after he died.[10]

Copper-alloy knife from Verulamium, Hertfordshire. The blade is decorated with curvilinear La Tène designs and the knife was probably made in the 1st century AD.

Lindow Man also sustained a throat wound, although in his case, this was accompanied by garrotting and blunt force trauma to the head. The Greek geographer Strabo provides a graphic description of throat-cutting among the Cimbri, carried out by women on prisoners of war. This is what he says:

> These women would enter the [army] camp, sword in hand,
> go up to the prisoners, crown them and lead them up to a bronze vessel
> which might hold some twenty measures. One of the women would
> mount a step and, leaning over the cauldron, cut the throat of a prisoner,
> who was held up over the vessel's rim.
>
> STRABO, *GEOGRAPHY*[11]

Strabo explains that the killers of these hapless captives were not only women but old women at that, 'grey with age', as he calls them. Whether or not he was engaging in some creative reporting, Strabo's testimony is of particular note because he was speaking of the territory of the Cimbri, a group of north European peoples occupying the far north of Germany and much of Denmark, precisely the region where Iron Age bog bodies, like Grauballe Man, have been discovered. If Strabo's words do no more, they encourage us to think about the context that may have surrounded Grauballe Man's spectacularly bloody death. Was his blood collected for some use or other, or was it simply allowed to soak away into the earth? His comments also make us consider the perpetrators of such violent killing, and to acknowledge the likelihood that both women and men were involved.

Other parts of bog victims' bodies also suffered stabbing injuries. The Yde Girl from Drenthe in the Netherlands was strangled but had a stab wound near her clavicle. One of the two young men found together at Weerdinge (also in the Netherlands) had stab wounds to his upper torso, so savage that his small intestine protruded from his body (PL. VII).[12] Another young man, from Dätgen in Schleswig-Holstein, was stabbed through the heart, his hair first being dressed in the so-called Suebian Knot, which, according to Tacitus, was the mark of a free man of some consequence in Germanic society (see illustration overleaf and discussion on p.22).[13] Again, perhaps Strabo can help flesh out the circumstances of such killings, commenting that among the Gauls there used to be a divinatory custom that involved stabbing a man in the back and interpreting the future from the manner of his death throes.[14]

Blood-killings are special, for they involve crossing the body's boundaries and causing inside to become outside. By penetrating the skin, a liminal membrane is broached and the confines of the body have lost their integrity. Blood can be regarded as both a pollutant and a purifier. Killing by stabbing also possesses peculiarly theatrical properties. The wounds, the bright red spouting arterial blood and the agonized and terrified cries of the dying all add to the spectacle of violent death. Sharp instruments, sometimes weapons of war, are involved, and the spread of blood inevitably involves any watching spectators in the act of killing. Quantities of liquid escape from a solid body, seemingly with a life of their own as they spurt from wounds; the red colour is a violent contrast to the pale flesh of the victim. The Iron Age British love of red glass, enamel and coral as an embellishment to weapons and other prestigious objects may be relevant to the importance of symbolic blood both in warfare and in everyday life. The Kirkburn sword from Yorkshire was decorated in bright red spots of molten glass that were surely deliberately evocative of freshly spilled drops of blood,[15] very like the genuine blood spatters that would have covered the blade and handle of a sharp-edged stabbing blade (and the red glass was a viscous liquid when inlaid onto

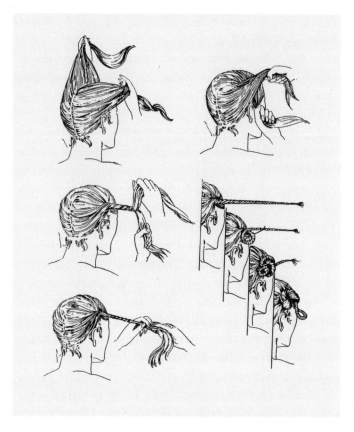

Stages in creating a Suebian knot, the distinctive male hairstyle
mentioned by Tacitus, and worn by the bogmen from Osterby
and Dätgen in Schleswig-Holstein.

metal, just like blood). Finally, this mode of killing enabled a particularly
intimate connection between the body and the bog: the mingling and
exchange of fluids between them.

BLUNT FORCE TRAUMA

Until 2001, it was thought that Grauballe Man had suffered a fractured
skull before his throat was cut. However, the latest forensic analysis shows
that this head injury occurred after death and was probably the result
of accidental damage caused by the pressure of peat or at the time of
excavation.[16] One other injury, though, does seem to have been inflicted
pre-mortem by a heavy blow from a blunt instrument: an open fracture

to his left shin that Grauballe Man may have suffered at about the time of his death, probably as part of the abuse associated with his killing, and maybe either due to torture – in order to increase his pain – or to disable him, either for some symbolic purpose or simply to prevent him from escaping.[17]

Some bog bodies did sustain deliberate head injuries as the result of blunt force trauma while they were still alive. Lindow Man is a prime example of someone who suffered at least two blows to his head, one on the crown and one on the back of his scalp. Both injuries were probably inflicted by someone using an axe.[18] Examination using a stereoscopic dissecting microscope revealed swelling around the margins of the blows, indicating that they were inflicted some time before death, allowing time for bruising and the collection of protective fluid around the injuries. The more serious blow was the one that landed on the crown of the victim's head, so vicious that it not only fractured the skull but also pierced the dura (the membrane around the brain) and drove pieces of bone deep into the brain. This was a fatal injury but, although Lindow Man would have lost consciousness immediately after the blow, he could have survived for some hours. The *coup de grâce* was the noose that throttled him, coupled with a severe cut to the throat, inflicted with a sharp-edged knife, the clear intention being to sever the jugular vein. Each of these three injuries would have been sufficient to kill him, begging questions about 'overkill' violence that are addressed later in this chapter and in the next. The combination of tightening the noose and cutting the throat would have had the effect of causing a fountain of blood to spurt from the throat wound at high pressure.[19] The precision with which the throat was cut indicates that such a spout of blood was clearly intentional, to project a message (as well as blood) to those watching and to enhance the theatricality of the killing. What is more, such ability to 'play' with the human body argues for sound anatomical knowledge on the part of the perpetrators.

The blunt force trauma sustained by the Lindow and Grauballe bodies is replicated in other bog people, notably those from Borremose in Denmark, where three Late Bronze Age or earliest Iron Age bodies, those of a man and two women, were discovered separately between 1946 and 1948. Like the Grauballe and Lindow bodies, Borremose Man was placed in the peat naked. The rope around his neck shows the manner of his death, but the jury is still out on whether the severe fractures to the back of his skull were deliberately inflicted either before or immediately after death or were the result of subsequent peat damage. But the two women also found at Borremose both had severe head injuries too. There is evidence that one of the females had been scalped and her face crushed and some facial bones removed, perhaps deliberately. All three sustained other signs of abuse before their deaths; two had had their right legs broken.[20] These are just a few of many instances where prehistoric bog victims were the recipients of savage blunt force injuries inflicted by the blows of axes, the butts of spears, the hilts of swords or, possibly, heavy pieces of wood.

HEADS WITHOUT BODIES AND BODIES WITHOUT HEADS

> The Boii stripped Postumus's body, cut off the head and carried their
> spoils in triumph to the most hallowed of their temples. There they
> cleaned out the head, as their custom is, and gilded the skull, which
> thereafter served them as a holy vessel to pour libations from and as
> a drinking-cup for the priest and the temple-attendants.
>
> LIVY, *AB URBE CONDITA*[21]

Livy was a Roman historian who lived in the time of Augustus (late 1st century BC – early 1st century AD). Much of his great history of Rome has been lost but the surviving books contain detailed information about the wars between Romans and north Italian Celtic tribes. Postumus was a Roman general who led campaigns against the Boii, a powerful tribe living in the Po Valley; he was captured and executed by them in 216 BC. Diodorus Siculus, a broad contemporary of Livy, records that it was customary for the Gauls (he does not say precisely where) to behead their fallen enemies, sling the heads from the harness of their horses and bear them home in triumph, as precious war booty.[22] It is likely that Diodorus's information related to customs of southern Gaulish tribes. Archaeological evidence clearly indicates that the Saluvii of the lower Rhône Valley were heavily involved in head-taking. Genuine skulls have been found in temples such as Roquepertuse and Entremont, together with carvings of disembodied heads.[23]

Southern Gaul is a long way from the north European heartlands of bog body deposition. However, the presence of headless bodies and severed heads in northern marshes does beg questions about the customs and practices that underpinned them. Lindow III's head was taken off and his body and head buried separately, some distance apart, though both in the peat bog at Lindow Moss.[24] Decapitation is likely to have been the cause of death and, as soon as the man was dead, his body was deliberately pushed beneath the surface of the bog. The singular treatment of this body is interesting, for the deliberate disintegration of the corpse raises all kinds of issues associated with the apparent urge to rob its owner of identity, to humiliate him and, perhaps, to neutralize a specific power perceived to be present in this individual. But it should be acknowledged that fragmentation of body parts in prehistoric contexts can have other, more symbolic or ideological purposes, such as reverence for the head and the power it conveys, or the making of statements about personhood.[25] Decapitation is a quick, if very violent method of execution (provided that it is not bungled, as were some Tudor and Elizabethan beheadings). In Lindow III's case, this mode of killing, involving the removal and separate interment of the head, may even have been a mark of honour. But, just as burial in bogs served to freeze-frame bodies in the present and prevent them from decaying and releasing the soul for the afterlife, so the taking of Lindow III's head might equally signal a further need to interrupt the natural order of things, where body and head would decay together.

Lindow III was special in other ways, too. His surviving right hand possessed a vestigial extra thumb, and this sixth digit would originally have been present on both hands. This marked him out as different, odd, a deviant from normal physicality. Did this account for his beheading? The other oddity about Lindow III is a residue of heavy metals on the skin, suggesting that his body was decorated with mineral-based paints at some time in his life.[26] There is a rich seam of classical literary reference to body art among the northern barbarian peoples, particularly Britons. For instance, Julius Caesar, Pomponius Mela, Pliny the Elder and Martial all make mention of painted Britons: Martial calls them 'sky-blue Britons'.[27] We will revisit the issue of body painting later because, apart from anything its presence may say about status, there is some evidence that it may have played a part in killing ceremonies.

Lindow III was decapitated and his head buried elsewhere in the same bog; Oldcroghan Man in Ireland was also beheaded but his head is lost.[28] But sometimes only the heads of bog victims have been recovered. This may be because the rest of the body has never been found, or it may be that those responsible for the beheading of the individual might deliberately have sought to dispose of the body in a totally separate place, or even abandoned it to be scavenged. The decapitated head of a 55–60-year-old Iron Age man, found in 1948 at Osterby in Schleswig-Holstein, was carefully wrapped in a deerskin pouch and secured to the marsh-bed with wooden stakes. He had died in the late 1st century AD from a blow to the right temple (the skull bones are particularly thin there) and then his head was severed with a sharp knife or sword at the second cervical vertebra. The striking feature was the full head of hair that had been twisted into a Suebian knot at the right side of his head.[29] Tacitus's comment, that such a hairstyle was reserved for German citizens of rank,[30] suggests that this man was not a slave, although he might have been a prisoner of war or even a hostage. The most distinguishing feature exhibited by the disembodied head of a man from Worsley Moss in Lancashire was a deformed right ear. The beheading weapon had gone into the neck at precisely the same position as Osterby Man, at the second vertebra. But in addition, the remains of a tight noose were also present on the Worsley head, whose owner died in the Roman period.[31] Like Lindow II, Worsley Man appears to have suffered more than one death, by strangulation and decapitation; what is more, before he died he was hit on the head with sufficient force to fracture the crown of the skull. The primary reason for cutting the head off was thus not to kill but to make another statement. The shrunken and malformed ear may have been congenital but it could have been formed through injury, like the 'cauliflower' ears suffered by professional boxers.

CUTTING OFF THE BREATH

The traitor and deserter are hanged on trees....

TACITUS, GERMANIA[32]

The majority of ancient bog bodies met their deaths by strangulation: by hanging or garrotting. In the cases of Lindow II and Worsley Man, the noose appears to have formed part of a complicated procedure whereby breathing was interrupted both by throat-cutting/beheading and by constriction of the airways by a rope. All these actions centred on the head and neck and the desire to separate one from the other. In Grauballe Man's killing, his throat was cut so violently as almost to cause head removal.

Hanging and garrotting are different methods of producing the same effect, robbing the victim of life-breath without bloodletting. Throat-cutting and decapitation have the same result but with appalling blood loss. The concentration on the head and neck of victims resonates to a degree with the use of multiple neck chains as a means of ferrying prisoners about. Roping or chaining people together by the neck serves to make a visual division between the head and the body, to constrict the neck enough to render prisoners docile but not to kill them. The whole business of putting people into multiple chain gangs is described in graphic detail by Michel Foucault in his discussion of 19th-century French practice at the Bicêtre prison. Here, the head warder (known as the *artoupan*) took on the role of blacksmith, and the procedure of heating the metal and hammering the rings while placed around the prisoners' necks added very real risk of serious or even fatal injury to the hapless victims.[33] Iron gang-chains are recorded in the British Iron Age, as we have seen for instance at Llyn Cerrig Bach on Anglesey, where two sets, the more complete one for five necks, were found in 1943 together with a whole range of votive objects deposited in the 1st century AD in a small marshy lake.[34] The parallel between strangulation and these gang-chains is both symbolic and real. Tacitus records an incident at Rome during the terror years of the emperor Tiberius and his henchman Sejanus, when Julius Celsus, charged with conspiracy, loosened the chain binding him and managed to strangle himself with it.[35]

There is something peculiarly dramatic about the sight of an inert, swinging body, the head lolling on its broken neck. Hanging is often public, designed both as a spectacle and deterrent, but garrotting can be a private business, involving stealth and secrecy. A particularly gruesome method of restraint practised on one Iron Age bog body was something possibly set up to effect either actual or symbolic auto-asphyxiation. The young boy from Kayhausen in North Germany was stripped naked, his feet bound and his hands tied behind him with a complicated arrangement whereby the same cloth was used to bind his hands, legs and neck, in a sort of ghastly hog-tie. If this occurred before death, the result of any attempt to free his hands would have pulled on the bonds so that the band between his legs would tighten agonizingly on his genitals and simultaneously throttle him.[36] The use of what appear to have been the boy's own clothes to restrain and potentially kill him makes the whole procedure intensely and deliberately personalized. The same is true of the way the Yde Girl from the Netherlands was strangled, with her own girdle, as was another pubertal child/adult from Windeby, whose *sprang* (belt), originally perhaps worn as a hairband, was round the lower face or neck at the time of death.[37] Both these bog victims were adolescents,

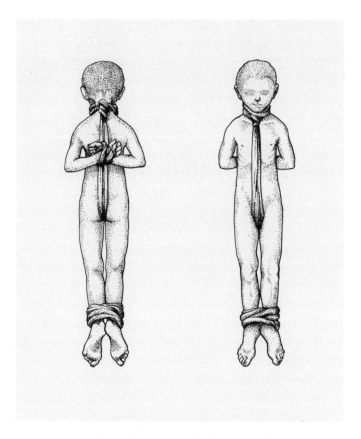

Drawing of the Kayhausen Boy, an adolescent killed and bound
in a hog-tie linking his genitals, hands and neck. From a peat bog
in Lower Saxony, 2nd/1st century BC.

between 12 and 14 years old, and both suffered from disabilities that
would have hampered their mobility. Were their garments deliberately
chosen as weapons, in order to present their own possessions as turning
against them, in an ultimate expression of degradation?

Whether or not the body is strung up, strangling is a unique way of
killing. It does little in the way of visible damage, although it often breaks
the hyoid cartilage and sometimes snaps the neck. It is a 'clean' method of
doing away with someone, without cutting the skin or causing blood loss. It
makes no noise, apart from the subdued choking made by the victim, and
not even that if done quickly. The use of special knots for the Lindow and
Tollund deaths suggests that professional 'hangmen' were employed and a
certain formulaic dimension to the events.

DROWNING

After that, the car, the cloth and, believe it if you will, the goddess herself
are washed clean in a secluded lake. This service is performed by slaves
who are immediately afterwards drowned in the lake.

TACITUS, *GERMANIA*[38]

Mercurius Teutates is appeased in this manner among the Gauls: a man
is lowered head first into a full tub so that he drowns there.

9TH-CENTURY COMMENTARY ON LUCAN, *PHARSALIA*[39]

Tacitus's text above refers to ceremonies associated with an annual
Germanic festival in honour of the earth-goddess Nerthus. The second
quotation is from the early medieval Bernese commentator who clearly
had access to more of Lucan's original poem *Pharsalia* than survives to
the present day. It describes the three great Gallic gods mentioned by
Lucan – Esus, Taranis and Teutates – and makes the connection between
them and their Roman equivalents. The text is important for it attests to
deliberate modes of killing as appropriate to particular circumstances,
a theme to which we will return.

Drowning is a fitting death for bog people because the means of killing
are so conveniently present. Several ancient bog victims show no specific
evidence for the manner of their dispatch: no injuries, wounds or nooses.
In these instances, it is fair to assume that some at least were drowned. Of
the two bodies from Windeby in North Germany, one – a man of mature
years – had been strangled, his corpse weighted down with stones and
branches. The second, much younger victim was similarly pegged down in
the swamp and may well have been drowned. Part of the latter's hair had
been shaved off, just as was true of the Dutch Yde Girl and another female,
from Huldremose in Denmark (PL. X), whose long hair had been cut off and
placed by her side (again like the Yde Girl's). But, significantly, in the case
of the Huldremose Woman a long skein of it was wrapped tightly around
her throat, as if acting as a symbolic (or indeed genuine) garrotte.[40] This
unfortunate bog victim had suffered a mutilating injury before she died:
her right arm had been hacked off. There were other signs of shaming and
abuse, including cuts to her left leg, and her left arm was bound to her body
with a leather thong. Without her right arm and with her left immobilized,
it would have been all too easy to drown her.

SECRET TOXINS

> Most of Britain is marshland…The barbarians usually swim in these
> swamps or run along in them, submerged up to the waist. Of course, they
> are practically naked and do not mind the mud…They also tattoo their
> bodies with various patterns and pictures….
>
> HERODIAN, *HISTORY*[41]

The Greek historian Herodian made his comments about 'barbarous
Britannia' in the late 2nd to early 3rd century AD, when Britain had been
part of the Roman Empire for two centuries. As I have argued elsewhere,[42]
Herodian's observations say more about the author and his ignorant
prejudices than about the reality of life in Roman Britain. However, there
is interest in the linking of bogs and decorated bodies. This has relevance
because traces of minerals – such as nickel, manganese, phosphorous and
aluminium – on the Lindow bodies[43] are likely to indicate they wore body
paint, whether as 'the norm' or as part of ceremonies associated with their
deaths. There is scant evidence for other painted bog bodies, although one
recorded (but since lost) from Schwerinsdorf, Lower Saxony, apparently had
elaborate decoration on the front and back of his body.[44] I mention body art
here because heavy metals on the skin have the capacity to penetrate and
release dangerous toxins into the bloodstream. It is by no means impossible that Lindow III was suffering the ill effects of poisonous chemicals
that may have caused physical and mental changes and, indirectly (and
slowly), may have contributed to his death. (Woad, said by Caesar to have
been used by the Britons to decorate themselves, gives its users a 'high').

Other toxins may have been ingested by bog victims. As we saw in
Chapter 3, Lindow II had a small but significant quantity of mistletoe
in his stomach.[45] Mistletoe is generally deemed to be poisonous, but
in small doses can have a therapeutic, calming effect on the brain and
nervous system. The presence of a token amount of mistletoe in Lindow II
may have been designed to sedate him or symbolically to poison him. Of
course, Pliny's famous account of the Druidic oak-and-mistletoe ritual[46]
has led to connections being made between Lindow Man and the Druids
(see p.59).[47] While the ingestion of mistletoe alone may not be sufficient
to implicate the Druids in Lindow Man's death, they – or other religious
officials – might well have been involved in killing bogmen, particularly
if the latter were ritual victims (see Chapter 9).[48]

The ingestion of mistletoe by Lindow Man leads to consideration of other poisons that might have contributed to bog victims' deaths, or at least their physical and psychological state when they were killed. As we have seen, the intestines of some bogmen, notably those from Grauballe and Tollund, contained ergot. But scholarly opinion is divided as to whether or not sufficient ergot was present in the bodies to be truly toxic (see p.60). Although the levels of ergot present in Grauballe Man did not kill him (and we know, in any case, that he died from a slit throat), they may have affected his behaviour. What is more, if he had ingested similar amounts over a long period of time, this might at least have weakened him.

THE MANNER OF THEIR DEATHS AND WHY THEY DIED

Might there have been connections between the manner of these bog people's deaths and why they were killed? There were surely reasons why some were beheaded, some allowed to bleed to death, while others were hanged or drowned. The Bernese scholiast on Lucan's *Pharsalia* speaks of the association between different ways of killing and the different gods to whom victims were offered.[49] He is clear that Lucan's three Gallic gods Esus, Taranis and Teutates were propitiated by human deaths. But to comment on human sacrifice here is to anticipate its rightful place of discussion in Chapter 10. What is clear from this chapter on the modi operandi involved in the killing of bog victims is both the range of injuries but also the similarities of behaviour on the part of the perpetrators, for example in the recurrent use of special knots on victims of strangulation. What is perhaps most striking is the amount of violence that is often involved, and that is the focus of the next chapter.

CHAPTER 7

Instrumental Violence: Abuse with Purpose

> Now you feel quite dry and cool,
> But grossly your mouth is grimacing
> The death-cry, when you were drowned in the bog
> Bogged down by the executors' stakes.
>
> STEEN STEENSEN BLICHER, *QUEEN GUNHILD*[1]

The subject of Bilcher's poem is the Iron Age bog body from Haraldskaer ('Queen Gunhild') in central Jutland. He constructed it so that alternate verses told her story 'then' and 'now'. The extract above is a fitting start to this chapter because it sums up the pain, fear and indignities endured by bog victims and their multiple suffering. In four simple lines, the poet paints a vivid and disturbing picture of a terrified woman, crying out in anguish as she went into the bog, her asphyxiation emphasized by the timbers that skewered her into the marsh and made sure she never floated free. 'Queen Gunhild' had been discovered less than 10 years before Bilcher composed his poem about her; at that time, it was still thought that she had been drowned, and that her body had been pinned down while she was still alive. Now we know that she had been strangled and only then placed in the swamp, and that the stakes pegging her down were driven into her body when she was already dead. Even so, the piercing of her dead flesh and the force required to drive a sharp stake through her knee-joint argues for post-mortem violence almost as disturbing to the modern western mind as if it had occurred when she was breathing.

The term 'instrumental violence' expresses the kind of abuse to the human body that has a specific purpose, an end product that somehow transcends the violent act itself. So, in the case of bog bodies, it could be argued that extreme violence was the result of perceptions that such force was somehow necessary in order for the killing of an individual to be efficacious. For example, the violent behaviour of attackers could be attributed to the fear of the victim or revenge for his or her misconduct, or designed to send a symbolic message either to the community or to the gods. An example that takes in all of these possible reasons for instrumental violence is that of the *pharmakos* or scapegoat: in ancient Greek tradition, someone was chosen to take responsibility for all the ills afflicting a town, driven out and stoned or drowned, thus ritually cleansing the community (PL. XI).[2]

The focus of this chapter is on the evidence for the sometimes excessive and sustained violence inflicted by the killers on their bog victims. The violence appears to have been totally personal, directed at specific individuals, but that does not necessarily mean that the rest of the community was not caught up in the act or symbolically connected to it. Some of the bog people appear to have suffered abuse over a period of time before their eventual death, others received multiple peri-mortem injuries, any one of which would have been sufficient to kill them. Why did such long-term abuse and 'overkill' violence happen? Why was it necessary to inflict such terrible damage on people if the ultimate purpose was simply to end their lives?

'OVERKILL' VIOLENCE: SOME OF THE VICTIMS

It is a commonly held view that 'human nature' is inherently violent, and that this tendency is a product of our genetic programming and evolutionary history.

WAKELY, 'IDENTIFICATION AND ANALYSIS OF VIOLENT AND NON-VIOLENT HEAD INJURIES IN OSTEO-ARCHAEOLOGICAL MATERIAL.'[3]

Lindow Man from northwest England and Oldcroghan Man from central Ireland each exemplify a concentration of violent injuries that resulted in death. They differ, though, for the violent acts perpetrated on Lindow

Man appear to have happened all at once, just before he died, while many of Oldcroghan's injuries seem to have been inflicted just after he died and before he was put into the bog.

For he who lives more lives than one
More deaths than one must die.

OSCAR WILDE, *THE BALLAD OF READING GAOL*

By reading the marks of violence on Lindow Man's body, we can try to construct a narrative of the multiple manner of his death and, by implication, what kind of person he might have been in life. Was it possible that the 'overkill' or 'triple death' that he suffered was because he lived 'more than one life', as Wilde put it? The poem quoted above is a bitter expression of resentment concerning the then attitudes to homosexuality, and the double lives that were forced upon hidden same-sex couples. But it is possible to extend Wilde's observation and to pose the question whether an individual who had more than one persona (for example as a shaman, or 'two-spirit' person,[4] someone who moved between the earth world and spirit world) when alive might be killed in multiple ways in order to reflect that multifaceted life.

The first part of the killing ritual might well have been the baking of the griddle cake that formed Lindow Man's 'last supper'. Once he had eaten it and, with it (or in it), a small quantity of mistletoe, he was stripped but for an armlet of fox fur and led out to a remote wetland place, probably specially chosen beforehand. I suspect that at least two individuals were responsible for his death, for he was a powerful, fit young man, in the prime of life. The vicious blows to the top and back of his head stunned him but did not lead to his immediate demise, although his skull was fractured and fragments of bone driven deep into his brain (PL. IX). The position of the wound on the crown of the head would suggest that it was caused whilst the deceased was in a standing or kneeling position.[5] The narrow, sharp-edged blade that could cause such a traumatic injury was probably used to deliver two blows in quick succession. It is all too probable that Lindow Man's attacker knew exactly the amount and type of force trauma needed to stun his victim but not to kill him. The next stage was the summit of the theatre involved in the act of killing Lindow Man, and the forensic evidence points to a complex procedure. Once the victim was rendered immobile by his head injuries, someone moved up close behind him and looped a sinew rope around his neck, forming a ligature with two twists at the back, suggesting that the man was garrotted, the noose tightened by means of a stick or other implement that was used to wind and therefore shorten the rope so as to throttle him, but perhaps not quite tight enough to break his neck immediately. At virtually the same time, his throat was cut at the right side with a sharp blade, probably by somebody else, clearly with the intention of severing the jugular vein.[6] The tight noose, the heightened blood pressure thus caused, and the throat-slitting all would have combined to cause a fountain of blood to spurt from the neck wound that would have covered both the victim and his killers in a veritable bath of blood. Even then, the violence was not over, for bruised tissue at the base of the victim's spine indicates that he was dealt a vicious knee-blow to his back, causing him to fall face down into the bog, where he was quickly submerged and buried, probably during cold weather that would, like the water itself, inhibit the process of decay.

The sequence of events that led to Lindow Man's death is chilling enough. But consideration needs also to be given to the skill and anatomical knowledge that the killers must have possessed. They knew just how much injury the man could sustain while still keeping him alive for the final gush of blood. This argues not just for skill but for the need both for the maximum spectacle and for total control over life and death. The attackers were playing with time, able to suspend and manipulate the death process, and I am sure that this was a significant element in the entire procedure, right from the selection of the victim, the food he was given and the stripping of his clothes to the moment that his near-lifeless body sank into the bog water.

Although the injuries and sequence of events were somewhat different from Lindow Man's, the several traumas suffered by Oldcroghan Man indicate similar levels and varieties of extreme violence, far in excess of what was needed to kill him. The processes that led ultimately to his death involved savage slashing blows that decapitated him and cut him in half, possibly with a sword although, given the small size of most Irish La Tène swords, a sharp iron axe is more likely to have been the weapon used. But the abuse did not end there, for his upper arms were pierced, the holes threaded with hazel withies, and his nipples sliced. Like Lindow Man, he was naked but for an armlet, this time made of leather and ornamented metal. The sheer size and powerful build of Oldcroghan Man makes it almost certain that several people were needed to restrain and overpower him (unless, of course, he was sedated, or went willingly to his excruciating torture and death.)[7] The injuries to his nipples seem to represent a very particular form of somatic abuse. The Irish archaeologist Ned Kelly,[8] who has led research into the body, believes that this relates to a ritual associated with early medieval Irish kingship. But Oldcroghan died in about 300 BC, and the textual references to kingship ceremonies are nearly a thousand years later, so I am sceptical about such connections. The slicing of the bogman's nipples perhaps more likely represents an act of humiliation perpetrated on the already mutilated dead body before it was consigned to the swamp.

Mutilation, before and after death, is a recurrent feature of ancient bog bodies, and is a mark of extreme violence. As the term implies, it involves changing the body irreversibly. Some acts involved dismemberment, as was suffered by the Danish woman from Huldremose, whose right arm was chopped off while she was still alive[9] (the cutting off of her hair was also a form of mutilation; PL. X). Such an injury to a limb perhaps resonates with the deliberate fractures suffered by other bog bodies, such as Grauballe Man (see Chapter 6). Another Danish woman, from Borremose, was facially disfigured, by crushing and removing some of the bones. This would have been an especially gory procedure, involving huge amounts of blood. It is tempting to view this treatment as akin to the Roman custom of *damnatio memoriae*, which involved the erasure of facial features on the statues of hated (deceased) emperors or the blotting out of their names on inscriptions, in order to 'rub them out', deny their identity and the very fact that they had ever lived. The removal of faces on statues of discredited prominent people has a long history in antiquity: stone images of both the Assyrian kings Tiglath-Pileser III and Sennacherib often had their faces thoroughly picked out from their sculptures.[10] The difference between *damnatio memoriae* among the Assyrians and the Romans, on the one hand, and what happened to the Borremose woman, on the other, is that whilst the *damnatio* facial abuse was inflicted by proxy, on the images of the hated, on the Borremose body it was applied to the person herself.

In his book *Violence and the Sacred*,[11] the French anthropologist René Girard narrates a mythic tale of the Tsimshian native Americans of the Pacific Canadian coast, which involved a pair of star-crossed lovers, each a member of the chieftain's kin. The girl was unsure of her young cousin's love and demanded that he prove it by disfiguring his own face. Unsurprisingly, the girl then spurned him because he was ugly. In his despair, he went to 'the land of Chief Pestilence' and its leader, the 'Master of Deformities'. His beauty was restored by means of a kind of death and rebirth ritual in which he was boiled, his bleached bones harvested and his body reconstructed whole. His callous girlfriend fell in love with him all over again, and he now demanded the same proof of love from her. She obeyed him and mutilated her face, and he, in his turn, rejected her on account of her wrecked looks. She trod the same path as her lover, turning in her despair to the land of Pestilence and its awful chief. But her fate was horribly different. Her cousin had refused to join the tribe of Deformity, all of whom were mutilated and crippled, but she made the mistake of agreeing to become one of them. Immediately, all the disfigured tribespeople fell upon her, 'crippling and mutilating her and then casting her out to die'.[12]

The Tsimshian myth serves to remind us of a whole host of perceptions and 'freights of attitude'[13] of which we are entirely ignorant when trying to understand the treatment of Iron Age bog victims. But in considering the kind of excessive violence that leads to dismemberment and the other mutilating injuries sustained, it is worth posing the question of whether this specific form of violence had any connection with the natural deformities or other disabilities suffered by a significant number of the Iron Age individuals who ended up being killed and deposited in swamps (see Chapter 8). The idiopathic scoliosis (extreme curvature of the spine) endured by the Yde Girl and the hip malformation of the Kayhausen Boy are just two examples of many. It is almost as though certain aspects of the violent abuse inflicted on bog bodies – the leg fractures and dismembered limbs – were conscious reflections of natural or accidental deformities. Another issue that arises in consideration of victims such as Lindow Man and Oldcroghan Man, who were the object of so much violence, is the possible analogy with *sparagmos*, an ancient Greek term used to describe the kind of frenzied dismemberment inflicted by groups upon humans, like Pentheus in Euripides's drama *The Bacchae*, who was torn apart by maenads while they were maddened by the god Dionysus.[14] Euripides wrote his play during the war between Athens and Sparta in the late 5th century BC, and used it to explore the chaos and social dysfunction caused by civil war and to draw analogies between the destruction of normal human values as played out in the drama and in the two great city-states

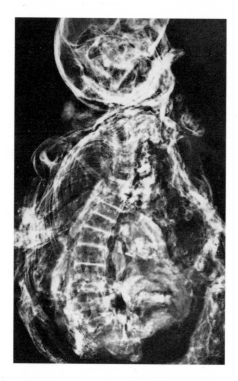

X-ray of the Yde Girl's upper body showing the pronounced and
disabling curvature of her spine, a condition that would have caused
her to walk painfully and with a lurching gait.

at the time of the conflict between them. The disaggregation of human
bodies – dismemberment, decapitation, piercing of limbs – was enacted
in the context of immense emotional (and perhaps also socio-political or
even religious) disturbance. Is it possible to see the apparently sadistic
treatment of bog victims as analogous in some way?

There is another possible reason why some of the bog bodies were
mutilated. In his book *Greek and Roman Necromancy*,[15] the classical historian Daniel Ogden discusses the treatment accorded some corpses, which
included savage post-mortem mutilation. This was apparently done to
victims of murder in order to protect the perpetrators from the ghostly
retribution of their vengeful spirits, to hobble their ghosts, an idea I briefly
introduced earlier in the book (see Chapter 5). Abusing the body in this
way was perceived to weaken a ghost so that it did not possess the strength
to retaliate. Is it possible that something broadly similar was behind at
least some of the mutilations carried out on bog victims? Even if these

people were killed for religious purposes (as argued particularly in Chapter 10), killing is likely to have been hedged about with taboos and anxieties, perhaps not least because of worries about revenge. Such fears of the untimely dead might even explain why they were given special watery interments: because their unquiet spirits matched the dangerous marshes in which they were placed.

ON THE CUSP OF EXISTENCE

In focusing on the way Lindow Man died, the issue of control was touched upon, together with the deliberately sustained liminality of the corpse, kept hovering between life and death. We can pursue this a little further by looking at other aspects of bog deaths. Bogs themselves are liminal places, oscillating between land and water, often with a skin of green algae on their surfaces and presenting a false image. The stripped body of a bog corpse exposes the skin directly to the bog, and skin itself is a border, a wrapping containing the organs, blood and tissue. The violence meted out to victims, especially those attacked with knives or other weapons, caused blood to leak out and bog water to percolate in, in a mutual exchange of inner and outer fluids, thus blurring the boundaries between human and swamp. The fragments of *Sphagnum* moss in Lindow Man's stomach 'suggest that he may have made one last gasp for air as he lay face down in the mire'.[16] The gaping mouth of a victim of asphyxiation again presents a liminal space, interrupting breath and causing the normally contained and hidden tongue to be exposed to the air.

If bog victims like Lindow Man were deliberately kept hovering between life and death for extended periods, there must have been an underlying purpose. It could have been simply punitive, the result of a vengeful community revelling in its capacity to 'make good' the evils done to it. But what maybe reflected instead is the special nature of the victims themselves. Powerful, influential individuals may have required overwhelmingly powerful killing. If there were religious intentions associated with these deaths, it may have been considered that the gods could only be appeased for wrongs done if the manner of death was extreme. It may also have been perceived that victims had to be prevented from going into the next world not only by freeze-framing them in the preserving environment of the swamp but also by the over-thorough methods of their destruction.

BOG BODY VIOLENCE IN CONTEXT

Do you believe violent death leaves a kind of surge of energy behind
it which is really what's meant by ghosts?

BARBARA VINE, *KING SOLOMAN'S CARPET*[17]

This question, raised by a character in one of Vine's psychological thrillers,
is pertinent to the excessive physical abuse suffered by some Iron Age bog
victims. It is possible to argue that the extreme violence exhibited by some
of the bog people was the result of a perception that violence itself carried
an energy field and rendered the killings more symbolically effective, particularly if (as suggested in Chapter 10) they were ritual, even sacrificial,
victims. It is necessary at this juncture to widen the net beyond the bog
bodies themselves to consider how they fit into the broader context of
evidence for ancient violence, as demonstrated by the study of skeletal
remains. Of course, bones tell a much more limited death story than flesh-
and-blood bodies but, nonetheless, they can still possess the fingerprint
of violent killing.

The well-known hillfort at Danebury in Hampshire, excavated by
Barry Cunliffe in the later 20th century, revealed stark evidence for the

The skeleton of a young man interred in a disused grain silo
at Danebury, Hampshire, perhaps as a thank-offering to the gods
for looking after the seed-corn over the winter.

disposal of people who had met untimely deaths, the result of arguably deliberate attacks. As we saw in Chapter 2, they were found in pits that had been first dug for the storage of grain, then cleaned out and used as repositories for the bodies of humans and animals as well as other things. More than 25 complete bodies, mainly of young adult men, were placed in these silos,[18] and some of them showed signs of extreme violence. One man's body had been butchered, like the carcass of a food animal: someone had used a thin sharp blade to cut the pelvis and the heads of both femurs from his torso while they were still fleshed. If this savagery was not the cause of death, it occurred soon afterwards. Other people whose remains ended up in the pits included those whose bodies were crushed by rocks or lumps of chalk, or whose heads had been battered in.[19] There is even the grisly possibility that the corpse whose pelvis was butchered was the victim of cannibalism.[20]

There is a range of other evidence for the dismembering and chopping up of people in British Iron Age contexts. Some of the most horrific violence recorded happened at Wandlebury in Cambridgeshire, where both children and adults were hacked about before being deposited in pits. One woman had sustained a plethora of limb fractures; her legs were taken off at the pelvis and the pelvis itself crushed by blocks of flint.[21] At Hornish

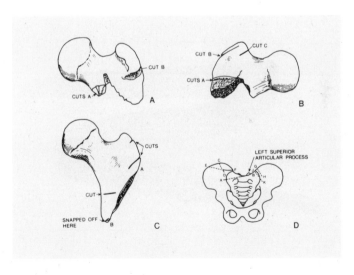

The butchered human pelvis from a disused grain storage pit at Danebury, Hampshire. Its presence raises the possibility of ritual cannibalism in the British Iron Age.

in the Western Isles, the body of an adolescent boy was carefully divided into quarters, each piece buried in a pit at the corners of a rectangular Iron Age house (see p.188).[22] These are just some of the more spectacular examples of the violence done to human bodies as reflected in their skeletal remains. It is not usually possible to be certain whether such horrific injuries were the cause of death or whether the mutilations and dismemberments were carried out post-mortem. But in either case, the violence meted out to living body or lifeless corpse was significant and highly motivated, and serves – perhaps – to provide a context for what happened to some of the bog bodies.

Animals as well as people could be victims of excessive violence. A man was buried in a late Iron Age cemetery at Tartigny in northern France, accompanied by various animal body parts, as well as a dog that had been disembowelled and skinned.[23] A similar thing happened to a dog found at the late Roman Lankhills burial ground near Winchester.[24] The practice of delivering extreme violence extended to objects, too. Great force was exercised in order to bend swords into snake-like contorted shapes at the sanctuary of Gournay-sur-Aronde in northern France in the 3rd century BC (see pp.173–74).[25] Roman amphorae – the tall, double-handled, narrow-necked jars used for storing quantities of

An iron sword, one of several weapons deliberately 'killed' by being twisted out of shape, from the 'war sanctuary' at Gournay-sur-Aronde, northern France, 3rd century BC.

red Mediterranean wine – were deliberately smashed in huge numbers at the late Iron Age township of Corent in the Auvergne; others were 'beheaded'. The pinkish colour and rather human shape of these vessels, together with their blood-like contents, might have led to them being perceived as surrogate people, and their destruction may have been a form of substitutive violence.[26] The spectrum of deliberate, extreme and instrumental violence, then, was by no means confined to the bodies in the bogs; it extended to other people, animals and even to weapons and wine-jars.

VIOLENCE AND MAGIC

In former times, the Lambadis, before setting out on a journey, used
to procure a little child and bury it in the ground up to its shoulders,
and then drive their loaded bullocks over the unfortunate victim.
In proportion to the bullocks thoroughly trampling the child to death,
so their belief in a successful journey increased.

WHITEHEAD, *THE VILLAGE GODS OF SOUTH INDIA*[27]

This quotation comes from the account of Bishop Whitehead of his missionary sojourn in India in the early 20th century. He observed and recorded a range of magical practices of which perhaps the most spectacular (and to our minds horrific) was this ritual custom of the nomadic Lambadis. Whitehead was describing a magical connection between a ritualized action and a desired outcome. The sacrifice of a child, by animals that were essential to the tribe's peripatetic way of life, was believed to bring blessings from the spirits and so achieve success in journeys for which those animals were a key element

In his book *The Pagan Religions of the British Isles*, the historian Ronald Hutton defines magic as the use of spiritual forces by people to exert control over the natural world.[28] The main difference between religion and magic is that of control. Religious belief involves a subordinate relationship between gods and humans, the former perceived to exist entirely independently of human worshippers. But where magic is concerned, people are in the driving seat and the spirits are manipulated in order to achieve a desired result. I include a section on magic here because of current research into a particular group of ancient figurines that have been classified as being of magical purpose and associated with the widespread

Romano-British *defixio* (curse tablet) from Telegraph Street, London. The message refers to a woman called Tretia Maria. The holes pierced in the lead were for nails to 'fix' the spell onto the victim and ensure it did not rebound on the spell-caster.

practice of using *defixiones* or curse tablets as a means of exacting spiritually engendered, and excessively savage harm upon wrongdoers.

The majority of these figurines – often made of lead – belong to Mediterranean and Near Eastern antiquity, but a few have been identified in the western Roman provinces, including Gaul and Britain. An example dating to the later 2nd century AD was found at the great Roman palace of Fishbourne in Sussex. It was made of lead, and exhibited signs of deformity in the differing lengths of its legs.[29] The importance of these figurines lies in the violent treatment accorded them. They are sometimes decapitated or dismembered, often twisted out of shape, as if tortured, bound or pierced with pins. Two hollow figures from Straubing (Roman Sorviodurum) in Bavaria contained seeds.[30]

While there is no reason whatsoever to make a direct connection between these magical figurines and north European bog bodies, there is possible broad relevance in terms of the violence inflicted upon each group of material (images and real bodies). The analogous treatment of both bog corpses and the magical figurines (even down to the seeds inside the Bavarian examples) leads me to question whether the violence present on the bog bodies may have been 'instrumental' not only in terms of killing and suffering but also – possibly – in terms of magic. Was the amount and manner of the violence sustained by these people commensurate with a need for the killing to have a magical power, in order to shape future events or neutralize negative forces? Were piercing, binding, decapitation, dismemberment and even disability seen as part of elaborate magical rituals designed to harness and control the spirits of the marshes or even the souls of the dead themselves?

VIOLENCE AND THE SACRED

All violence is sanctioned by someone, even if only
by the perpetrator. Victims will, in general, take the position
that violence is non-sanctioned.
JOHN CARMAN, 'GIVING ARCHAEOLOGY A MORAL VOICE'[31]

The process that led ultimately to the deposition of human corpses in bogs, after their untimely and often violent deaths, involved several episodes, certain of which might have occurred sometime before the killing. The ingestion of special, often unpalatable, food whose presence is found in the preserved gut may not have been one event. The victim may have been fed in this way for days, weeks or even months leading up to the death day. The violence inflicted upon the bog body may similarly have been systematic and of long-standing, as witnessed by the partially healed fractures, the result of old injuries (PL. XI). If the deaths did not occur as simple murder, for gain, hatred or revenge, then the violence may well have been 'sanctioned' by the community, or at least by some sections or powerful individuals within it. Sanctioned violence may have come about in the context of warfare, punishment or ritual behaviour. And if ritual were to have been involved in bog body deaths, the violence *may* have been associated with human sacrifice (see Chapter 10).

But there may have been other ritually motivated intentions wherein the violence, abuse, destruction and morphing of living (or dead) bodies by mutilation might have been the primary purpose, rather than the death itself. In *Violence and the Sacred*, René Girard comments that in choosing a single victim that can be treated with extreme brutality, society can deflect onto that victim the pent-up violence that could otherwise harm the rest of the community.[32] So, according to Girard, violence towards an individual can be vented in the manner that causes the least damage to society. If we take this idea further, it could be argued that the greater the amount of force and injury, the more efficacious this deflective mechanism may be. Ritualized violence can thus be used as a safety valve, as a means of getting rid of unhealthy anger or friction and of restoring calm and balance within a community.

Ritual violence may not necessarily occur within the enclosed context of a connected group of people. It may, instead, be directed outwards to other communities. Like single combat, which was a military device used in many ancient societies to avoid mass destruction of troops, it may be that one group could act out its aggression towards its neighbours or to foreigners by venting it upon a single neighbour or foreign individual, maybe a hostage, particularly if the community perpetrating the violence felt threatened by external forces. In this way, the violent killing of a person might be freighted with punitive, deterrent and ritual purpose. If a bog victim sustained multiple injuries, as was the case with Lindow Man and many others, it is entirely possible that such injuries reflected surrogacy, wherein the individual person stood for the many.

The ancient author Dio Cassius described an episode in the great rebellion led by Queen Boudica against the Romans in AD 60, in which the Britons engaged in terrible atrocities against the Roman settlers living in London during its sacking. This is what he says:

> Those who were taken prisoners by the Britons underwent every
> possible outrage; the most atrocious and bestial committed was this:
> they hung up naked the noblest and most beautiful women, cut off
> their breasts and sewed them into their mouths so that they seemed to
> be eating them. Then they impaled them on sharp stakes which ran the
> length of their bodies.[33]

If Dio was not exaggerating, these acts did not simply represent mindless brutality against vulnerable members of a hated enemy but a particular revenge-torture in direct retaliation for the raping of Boudica's daughters. But it possessed a ritual angle in that these atrocities occurred within the sacred grove of Andraste, the Britons' goddess of victory.[34] In Tacitus's account of the behaviour of Boudica's forces during the rebellion, he comments that 'they could not wait to cut throats, hang, burn, and crucify – as though avenging, in advance, the retribution that was on its way.'[35]

While it is generally accepted that a victim of violence does not sanction the treatment received, it is possible that in certain instances, consent was involved. In the ritual behaviour surrounding the *pharmakos* in the ancient Greek city of Massilia (Marseille) in southern Gaul, the victim was a poor man who not only consented to be selected as the scapegoat but actually volunteered. This may not have been through any altruistic motive but because, for the year leading up to his death by stoning or drowning, he lived a life of extreme luxury, thus symbolically raising his status within the city, so as to make the atonement ritual all the more effective.[36] The *pharmakos* was associated with a general cleansing ritual but, if bog victims were to have fulfilled a similar role, it could be that they were atoning not for the evils or misfortunes of an entire community but to wipe out the pollution caused by their own behaviour. This is reminiscent of Oscar Wilde's allusion to double lives leading to double deaths, in the *Ballad of Reading Gaol* (see p.132). Personal or collective pollution and the need to counter it by ritual means might account for the violence to which bog bodies were sometimes subjected.

There is considerable evidence to suggest that the excessive and multifaceted force inflicted upon ancient bog bodies – whether by blunt force trauma, strangling, stabbing, decapitation or a combination of injuries – was something over and above what was necessary to take away their lives. The evidence is heavily weighted towards some kind of ritual interpretation, whether associated with atonement, neutralizing pollution, surrogacy (the one for the many), honour killing or magic. This chapter has not considered the one interpretation that makes a great deal of sense: human sacrifice. That is the subject of Chapter 10. Before discussing this controversial issue, however, it is necessary to focus sharply on the protagonists in the killing drama: the victims and their killers. Why were particular victims chosen to be ceremonially done to death? What criteria were used in their choice? Can we discern patterns based upon age, gender, status, state of health or deviance from the 'normal', such as disability? Who was involved in the killings? Were they individual acts or was collective responsibility taken for the violence? Were these actions the preserve of a priesthood or another group within the community? All these questions are considered in Chapters 8 and 9.

CHAPTER 8

The Chosen Ones

Posidonius says that there is a small island in the ocean, not far from
the land, lying off the mouth of the Loire; and the women of the
Samnitae inhabit it; they are possessed by Dionysus and propitiate
the god with initiations and other sacred rites; and no man may land
on the island, but the women themselves sail out from it and have
intercourse with men and then return. It is their custom once a year
to remove the roof from their temple and to roof it again the same day
before sunset, each woman carrying part of the burden; but the woman
whose load falls from her is torn to pieces by the others, and they
carry the pieces around the temple crying out 'euoi', and do not cease
until their madness passes away; and it always happens that someone
pushes against the woman who is destined to suffer this fate.

STRABO, *GEOGRAPHY*[1]

In common with other writers of the late 1st century BC and 2nd century AD,
such as Julius Caesar and Diodorus Siculus, the Greek geographer Strabo
quarried the earlier work of Posidonius, a Greek Stoic philosopher who has
the merit, as a reasonably authentic historical source, of having visited Gaul
himself in about 90 BC.[2] Clearly, however, the Greek god Dionysus, as such, is
unlikely to have been worshipped in Gaul; as so often occurred when classical writers described 'barbarian' religion, Strabo (and/or Posidonius) equated

Reconstruction drawing of Strabo's Loire Island sanctuary, in which priestesses
sacrificed the one of their number who was nudged into dropping her bundle
of thatch during their annual re-roofing ceremony.

a Graeco-Roman god with a seemingly equivalent local Gallic deity. What
is important in this passage is not so much the detail of the island and its
temple, nor even its single-gender occupancy, but the choice of a particular
woman to be ritually slaughtered in order to bless the reconsecrated shrine.
This person was a priestess but one whose death was validated, and indeed
precipitated, by a perceived and manipulated act of contamination or taboo.
The victim was in a liminal state: holy but unclean, a member of the religious
community but put outside it by deliberate exclusion. The predestined aspect
is telling: she was presumably chosen in advance of the re-roofing ritual by
her 'sisters', so that she would fulfil the necessary criterion for her death
and dismemberment. The reason for choosing her is not explained. Was it
because of some misdemeanour? Did she have a particular characteristic –
age, appearance, blemish, behaviour – or was it simply *her* turn?

The Loire island ritual serves to introduce the issue of selection of people
destined to become victims of violence and deposition in remote marshy
places. Like the Loire priestess, the bog victims did not die natural deaths
but were deliberately killed. Many of them were stripped naked, several suffered extreme physical trauma (PL. X), and nearly all of them were interred
without any personal possessions or grave furniture. Each person treated
in this way was chosen for a reason. It is possible that they were randomly
selected by lot but perhaps more likely that they possessed some quality or

particularity that marked them out as being special and suitable for deaths that fulfilled some purpose within the community. If we follow Strabo's model, that purpose is likely to have had ritual connotations.

CHOOSING BY LOT

For auspices and the casting of lots they have the highest possible regard. Their procedure in casting lots is uniform. They break off a branch of a fruit-tree and slice it into strips; they distinguish these by certain runes and throw them, as random chance will have it, on to a white cloth. Then the priest of the State, if the consultation is a public one, the father of the family if it is private, after a prayer to the gods and an intent gaze heavenward, picks up three, one at a time, and reads their meaning from the runes scored on them.

TACITUS, *GERMANIA* [3]

Could bog victims have been chosen by lot? Tacitus's remarks about lot casting relate to the very part of northern Europe in which most of them have been discovered. I can imagine a scene in which representatives from all sections of society – young, old, fertile women, adolescents,

Reconstruction drawing of a Germanic priest casting lots
to predict the will of the gods, as described by Tacitus.

farmers, elders, blacksmiths, warriors, foreigners, prisoners and slaves
– were gathered together for the lot-casting ceremony. Perhaps a priest
questioned them all about their role in their community and their perceived value to it before signing a lot-strip with that person's mark,
casting it onto a cloth and 'reading the runes'. If the death rituals were
connected with the propitiation of the gods, it may be that, despite the
'randomness' of the choice, the priest might have engineered it so that,
for instance, if it was a poor harvest that triggered the event, the most
appropriate individual – a farmer or a woman with at least one child (or
even pregnant) – was selected for bog death. Maybe the choice of fruit-
bearing trees for making the lot sticks might have been significant if
a failed harvest were threatened.

ISSUES OF NAKEDNESS

Now you lie naked, arid and foul,
With your bald head
Blacker far than the oak stake
With which you were wed to the bog.

STEEN STEENSEN BLICHER, *QUEEN GUNHILD* [4]

The practice of stripping certain bog victims before their interment in the
mire has been raised in earlier chapters. But here I want to reflect upon its
possible association with selection and, in particular, with the matter of
gender. For nakedness above all reveals a person's sex. It could be argued
that the act of divesting a chosen victim of their clothes made a deliberate statement both to the living witnesses of the event and to the bog
itself, thus forming a direct and intimate connection between the victim,
the killer, the spectators, the site of interment and the spirits perhaps perceived as dwelling in the marsh.

Nakedness not only brings gender to the forefront of revelation, but
also creates an ambiguity between private and public. In Tacitus's treatise
Germania, he emphasizes the strict morality of the northern peoples and
the chastity of their women.[5] He also comments, though, that Germanic
female dress often left bare the part of the breast closest to the shoulder.[6]
In her discussion of Scandinavian miniature gold foil figures of the 8th
century AD, Ing-Marie Back Danielsson[7] argues that naked images allow for
the intimate gaze as well as manipulation of sexual body parts. Unclothed

bog bodies were on view, without privacy and visually very firmly gendered. It is not usually possible to be certain whether these victims were stripped before or after death. Whenever it happened, it was for a purpose that was not linked to personal gain on the part of the killers, for the clothes were often placed near the body. Perhaps baring the bog victims was a way of allowing the bog to penetrate and clog the bodies' orifices.

A shaven head is also a form of nakedness. It was perhaps more traumatic for women than for men, not only because the latter more frequently suffer natural baldness from early middle age onwards but because hair played (and still plays) such a key role in perceptions of feminine beauty. Several north European bog people had the hair shaved from their scalps before their interment, including mature adults and adolescents of both sexes. One of the most dramatic instances was the young girl from Yde in the Netherlands, whose long blonde hair was intact on the left side of her head whilst it had been yanked out on the right. At least three other bodies from the Drenthe region of the Netherlands were also found to have had their hair close-cropped or shaved on the right side only.[8] So not only did

The Yde Girl, as found, a noose made from her own belt around her neck and her surviving hair beside her head.

these people suffer the mutilation of sudden hair-loss, but that humiliation included lopsidedness, making the person's appearance all the more bizarre. If, as in the Yde Girl's case, the hair had been torn out of the scalp rather than shorn, the resultant agony would have contributed to the acute misery suffered by the victim.

Head-shaving may have a range of purposes. In antiquity, it often marked the rite of passage from childhood into puberty and adult status. In classical Greek coming-of-age rituals, adolescents offered part of their hair in self-dedication to the gods.[9] Ancient Egyptian boys and girls traditionally had their heads shaved but for a single side-lock that was cut off at puberty, thus following the imagery of the child-god Horus.[10] These practices might be seen as broadly analogous to pubertal rites practised among Nigerian Yoruba communities, where adolescents have their hair shaved off to symbolize their rebirth as adults.[11] This kind of *rite de passage* could be relevant to the Yde Girl and the similarly aged child from Windeby (in his/her case it was the left side that had been shaved),[12] but it doesn't work for the mature woman from Huldremose in Denmark, whose hair was shorn and wound round her neck.[13] Perhaps she had entered another *rite de passage*, that of menopause, her status changing to one no longer of child-bearing capacity and even, therefore, her symbolic gender changing from female to asexual.

Tacitus reminds us that among the ancient Germans, head-shaving could be done to shame, humiliate or disfigure errant wives and draw public attention to adulterous behaviour.[14] In a modern context, a powerful scene in the film *Ryan's Daughter* shows the punishment of tarring and feathering meted out to a young Irish wife after the discovery of her affair with a British army officer. Her head was shaved, dipped in tar and adorned with chicken feathers. Even more shocking was the treatment of Jewish captives in German concentration camps during the Second World War, whose heads were brutally shaved. In Sara Nomberg-Przytyk's diary of her time in Auschwitz, she writes 'It did not bother them that we were women and that without our hair we felt totally humiliated.'[15]

Nakedness and head-shaving both act to leave an individual vulnerable, physically and emotionally fragile. But they also allow direct contact between human skin and the 'skin' of the bog. Special people – perhaps those at the interface between life stages – may have been treated in this way because it was deemed that particular power emanated from their bodies and it was perceived important that this was transferred to the water in which they were immersed. In a view of life and death perhaps broadly analogous to the Christian doctrine of 'dust to dust', it is possible that certain bog victims needed to go to their miry graves as naked and hairless as when they were born. Maybe we are witnessing reciprocal transformation ceremonies in which an exchange of matter between bog and person was being played out. This might be doubly important if the naked bodies deposited in the swamp were tattooed or painted, for the art is likely to have been highly symbolic and charged with energy that needed to be transferred.

SPECIAL BODIES

You were flaxen-haired,
undernourished, and your
tar-black face was beautiful.
My poor scapegoat.

SEAMUS HEANEY, *PUNISHMENT*[16]

The theme of *Punishment* is the Iron Age bog body of an adolescent from Windeby in North Germany. The important word in this extract from Heaney's poem is 'undernourished'. Growth had been stunted and interrupted, so he/she would have been undersized and unusually slight; the child may have stood out from its fellows as being unnaturally fragile. Physical differences do seem to have played a role in the choice of bog victims. Time and again, forensic analyses have demonstrated abnormalities that would have marked these individuals as deviant from the rest of the community. (In the case of the Windeby Child, it may even be that his or her gender ambiguity was an issue (PL. IV).)

Dionysius of Halikarnassos, whose work *Roman Antiquities* was written in the late 1st century BC, described how Romulus, founder of the city of Rome, issued a decree concerning the raising of children. He instructed parents to bring up all their male offspring and the female first-born, and not to kill any child unless it suffered from a physical deformity. He also decreed that parents of such malformed infants were allowed to abandon their babies by exposing them out of doors, provided that they allowed five neighbours to examine them beforehand.[17]

But in the Graeco-Roman world generally, congenital deformity or other physical abnormality was regarded as a divine blight, born of the gods' ill will towards the parents.[18] Disability was not sympathetically treated but regarded as an unfortunate deviation from the gold standard of human perfection. Aristotle went further than the later writer Dionysius, arguing that parents should be banned from rearing such children.[19] In rare instances, an adult with an acquired disability might use it to their advantage. A case in point is Julius Caesar, who suffered from late-onset epilepsy.[20] In typical Caesar fashion, he exploited his disease, commenting that it marked him out as being especially blessed by the gods.

There is no literary testimony for the attitudes of northern peoples in antiquity, such as Britons, Gauls and Germans, towards bodily difference. However, the repeated occurrence among bog victims of individuals who had survived, or been allowed to survive, to adult or sub-adult age with congenital deformities or differences suggests a somewhat less draconian response to somatic deviance than is evident in the classical world. It is possible only to identify certain physical abnormalities in the bog people; differences of mind are, of course, impossible to detect, as are deafness, speech impediments and even most forms of blindness.

Of the many types of physical divergence represented by bog victim populations, the most striking are those associated with mobility, particularly amongst adolescents. In a chapter entitled 'Half-Lives' in his book *The Eye of the Beholder*, the classicist Robert Garland discusses attitudes to the disabled in the Graeco-Roman world, commenting on the ambivalent fascination and repulsion with which they were regarded. The emperor Claudius probably suffered from a form of cerebral palsy: he limped heavily and spoke with a stammer. According to Suetonius, Claudius's mother Livia 'often called him a monster: a man whom Mother Nature had begun to work upon but then flung aside'.[21] Nonetheless, Claudius survived to become one of the most influential of the Julio-Claudian emperors, and ruled the known world for more than a decade, adding Britain to the portfolio of his empire.

The young girl strangled with a woollen girdle from Yde in Drenthe in the northern Netherlands was discovered in a peat bog in 1897. Radiocarbon dating carried out on the body in 1988 indicates that she died and was placed in the swamp in the 1st century AD. She was about 16 years old when she was killed, a small teenager, only 1.4 m (4 ft 7 ins) tall, with long blonde hair. CT scans and X-rays showed that she had suffered pronounced idiopathic scoliosis, severe curvature of the spine, which would have caused her considerable and constant pain and would have meant that she had walked with a curious lurching gait. Unlike many bog victims, she was found covered with the remains of a long coat, badly woven and very worn, with signs that it had been patched up on several occasions.[22] The body of the teenage boy from Kayhausen in Schleswig-Holstein, hog-tied and his throat cut in the 2nd to 1st centuries BC, suggests that he would have had similar difficulties in walking. This was due not to a spinal deformity but a diseased hip, in which an infection had eaten away the neck of the right femur.[23] Like the girl from Yde, the boy could have moved about only in great discomfort and with a very pronounced limp. Both these individuals would have stood out visually among other members of their community. Their continual discomfort may also have caused them to be surly and withdrawn, leading – perhaps – to their unwarranted reputation for witchcraft or ill-wishing and even to their blame for the community's misfortunes.

Even tinier than the Yde Girl was another body, of Roman date, from the Drenthe peat lands, that of an adult woman from Zweeloo. Most of her soft tissue has disappeared but her skeleton revealed severe limb deformities, resulting in abnormally short forearms and lower legs. This was the result of a rare form of dyschondrosteosis (dwarfism characterized by foreshortened limbs) that was not apparent in her infanthood but developed in adolescence.[24] So this woman would have presented not only as short in stature but as having the characteristics of dwarfism, with a torso long in relation to the limbs. It is a grotesque fact that in the Roman world, midgets fetched high prices in the slave market because of their rarity value: they were prized as oddities, to be displayed as curiosities

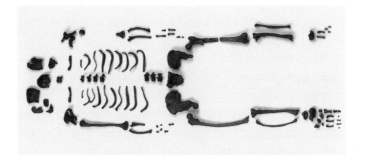

The Zweeloo Woman, from a peat bog in Drenthe, Netherlands.
She suffered from dwarfism, and died in the Roman period.

at dinner parties.[25] But if the Zweeloo Woman was singled out because of her tiny stature, the reverse might have been true of the huge man from Oldcroghan in Ireland. His great height and immense arm-span would have made him stand out in his community and, perhaps, this resulted in him being a target for ceremonial killing.

These are just a few of many examples of bog victims with physical abnormalities. Each of them would have found life extremely challenging and (with the exception of the Oldcroghan giant) probably would not have survived long without care from their family or wider community. Far from being a victim of Aristotelian eugenics, the child from Yde was nurtured and raised to sub-adulthood rather than being killed when her disability first became apparent. The woman from Zweeloo, too, was looked after for some years after her body developed its malformation. It is not possible to say with certainty how long the boy from Kayhausen survived after suffering the infection that destroyed his right hip, but it had had time to heal. So all three were kept alive, fed, clothed and given shelter by their kin and neighbours, even though they might have represented an economic burden to subsistence farming communities, until the time came for them to be killed and deposited in the swamps.[26]

It is worth a sideways glance here at evidence for other special deaths broadly contemporary with but separate from bog bodies. A striking instance relates to the burial of the burnt remains of a British chieftain who died in about AD 55 at Folly Lane, Verlamion (the Iron Age town preceding Roman Verulamium), now St. Albans in southeast England. The cremation was surrounded by a ditched enclosure, at whose entrance the bodies of three women were interred. They were all mature, almost certainly related to one another, and each of their skeletons indicated that they had suffered from conditions affecting their mobility: at least one of them had had tuberculosis that had spread to her lower limbs.[27] Why these women were buried here is unknown, but it is likely that their bodies were placed by the entrance as guardian-companions to the dead chieftain.

Other bog victims exhibited physical deviance that would have impacted less upon their ability to fend for themselves, but nonetheless would have distinguished them from their fellows. The 1st-century AD man discovered at Worsley Moss in Lancashire had been deliberately decapitated at the second cervical vertebra with a sharp-edged blade – a large knife or a sword – and forensic analyses revealed the presence of lacerations and skull fractures, at least some of which were probably delivered before death. Deeply embedded in the upper neck was a cord, almost certainly used to strangle the victim before decapitation. As we have already seen, the most distinctive feature of the man's head was a badly deformed right ear.[28] This would have been highly visible to others, and there is some evidence that he grew his hair long on the right side of his head, perhaps in an effort to conceal the deformity. It is also possible that the malformation of Worsley Man's ear led to his partial deafness.

Lindow III, who lived at roughly the same time as the owner of the Worsley head, was similarly beheaded, although this time archaeologists found the headless body rather than a disembodied head. He, too, had a 'non-functional' deformity: his surviving right hand displayed a vestigial extra digit sprouting from the outer edge of the main thumb, an abnormality that would have been present on both hands. This was indicated by the presence of two tiny extra phalangeal bones.[29] The deformity would not have presented him with dexterity problems, but – like the Worsley man's ear – it would have been highly visible to anyone who regularly spent time with him, particularly perhaps during communal meals. Both men were mature adults, in the prime of their lives; each would have been a useful member of the community, able to play a full part in warfare, farming and other tasks. The fact that both were beheaded prior to their deposition in swampy graves raises questions as to whether their particular deformities caused them not only to be deliberately killed, but 'doubly' killed by cutting their heads off, thereby making reincorporation in the next life impossible. Is it likely that both men were regarded as having special and dangerous powers, charged with such mental (or spiritual) force that particular efforts were needed to neutralize them by severing heads and depositing them at some distance from their bodies?

To try to understand what might have been going on with these decapitated bodies, we should concentrate on their particular abnormalities: an ear and a thumb. Let us hypothesize that each man possessed a distinctive status within his community. It may not be too fanciful to imagine that the Worsley individual had a role as a seer and a hearer, able to communicate with the gods and listen to what they told him. It is even possible, far-fetched though it might seem, that this individual 'heard voices' as a result of a neurological disturbance such as schizophrenia, and that such a peculiarity was explained by his kin as manifest in his weirdly shaped ear. It may even be that the withering of the ear was interpreted as the result of the scorching breath of the spirits whispering to him.

In much the same way, Lindow III's extra thumb might have been perceived as linked to spirit forces. Late Iron Age iconography may support the notion that thumbs and fingers possessed special significance, for certain images depict both exaggerated thumbs and extra fingers. On gold coinage issued by the Redones and Turones, northern Gallic tribes, female charioteers are shown with attenuated thumbs.[30] Similarly raised and exaggerated thumbs are present on a headless granite image from Lanneunoc in Brittany.[31] This last is especially striking because the forearms and hands are the only details on an otherwise completely blank human image. The 'seer's thumb' is a well-recognized theme or trope in early medieval Celtic mythic texts. In one Irish prose tale, a young hero, Finn, obtained wisdom by burning his thumb on the roasting flesh of the famed Salmon of Wisdom.[32] Thereafter, whenever he needed spiritual

Iron Age granite statue from Lanneunoc, Brittany. Both thumbs are exaggerated and upraised, calling to mind the Irish and Welsh legends of the 'seer's thumb'.

insight or divinatory powers, he only had to put his thumb in his mouth for inspiration. The extra digit on Lindow III's hand chimes with other imagery, too, notably a stone carving of a flute player from Pauvrelay à Paulmy in central Gaul, probably dating to the very end of the Gaulish Iron Age in the 1st century BC. Like the statue from Lanneunoc, the image is virtually featureless except for a large buffer-torc around its neck and two enormous hands that appear to grasp a long tube-like object. The figure's right hand had six fingers.[33] It is possible that the extra digit represents the consummate skill of the flautist, or the musician's physical oddity perhaps reflects his distinction as spiritually connected. Lindow III's tiny second thumbs may have been enough to mark him out as special, and maybe even brought about his death.

ISSUES OF STATUS

> Although Gaul is not a rich country, funerals there are splendid
> and costly. Everything the dead man is thought to have been
> fond of is put on the pyre, including even animals. Not long ago
> slaves and dependants known to have been their masters'
> favourites were burned with them at the end of the funeral.
>
> CAESAR, *DE BELLO GALLICO*[34]

The 'attendant killing' to which Caesar refers was common practice in many ancient societies, including those of the Vikings and the Scythians.[35] Those chosen to accompany the noble dead might also be of high rank, such as wives or warriors, but they might otherwise have been slaves, prized but regarded as things rather than as people. The three women buried in the enclosure ditch surrounding the cremated remains of the Folly Lane chieftain may well have been killed to be with their lord and wait upon him in the Otherworld.

The bog victims do not appear to have perished as the result of attendant killing, for they generally occur alone. It is just possible that where they were interred in pairs – such as the couples from Weerdinge and Hunteburg – one was killed to be with the main victim, but this is unlikely, given the absence of other grave goods, such as slaughtered animals, joints of meat and personal possessions that one might reasonably expect to find in such circumstances. If attendant rituals were involved in peat bog deposition of human remains, the deliberate and violent killing of the bog people would appear to reflect the burial of the companion without the main character in the funeral ceremonies, the noble deceased. The only way that makes any sense is if some kind of surrogate rituals were going on, whereby an attendant of a high-ranking individual was slain and deposited in a spiritually charged place as an appeasement offering, in order to avert the threatened death of their lord.

The physical attributes of the bog bodies send out mixed messages in terms of their rank. In any case, life status and death status may have been completely different, and even directly opposite one from the other. So the possible high rank enjoyed in life by fit, well-nourished men like Lindow Man and Oldcroghan Man, whose hands indicated that they had not habitually undertaken manual labour, could have been deliberately inverted in death. In a paper on the Neolithic complex of passage graves at Loughcrew, County Meath in Ireland, the prehistorian Andrew Cochrane explored the curious art forms on their walls and, in particular, the notion that they might represent the 'carnivalesque'.[36] This term is used to define the thinking behind carnivals, a community's conscious desire to 'subvert, distort and invert habitual or established life'.[37] Cochrane put forward the notion that what is going on is the release of a safety valve whereby the social norm is temporarily turned on its head, madness becomes sanity, unbridled lust is legitimized and status is reversed. In the Roman world, the 'carnivalesque' was expressed in the annual Saturnalia, perhaps the most popular ceremony in the Roman festival calendar, held at the time of the winter solstice in late December. This involved many carnival-like activities, but the best-known practice was the domestic inversion of rank, in which the servants were waited on by their masters.[38]

It is possible to approach bog body deaths using this lens of 'carnivalesque', in which the violence and degradation meted out to certain individuals was at total variance with their life status. For instance, the nakedness, absence of grave goods and humiliating ways of killing might have been deliberate inversions. In this sense Lindow Man might have been a great warrior, defending his community, but his death presented him as the opposite, an abject, passive victim of sustained and perhaps frenzied violence. According to such a model, what he was in life had a direct and perverse relationship to his mode of death and disposal. In a sense, this is the scapegoat in reverse: while the latter was of low life status that was artificially elevated to prepare him for death, Lindow Man and his fellows were ceremonially stripped of their rank and their very identity. Perhaps communities that practised bog killings had an emotional need to let go on certain occasions, to behave in ways that were otherwise unacceptable, in order to release tensions at moments of great crisis or in structured and regular ceremonial events. The violence dealt out to these bog victims was not simply random: its efficacy for the community was surely – at least to a degree – dependent upon the chosen person.

The ultimate inversion of status is perhaps evident in the case of ancient prisoners of war. In Iron Age Europe warriors enjoyed high rank among their own people. Yet when captured, their rank became ambiguous: they were non-citizens, foreigners, enemies and often representatives of defeated adversaries. Tacitus speaks of the killing of war captives in the sacred groves on Anglesey.[39] Plutarch's *Life of Themistocles* contains an account of Persian war captives who were particularly prized for their nobility, their youth and good looks. Yet when the Greek prophet Euphrantides ordered the Greek commander to kill them to honour the god Dionysus, Themistocles obeyed, although he felt repugnance in so doing. The point here is that, however high their rank, the Persian prisoners of war had no real status; their fate was entirely in the hands of the victors.[40]

People of low rank were also singled out for special death rituals. Caesar speaks of the particular value of criminals,[41] remarking that they had more currency as dedications to the gods than the innocent. But maybe, like foreign war captives, villains too possessed ambiguous status: there is no reason to suppose that the wealthy and the noble were incapable of misconduct. But the malnourishment shown by the Windeby adolescent's body suggests that (s)he was not of sufficiently high rank to be properly fed, whether because of famine or slavery.

EFFICACIOUS DEATHS: EFFICACIOUS CHOICES

His slave girls were asked who wished to die with him; one volunteered
to be burned with him. 'In these ten days she drinks and indulges in
pleasure; she decks her head and her person with all sorts of ornaments
and fine dress and so arrayed gives herself to the men.'

FROM THE *RISALA*[42]

This extract from a 10th-century account of a Viking funeral that took place in the middle Volga region reminds us that at least some of the bog victims might have gone willingly to their deaths in order to honour an illustrious person or to benefit their community by propitiating the gods. Bog people were clearly chosen with care and at least some of their vital statistics – age, status and physical state – were almost certainly relevant factors in their selection. There may have been others that have left no archaeological trace: voice or mental state, for instance. Some may have been shamans or priests, too powerful to be accorded normal burial rites, or sorcerers who gave off negative energy that had to be neutralized. In some Romany traditions, the dead have their nostrils and other bodily orifices plugged so as not to let the spirit out.[43] Could it be that something essentially similar happened to bog victims? Was the bog itself seen as a way of clogging the body's openings so as to imprison the spirit and stop it walking (and talking) after death?

We are edging ever closer to notions of human sacrifice, the focus for Chapter 10. But first we need to examine the identity of those who perpetrated the killings. Who commissioned the deaths and who got their hands dirty in carrying out the actual killing?

CHAPTER 9

Natural Born Killers

The two privileged classes are the Druids and the knights. The Druids are
in charge of religion. They have control over public and private sacrifices,
and give rulings on all religious questions...In almost all disputes,
between communities or between individuals, the Druids act as judges.
If a crime is committed, if there is a murder, or if there is a dispute about
an inheritance or a boundary, they are the ones who give
a verdict and decide on the punishment.

CAESAR, *DE BELLO GALLICO*[1]

In this passage, Caesar makes an important point concerning the centrality of the Druids in both religious and judicial procedures. His singling
out of only two groups of people who 'mattered' in Gaulish society in the
1st century BC suggests that any crucial event within communities would
be orchestrated by either Druids or knights. Diodorus Siculus similarly
speaks of the need for a 'philosopher' to be present at any religious ceremony.[2] In his *Germania*, Tacitus, too, stresses the need to have priests
present at both religious and criminal proceedings.[3]

The previous chapter was concerned with the selection of victims to be
killed and consigned to the bogs of northern Europe. This one engages with
the issue of responsibility. Who were the killers? Were they professional or
private individuals, chosen because they had been wronged, belonged to the

victim's family or, perhaps, were singled out by lot? To what extent did entire communities take collective responsibility for bog victim deaths? While it falls to Chapter 10 to explore bog killings within the context of possible human sacrifice, it is necessary to mention the topic here, too, for if we are to connect the Druids with the deliberate killing or execution of victims, the testimony of classical authors demands that sacrifice is taken as a serious issue. Caesar specifically alludes to the practice of human sacrifice by the Gauls in order to propitiate the gods (under circumstances where it was necessary to save a life by offering the gods another in exchange).[4]

We need, however, to be careful in using Caesar as a source. Although he makes strong links between Gallic and British practices, and specifically refers to the presence (and even the origins) of the Druids in Britain, where bog bodies are known, the majority of these marsh victims have been discovered in northern Europe – in North Germany, Denmark and the northern Netherlands. Caesar himself commented that 'the customs of the Germans are very different from those of the Gauls. They have no Druids to supervise religious matters and they do not show much interest in sacrifices.'[5] This is in direct contradiction to Tacitus's *Germania*,[6] in which he points out that priests were wholly responsible for capital punishment and flogging. He adds the interesting statement that the infliction of such punishment symbolized more than simple retribution but was demanded by the gods.

Despite differences in the detail of their reporting, Caesar, Strabo, Diodorus and Tacitus all make links between the ritualized killing of human beings and professional religious officials. The identification of such individuals is therefore key to understanding the context in which bog deaths may have occurred. But alongside the argument for the involvement of priests, whether they went by the name of Druids or had other titles, it is also crucial to consider other possible types of bog victim killer. Who they may have been must have depended, in part at least, on why the deaths occurred. If they were punitive executions, then priests may, as Caesar and other ancient writers indicate, have been present either to supervise or to engage as active participants. But the wronged persons or their families are also likely to have been heavily involved, particularly where honour was concerned.[7] And just as some victims may have been chosen by lot, so too – in certain circumstances – may the killers have been selected (in a manner not all that far removed from the modern British legal system of jury selection).

ARCHAEOLOGIES OF IRON AGE PRIESTHOOD

FATHERS OF INSPIRATION

The Musée Rolin in Autun, Burgundy, contains a miniature marble altar dedicated to 'Augustus' (a title used for many Roman emperors, not just the first emperor, Augustus) and a local Gallic god named Anvallus. Nothing is known about this latter deity, whether he was a local spirit of place or whether he possessed a specific function. More interesting is the information given about the individual who had the altar made. His name was Norbaneius Thallus (a Gallic name), and on the very bottom of the altar he refers to himself by the title 'gutuater'. This was one of two similar altars from the city of Autun (Roman Augustodunum), tribal capital of the Aedui.[8] Others are recorded from Gaul, including one from Mâcon in the same region, which firmly links the title 'gutuater' with religious office. The Mâcon altar was commissioned by a Roman citizen named Gaius Sulpicius Gallus, who was the gutuater of Mars and priest of a local god called Moltinus.[9] A gutuater is also mentioned by Hirtius, the man who completed Caesar's *de Bello Gallico* after the dictator's death in 44 BC, in his discussion of rebellion among the central Gallic tribe known as the Carnutes.[10] What is fascinating about the term gutuater is that it is a Gaulish word meaning 'master of voice' or 'father of inspiration'. Such a title accords with the powers classical writers, such as Caesar and others, attributed to the Druids, including eloquence, curation of tradition and divination.

THE MAGICIAN'S HOUSE IN CHARTRES

In July 2005, work on the construction of an underground car park in the city of Chartres was halted by the discovery of Roman remains. What the builders had stumbled upon was the debris of a burnt-out house, dating to the 2nd century AD, which had collapsed and thereby preserved a cellar in which ritual events had clearly taken place. Concealed beneath the staircase, where they had been hidden for secrecy and safe-keeping, were sacred objects including lamps, incense burners and a large knife of the kind commonly used for sacrificing animals. Most telling was the group of *thuribula* (censers): three were found but, on the basis that they may once have marked out a sacred rectangular space, there were probably originally four of them. They were made of clay, their outer surfaces inscribed

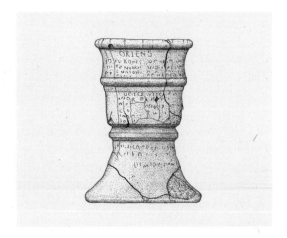

Inscribed *thuribulum* or incense burner from a Gallo-Roman underground
shrine at Chartres, France. The pot (one of at least three) is marked with lists
of sacred names, including the word 'Dru', which might refer to the Druids.

with phrases and lists of names, scratched on while the pots were leather-
hard (dry but before firing). The most complete vessel features the name
of the religious official involved in the ceremonies in this house-cellar: he
was Gaius Verius Sedatus, a Roman citizen of Chartres. The message on
the censer begins with Sedatus's summons to those whom he called *omni-
potentia numina* ('all-powerful spirits'), followed by a list of obscure and
perhaps magical names, but one of which is 'Dru'.[11] Could this word refer
to the Druids? If so, it is the only unequivocal mention of this priesthood
in any inscription anywhere and, indeed, the sole specific archaeological
evidence for the existence of the Druids. It would also seem to indicate that
the status of the Druids had changed from priests to gods.

The *thuribula* may have been used to burn aromatic and even psycho-
tropic material, inducing a state of trance or ecstasy in the celebrants.
The knife found in the same cellar suggests blood rituals of some kind.
Sedatus's description of himself on the censers was *vester custos* ('your
guardian'), as if he was in control of the spirits whom he was summon-
ing by name. The fact that these esoteric and probably magic-driven rites
appear to have been held in secret suggests that they were frowned upon
in the sober *romanitas* of a major Gallo-Roman city, particularly if led by
an upright Roman citizen. But we should remember too that Chartres was
the tribal capital of the Carnutes, whose territory was identified by Caesar
as the place where the annual Druids' assembly took place.[12]

REGALIA AND LITURGICAL OBJECTS

In many societies and religious systems, past and present, priests and other clergy differentiate themselves from the rest of the community by their possession of distinctive regalia, whether worn, carried or used. This is no place to dwell in detail on the archaeological evidence for Iron Age liturgical regalia.[13] However, a brief consideration of priestly paraphernalia serves to provide an image of how celebrants of cult events might have presented themselves. If bog killings were perpetrated within the context of religious ceremonies, they were in all likelihood orchestrated by clergy, who would have known exactly how to enact the ritual practices the culmination of which was a killing and then deposition in the bog.

Special headdresses were part of the ritual garb worn by Iron Age clergy. Many are recorded in Gaul, Germany and Britain but one is worthy of particular note because it was found *in situ* around the head of a man buried in a cemetery at Deal in Kent in the 2nd century BC.[14] This diadem was made of bronze and decorated with intricate engraved designs, and the man was clearly buried wearing it as a symbol of prestige and (probably) of his own office during life. It was not the only distinctive feature about the burial. He was about 20–35 years old, slim, his skeleton revealing of an almost feminine build. He was interred with a sword, the decorated surface of its scabbard face down, and his shield was deliberately broken before being placed in the grave. What is more, despite the presence of weapons, the position of a brooch found on the body indicates that he was buried wearing a long flowing robe. This may simply have been a funeral shroud, but it is more likely to represent a garment, and one more fitting for a religious official than a soldier. The treatment of the weapons suggests that they had been decommissioned or, perhaps, that they were present as a mark of 'full military honours' rather than reflecting the man's role as a warrior. More curious still was the position of the grave, for it was set apart from the rest of the cemetery. Was he buried on the margins because of his function as a priest or even a shaman, an edgy, dangerously powerful being who needed to be interred on his own? Was he the kind of person who might have presided over arcane rituals that may even have included sacred killing?

The Deal headdress was worn by someone who lived far away from bog body deposits. But another religious official, who wore an elaborate 'crown' when performing his religious duties, was buried in a grave at

The skull of the Deal Man, who died in Kent in the 2nd
century BC. He was interred with weapons but clothed
in a long robe and a decorated diadem.

Cerrig-y-Drudion in Denbighshire, not too far from Lindow Moss nor from
the ritual deposit at the swampy pool of Llyn Cerrig Bach on Anglesey,
from which human remains have allegedly been found. The Cerrig-y-
Drudion headdress consisted of a bronze and leather helmet-like device,
highly decorated with La Tène designs and sporting a long horsehair
plume. Radiocarbon dating of the leather, and the artistic style of the
ornament, date the object to the 4th century BC.[15]

The huge Bavarian oppidum at Manching was built by the Danube in
order to command an immense and complex trading network. Established
in about 300 BC, it had a population of about 10,000. It had regularly laid-
out streets and industrial districts, the latter associated particularly with
the production of pottery, ironwork and glass jewelry and the import
of wine. Among its people was a priest whose wand of office was a kind
of artificial tree.[16] It was made of a wooden rod covered with sheet bronze,
attached to which were delicate bronze leaves that would have rattled
against the stem when carried, and shivered in a breeze. The leaves were
distinctive and have been identified as those of *Ipomoea violacea* (a type
of morning glory), a plant whose seeds have hallucinogenic properties that
could have been used by shamans in attaining trance states. The 'cult-tree'
from Manching may thus reflect the presence of a religious practitioner

The 'cult tree' or priest's sceptre from the Iron Age town
of Manching, Bavaria. Attached to the wooden staff are
metal leaves that would have jangled when moved.

whose activities involved the inducement of out-of-body experiences,
either for him/herself or for worshippers. We are reminded of the *thuribula*
from Chartres, vessels that could easily have been used to burn psycho-
tropic substances within the claustrophobic confines of the cellar-shrine
presided over by Verius Sedatus.

Classical chroniclers of Gallo-British customs emphasize the role of
Druids and other priests in divination, the ability to predict the future
and the will of the gods by the enactment of rituals. Diodorus Siculus
and Strabo each speak of the Druids' role in divinatory practices that
involved ritual murder and the interpretation of the spirits' will by
observing a victim's death struggles.[17] Although it is difficult to identify
divinatory equipment in the archaeological record, one class of objects
suggests that this was their function. It consists of pairs of bronze
spoons usually buried in the graves of Iron Age Britons, but very occasionally ritually deposited in marshy places: the pair found at Crosby
Ravensworth in Cumbria had been placed in a peat bog.[18] The spoons
were clearly designed as pairs: the inner surface of one is plain but with
a hole drilled in it off-centre; the other is marked into quadrants by
central intersecting lines. It is not known exactly how they were used
but one idea, based on experiments,[19] is that the two spoons were placed

together, their inner surfaces touching, the one with the drilled hole on the top, and that liquid or powder was then blown through the hole and the pattern of scatter on the lower, quadranted spoon interpreted, rather in the manner of the casting of lots mentioned by Tacitus (see p.148).[20] Blood, ground-up plant matter, powdered bone or other materials may have been used, and experiments have shown that an efficient form of blowing tool was a small hollow bird bone. The context of deposition of the Cumbrian spoons provides at least a superficial connection between this equipment and the bog bodies. So it is possible that equipment like this was used in ritual practices associated with bog killings and with the choice both of victim and practitioner.

KILLING TOOLS

They used to stab a human being, whom they had devoted to death, in the back with a dagger, and foretell the future from his convulsions.

STRABO, GEOGRAPHY[21]

Forensic science has provided a great deal of information as to how bog victims met their deaths, and the kind of objects used to murder them. The nooses found around the necks of many tell their own story but, in the case of penetrative injuries and blunt force trauma, the weapons used are absent from the scene. If Grauballe Man had been the victim of a modern killing, police investigators would have been looking for a sharp-edged blade with a notch on one edge: a dagger, sword or large knife.[22] It is possible that certain victims, such as the man whose head was interred in a bog at Osterby, as well as Lindow Man and Clonycavan Man, were clubbed using sacred regalia, even sceptres, like the Romano-British one from Willingham Fen, Cambridgeshire (itself from a marshy environment), which was decorated with sacred imagery associated with solar symbolism.[23] There is no evidence to link this cult object with killing, but it would be appropriate for a religious official to use his or her sacred staff when presiding over ritual events such as bog death ceremonies.

One of the most distinctive Gallo-Roman divinities was Sucellus, the hammer-god. He was worshipped all over Gaul, the Rhineland and in Britain, too. His name means 'the good striker', and his main emblems were a small pot or goblet and a large long-handled mallet.[24] Two of his major centres of veneration were Burgundy and the lower Rhône Valley, around Nîmes. A bronze figurine from Glanum, near Marseille, depicts a mature, bearded god wearing a heavy Gaulish coat or *sagum*, and a laurel wreath around his head. His left hand cradles a pot and in his upraised right hand he brandishes a heavy mallet.[25] Devotees of the cult from the nearby Roman city of Nîmes dedicated a stone altar, with a large mallet carved on one surface, presumably to the same god.[26]

Interpretations of the functions and responsibilities of Sucellus have always focused on his benign role as a provider of prosperity. This is partly because in some regions he is accompanied by a female partner, Nantosuelta ('Winding River'), whose representations depict her as a peaceful protectress. But what if Sucellus's hammer had a more active and aggressive meaning? I wonder whether it might suggest a role that involved clubbing, stunning and killing. Sucellus's hammer would have been just the implement to inflict the blunt force injuries seen on bog bodies such as Clonycavan Man and Lindow Man. And such a weapon would have been ideal for smashing the facial bones of the unfortunate bogwoman from Borremose. However, such a surmise might be overly fanciful, and these injuries could have been dealt equally effectively by the hilt of a sword or even a shield boss. Indeed, a sword or dagger could have functioned as a double weapon for a bog victim such as Lindow Man, its hilt or pommel wielded to fracture the victim's skull and its sharp edge to cut his throat. The Irish Clonycavan Man was killed with a very special tool: his skull was split by a stone axe.[27] Identification of such a weapon raises all kinds of questions but the most seductive notion is that his killers deliberately chose an ancient implement, a Stone Age axe, in order to imbue the deed with ancestral *maiestas* (dignity and majesty). This is perhaps not as far-fetched as it seems: Neolithic flint axes have been found as offerings in Gallo-Roman sanctuaries.[28]

Sometime in the 2nd century BC, a man of high rank died in Gaul and was given a rich burial at Saint-Georges-lès-Baillargeaux, near Poitiers in Vienne. His grave was discovered in 1998, and was found to contain a set of bronze implements including a whetstone, three razors and a knife nearly 32 cm (over 1 ft) long.[29] The juxtaposition of these implements is interesting in the context of how certain bog bodies were treated, for not only were sharp knives likely to have been used to inflict stabbing, slashing or throat-slitting wounds but razors were also employed in shaving off the hair of victims such as the adolescents from Windeby and Yde. Of course, the knife from Vienne might have been used to butcher sacrificial animals, but it could also have been used on people, and its sharpness is emphasized by the presence of the whetstone. All the tools in the man's grave had rings for suspension, and may have been worn around the waist as a permanent reminder of his responsibilities as a priest whose job was to let blood for the gods.

Another rich Gallic tomb, this time containing the cremated human remains of someone who died in the 3rd century BC, was in the cemetery at Tartigny in Oise in northern Gaul. The grave was furnished with a cylindrical bucket, of the kind used to contain local ale, together with a sharp iron knife, a bowl (for blood?) and a double-functioning tool, one end of which was a kind of scalpel and the other a pair of pincers.[30] This person might have been a healer, the knife and scalpel used to lance and drain infected wounds and the pincers to remove foreign bodies. In the ancient world, healing and sacrificial rituals often went hand in hand. We have only to glance at Pliny the Elder's *Natural History*,[31] in which he described a Druidic ritual that involved killing two white bulls and gathering mistletoe from a sacred oak, in a curative ceremony aimed also at promoting the fertility of herds and crops. It is not impossible that bog body rituals were enacted within a context of symbolic purification and a desire to propitiate gods of prosperity: the 'famine food' found in the gut of some bog bodies may infer aversion rituals associated with the threat of failing food sources.

FROM COOKS TO KILLERS

PREPARING THE LAST SUPPERS

The elaborate treatment of bog bodies in the hours leading to their death and deposition argues for a careful and highly organized formula of ritual actions, all of which may have been crucially important in ensuring the symbolic efficacy of the killing. Particularly striking is the forensic evidence for the specially prepared meals whose residues have been identified in the stomach and gut of several bog bodies.[32] In the case of Lindow Man, the food he ate consisted of bread baked on a griddle and slightly charred from contact with the hot baking stone. The most dominant components of the bread were the bran and chaff of cereals, mainly hulled barley and wheat (the emmer and spelt varieties), together with the seeds of many different wild plants. The wheat bran and weed seeds had been finely milled and the barley chaff was prepared by crushing or pearling (in the latter method, some of the grain is left adhering to the chaff). Scientists used a technique known as electron spin resonance[33] to determine the temperature the bread reached when being cooked, about which was about 200°C for a brief period, thus ruling out the boiling of cereal grains for porridge (for that, a lower temperature of around 100°C would have been recorded).[34] This evidence, coupled with the poor raising properties of the ancient cereal strains used and the charring, indicates that Lindow II's final meal was unleavened bread.[35] Lindow III's gut contents provided poorer and smaller samples, but it was possible to determine that he, too, had eaten food with a cereal component, with the addition of crushed raw hazelnuts.

The intestinal tracts of both Lindow men show a marked lack of meat, with only minute traces identified. If we believe the testimony of classical writers on the carnivous habits of their 'barbarian' neighbours, and if we take into account the vast amounts of meat debris found on Iron Age archaeological sites, it is a reasonable assumption that the Lindow bogmen's final meals were atypical and could either have been deliberately poor fare or famine food reflecting crop failure and a population under stress.

The contents of Grauballe Man's gut revealed similarly diverse ingredients, in fact even more so because the remains of at least 60 varieties of wild and cultivated plants have been identified.[36] New analysis of the Danish bogman's last meal suggests that it may have been ingested as a kind of inferior 'muesli', probably with a rather nasty taste but reasonably nutritious, similar to the unpalatable gruel found in Tollund Man's innards.[37] Tollund Man's gut contained no trace of meat, but bone fragments were identified in that of the Grauballe body. The scientists working in 2001 and 2002 on the contents of his gut were sceptical about the special nature of this food, but two things are perhaps particularly significant: one is the presence of ergot, a hallucinogenic toxin (see Chapter 6); the other is the presence of *Sphagnum*, the major plant component of the bog in which he was interred. Remnants of the same material were found in Lindow Man's gut too. It is possible that the people responsible for preparing the pre-death rituals surrounding the killings of these men deliberately added part of the bog to their food in order to represent the infiltration of the swamp into the innermost parts of their bodies. That way, the bog embraced and wrapped itself around the bog victim but was also present within. Of course, in the unlikely event that Grauballe Man was still breathing when he went into the bog, he may have swallowed the *Sphagnum* in a final convulsive gasp.

JOINT ENTERPRISE: COMMUNAL FEASTING AND COMMUNAL KILLING

Their food consists of a small number of loaves of bread together with
a large amount of meat, either boiled or roasted on charcoal or on spits...
When a large number dine together they sit around in a circle with the
most influential man in the centre, whether he surpass the others in
warlike skill, or nobility of family or wealth.

ATHENAEUS [38]

No nation abandons itself more completely to banqueting
and entertainment than the German. It is accounted a sin
to turn any man away from your door. The host welcomes
the guest with the best meal that his means allow.

TACITUS, *GERMANIA* [39]

These passages from Athenaeus and Tacitus are testament to the love of
feasting among the Gauls and the Germans. For both, meat was central.
Elsewhere in the *Germania*, Tacitus is also firm on the Germans' preference
for cattle-keeping (and therefore meat-eating) rather than the cultivation of
crops.[40] This being so, it is again of keen interest that many Iron Age bog
victims appear to have consumed little or no meat in their last meals.

Communal banquets have a wider concern, for they were often associated with ritual activity in Iron Age Europe. Many pre-Roman Gallic temples
show signs that huge quantities of meat and alcohol were enjoyed as part
of religious ceremonies. These sanctuaries were also places of political
assemblies, and that may be why they were sometimes situated on tribal
boundaries. Gournay-sur-Aronde (see p.140) was positioned at the borders
of three tribal territories.[41] Here and at cognate shrines in northern Gaul,
such as Ribemont, Mirebeau and Acy-Romance, there is abundant evidence
for feasting in a sacred context.[42] In ancient Greek religion, all meat consumed was from sacrificial animals, and in Greek society, religious officials
had separate and varying roles; those who slaughtered and butchered the
offerings were separate from those who carried out the observances and
liaised with the gods.[43]

Feasting and the killing and consumption of animals in religious ceremonies are relevant issues when considering the contexts in which bog
body killings may have occurred and who was responsible. While there
is no evidence for the consumption of collective meals in the immediate

Reconstruction drawing of the Iron Age 'war sanctuary' at Gournay,
northern France. In the centre was a desiccation pit for sacrificed oxen.

contexts of the bogs in which victims have been found, such activities may
well have taken place elsewhere, and the bog deliberately chosen as set
apart, in *terra inculta*. Picking up on the question of location and the possible connection with territorial borders, mentioned already in the context
of Gallic shrines, Ned Kelly has put forward an argument for the association
between the deposition of Irish bog bodies and political boundaries.[44] He
bases his supposition upon later, medieval kingship and royal land division
but, although his thesis is persuasive, I am not convinced of the validity of
back-projection and the assumption that early historical territories in any
way matched the situation in the Iron Age. In any case, we have no firm
evidence for the presence of political boundaries in prehistoric Ireland,
although some linear earthworks might be so interpreted.[45]

The theme of ceremonial feasting, whether or not relevant to the
rituals surrounding bog killings, raises two important and related topics.
One concerns what triggered the occasion for the deaths, the other of community involvement. Tacitus's comment concerning the Germanic tribe of
the Semnones brings the two issues together:

> The oldest and noblest of the Suebi, so it is said, are the Semnones,
> and the justice of this claim is confirmed by a religious rite. At a set
> time all the peoples of this blood gather, in their embassies, in a

wood hallowed by the auguries of their ancestors and the awe of ages.
The sacrifice in public of a human victim marks the grisly opening
of their savage ritual.

TACITUS, *GERMANIA*[46]

The organized and ceremonial gatherings described by Tacitus are reminiscent of Caesar's discussion of the annual Druidic assembly in the territory of the Carnutes. Neither author provides information as to time of year, month or day of celebration. The gut contents of some bog bodies suggest late summer or winter killings and there may be seasonal reasons for ceremonies involving victims of bog killings, associated with anxieties about food supplies. But they may also have occurred within the context of regular ceremonies, such as those chronicled by Caesar and Tacitus, that were themselves rooted in seasonality.

This brings me to the question of collective involvement, of communal responsibility for the killing of human beings. It can only be a matter of speculation as to how many people were actually involved in the killings or, indeed, the numbers of spectators. Depending on the occasion, bog deaths might have been private or public affairs but, if they were conducted within the context of festivals or assemblies, the entire community, and even perhaps also neighbouring ones, was likely to have been present. But what about the actual participants? Were the killings carried out by one individual or several? Forensics might provide at least partial answers. As we saw in Chapter 7, the dispatch of Lindow Man probably required at least two people: the tightening of the garrotte around his throat and the slashing of his throat were clearly synchronized. The blows to the skull could have been done first, by one or other of the two, but to my mind the multiple injuries suggest acts that were both really and symbolically communal. The French anthropologist René Girard[47] argues that the cathartic nature of ritual violence is all the more effective if many individuals share the event, and a communal meal may have preceded or followed the killing. Collective responsibility may also have been a matter of expediency, a question of sharing the guilt for taking a life. The murder of Julius Caesar by his fellow senators in 44 BC was a form of deliberately collective killing, with each conspirator making a contributory wound. The perceived need to share responsibility for the killing of human beings might be rooted in fear of reprisals by other people or in order to avert divine retribution.

WERE THE DRUIDS INVOLVED IN BOG BODY DEATHS?

To begin with, Dumnorix proceeded to use every kind of
reason to support his request to be left behind in Gaul. He said
he was not used to sailing and was afraid of the sea, and also
that religious considerations prevented him.

CAESAR, *DE BELLO GALLICO*[48]

The anti-Roman Dumnorix shared the leadership of the Burgundian Aedui with his brother Diviciacus, Caesar's friend and ally. Coins inscribed with Dumnorix's name are known in the archaeological record, confirming that he was a genuine historical character and not a figment of Caesar's imagination. Cicero met Diviciacus in 60 BC when the latter came to Rome begging for its help against the predatory German ruler Ariovistus, who had expansionist policies and was seeking to annex the territory of several Gallic tribes, including the Aedui. Cicero had great respect for Diviciacus, particularly for his skill at divination, and referred to him as a Druid.[49] Given Dumnorix's protestation of his religious responsibilities (as expressed in the above quotation), it is possible that both brothers were Druids or that they each, at least, had priestly roles. After all, Caesar tells us that the Druids were in charge of all religious rites in Gaul (and that the priesthood had its origins in Britain).[50]

All that we can confidently assert about the Druids is that they were powerful religious leaders in Gaul and Britain. The testimony of Caesar and Cicero implies that Druids were not only accorded similar status to that of noblemen (whom Caesar called knights) but also that – on occasions – political and religious leadership could rest on the shoulders of one and the same individual. The ritual killing of people, including the bog victims, is likely to have been conducted by those who enjoyed senior rank within their communities, and so it is by no means impossible that the Druids, or their Germanic counterparts, were involved in at least some bog killings. As we saw in Chapter 3, the identification of mistletoe in Lindow Man's gut has the potential for bringing bog bodies and Druids even closer together, because of Pliny's allusion to the Druidic reverence for mistletoe.[51]

One group of objects may be relevant to the possible association between ritual killing and Druidism: the curse tablets (*defixiones*) that have been found on Gallo-British sites mainly of Roman date but some belonging to the very late Iron Age. These lead or pewter inscribed plaques (see p.142) contained messages to the divine powers urging that they right wrongs and punish malefactors.[52] *Defixiones* worked on the magical principle of 'fixing' spells on people. They had their roots in the Mediterranean world[53] and were, in essence, hymns of hate and revenge. The main reason for their consideration in the context of bog bodies is the savage nature of corporal punishment for wrongdoing demanded of the spirits. Some of the many curse tablets found in the Roman reservoir at the temple of Sulis in Bath show just how bloodthirsty these messages could be. One *defixio* asks that the miscreant's guts be eaten away; others speak of cursing with blindness, bleeding to death (including the request that a bronze vessel that has been stolen be filled to the brim with the blood of the thief), and the inability to pass water, to defecate or to ejaculate semen.[54]

A long and fascinating curse tablet, written in the 1st century AD, from Larzac in southern France, speaks of an *uidlua*, a Gaulish term for a seeress, whose name was Severa Tertionicna. She was in charge of the *duscelinata* ('evil death-song') mentioned on the tablet, which was aimed at related pairs of women, all listed by name. This priestess called upon a goddess called Adsagsona to exact revenge on these women. The *defixio* was steeped in femininity: the religious official, the goddess and the malefactors were all female, and it is likely that those who had initiated the curse were also women.[55] Moreover, the tablet itself was deliberately snapped in half and laid on top of a funerary urn inscribed with the name of the dead person, a woman called Gemma. Like the prayer iterated on the *thuribula* from Chartres, the Larzac curse has a rhythmical, poetic structure that suggests it was meant to be recited aloud. It is pure speculation to make any kind of link between the message conveyed by these *defixiones* and the violent deaths of bog bodies, but the two phenomena are connected by the utter savagery presented.

BOGS, PRIESTS AND SPIRITS

The people who were responsible for killing bog victims and consigning them to their marshy tombs must have been fully conversant with their local environments and undoubtedly made choices based upon the most efficacious swamps available. I suspect that special bogs were selected,

Pair of wooden images, one male, one female, from either side of a wooden trackway over a bog at Oldenburg, North Germany, 3rd century BC.

perhaps because of a particular miasmic quality or spiritual essence deemed to have a particular charge of meaning. Perhaps each bog possessed its own spirits. When the bog people went into the marsh, they would have been immediately embraced by it, sucked in and wrapped around, and the swampy water would seep into the body's orifices, thus claiming it fully for its own. So it was important that the right bog was chosen to receive a particular victim.

As we have seen bogs are liminal spaces, uncultivable land, and so beyond the borders of human control and order. It is possible that the killers also occupied a marginal position within their communities, not least because of their killing role and their handling of corpses, which perhaps rendered them polluted and at the same time strangely powerful. Whether or not they were Druids, the 'clergy' who supervised or enacted bog killings occupied a special place, close to the spirits but set apart from the rest of society: they were dangerous, to be feared and maybe shunned, with their bloody hands and secret knowledge.

There is no clear evidence as to how the bog spirits were perceived or manifest. But Iron Age wooden images in human form are known from north European marshlands. At least two gendered pairs are recorded,

The Ballachulish Woman: a wooden female figurine carved in the 7th century BC, and pinned down with hurdles into a Scottish peat bog.

from Braak and Oldenburg, both in North Germany. The pair from Oldenburg were carved in the 3rd century BC and stood guard over a trackway over a bog, at the most vulnerable crossing place.[56] Of similar date, the Braak pair stood more than man-high and dominated the small bog in which they were found (see p.43).[57] An earlier female image, from a remote Scottish bog at Ballachulish, Argyll, was carved from a piece of alder in the 7th century BC, and given eyes made of quartz pebbles.[58] She may have represented a bog deity, but the presence of hurdles that pinned her down suggests an affinity with bog victims, many of whom – like those from Windeby and Haraldskaer – were similarly treated. Perhaps the alder bog lady from Argyll was a surrogate victim. Maybe the person who carved her or commissioned her production was a religious official, a Caledonian priest who made a ritual deposition of a wooden substitute for a body of flesh and blood.

This chapter has focused on the perpetrators of bog body deaths; previous ones have considered the reasons they might have died, the violence they sustained and the kind of person chosen. Hovering in the background of much of this book has been the possibility of human sacrificial killings. It is the remit of the final chapter to confront this issue head-on.

CHAPTER 10

Bog Deaths &
Human Sacrifice

The Gauls believe the power of the immortal gods can be
appeased only if one human life is exchanged for another,
and they have sacrifices of this kind regularly established by
the community. Some of them have enormous images made
of wickerwork, the limbs of which they fill with living men;
these are set on fire and the men perish, enveloped in the flames.
They believe that the gods prefer it if the people executed have
been caught in the act of theft or armed robbery or some other
crime, but when the supply of such victims runs out, they even
go to the extent of sacrificing innocent men.

CAESAR, *DE BELLO GALLICO*[1]

Whether or not we can believe the detail of Caesar's descriptions of human
sacrifice among the Gauls (PL. XIV), his testimony and that of others, like
Diodorus, Strabo and Tacitus, at least provides an indication that such
extreme ritual behaviour was not totally beyond consideration.[2] Tacitus's
remarks about human sacrifice among the Semnones (see pp.174–75),
and the ritual drowning of the slave-attendants at the goddess Nerthus's
sanctuary (see p.127),[3] are of particular relevance because he was writing
about Germania, the territory that belongs to modern Germany, together
with Denmark and the Netherlands, precisely the most prolific areas for the

interment of ancient bog bodies. Caesar's narrative is of special interest, though, because of his description of the kind of human offering favoured by the gods. Why were wrongdoers considered more effective sacrificial victims than the righteous? Maybe it was their very marginality that gave them a special force or energy appreciated by the gods. Or perhaps human expediency – that of ridding the community of its miscreants – meant that people justified selecting such individuals, in a kind of ritually sanctioned capital punishment.

SACRIFICE

And Aaron shall lay both his hands upon the head of the live
goat, and confess over him all the iniquities of the children of
Israel, and all their transgressions in all their sins, putting them
on the head of the goat, and shall send him away by the hand
of a fit man into the wilderness.

LEVITICUS 16: 21

In essence, a sacrifice is something of value that is given up or given away in order to achieve a goal. The two major factors in sacrificial ritual are giving and separation. The offering has to be acceptable to the being in receipt of the gift; the sacrifice has to be separated from the profane world and be treated in a manner that connects it to that of the spirits, whether by burning, consumption in a meal shared between people and the gods, or burial. In a religious context, the sacrifice has a perpetrator and a recipient: the person or community doing the sacrificing on the one hand and, on the other, the god or spirit who receives the offering. The goal is to persuade the divine recipient, via the gift, to bestow something positive on the giver or to avert disaster. The biblical scapegoat condemned by the Israelite priest Aaron was an actual goat, left to starve in the desert. But the Gallo-Greek scapegoat (the *pharmakos*) was a human victim, laden with the misfortunes of townspeople and steeped in impurities (see p.145).[4]

In classical and biblical antiquity, most sacrifices chronicled in the ancient literature were of animals, almost always domesticates. In general, the animals had to be perfect, without blemish, and, for the Greeks at least, the chosen beasts had to 'consent' to their deaths, by lowering their heads in submission.[5] They were beautified – groomed

Detail of a painted Greek black-figure vase depicting the sacrifice of the
Trojan princess Polyxena, whose throat was cut by Neoptolemus.

and their horns decked with flowers[6] – rather in the manner of the Greek
(human) scapegoats. Some wonderful evidence for ancient Italian animal
sacrifice comes from the Umbrian town of Iguvium. Here, in the 15th
century, a group of seven inscribed bronze tablets, dating to between
200 and the 1st century BC, was discovered. Their texts provide intricate
detail of sacrificial procedures, including the selection of animals for
their colour, age, gender and reproductive condition. Sacrifices at each
of the three town gates demanded different rituals and different criteria
for the selection of the victims.[7]

As in many ancient societies that practised animal sacrifice, the creatures are likely originally to have been surrogates, substitutes for the
people who had once been the victims of ritual killing either in genuine
antiquity or in myth. A Greek vase painting dating to the 6th century BC
(and already encountered in Chapter 6) depicts the sacrifice of Polyxena,
daughter of King Priam and Queen Hecuba of Troy, by Neoptolemus
at Achilles' tomb.[8] Euripides's play *Iphigeneia in Aulis* and Aeschylus's
Agamemnon tell the story of how King Agamemnon sacrificed his daughter Iphigeneia in order that the goddess Artemis would permit the Greek
fleet to set sail for Troy.[9] According to Greek myth, both Polyxena and
Iphigeneia were put to death within a context of 'doom-laden anxiety,'[10]
in desperate attempts to get the gods on the side of the sacrificers. Both
victims were royal virgins, young, pure and of incredibly high value, in

terms of their lost potential for forming alliances through marriage and their capacity to produce royal offspring.

In ancient Rome, human sacrifice was not made illegal until 97 BC. It was always rare and, like the situation in the Greek world presented in mythology, only enacted during times of heightened and extreme stress. Pairs of Greek and Gallic men and women were sacrificed by burial alive in the Forum Boarium in Rome in the later 3rd century BC, when Rome was engaged in a desperate war with Carthage.[11] This sacrifice was carried out having consulted the Sibylline Books, prophetic texts that advised Romans on matters of great moment. These were aversion sacrifices, enacted in order to avoid disaster. But most Roman writers referred to human sacrifice as being outlandish, weird and uncivilized. Several ancient authors described its practice among the Gauls, Germans and Britons with a mixture of distaste and voyeuristic fascination. Their comments are examined later in this chapter.

WATERY DEPOSITION AND THE SACRIFICE OF THINGS

Human and animal sacrifices are usually perceived as gifts to the gods. The same is true of inanimate objects. In later prehistoric Europe, a recurrent practice over wide areas and time zones was the deposition of valuable objects in watery contexts.[12] Helmets, swords, shields and spears were consigned to rivers, pools and bogs. Some, like the Battersea Shield, cast into the Thames in Londinium (what later became London) in the 1st century BC, were primarily decorative; the shield was so thin and fragile that it could never have seen service in battle.[13] Apart from military gear, cauldrons were favoured objects for ritual deposition in swamps and lakes, often in pairs. Mostly these were plain globular vessels of sheet bronze, like those from Llyn Fawr in Glamorgan, deposited in the 7th century BC, when they were already a hundred years old, along with other high-status objects.[14] The most famous ritually deposited cauldron, though, was anything but plain: it was made of gilded silver, richly decorated with images of gods and cult scenes, and carefully placed, dismantled into its 13 constituent plates, on a dry islet in a peat bog at Gundestrup in Jutland in about 100 BC.[15] Cauldrons were used for boiling meat, in high-status communal feasting events; the intended gifts to the bogs could have been the vessels themselves, their contents or both. In Irish peat bogs, the wooden containers filled with butter (see Chapter 1) might have been similarly deposited for votive purposes, but perhaps instead merely to keep them cool. However, the persistent deposition of querns (stones used for grinding corn) in Irish bogs suggests that food offerings were habitually being made to the marsh spirits.[16] Should the human bodies found in bogs be seen as simply another form of divine gift, even food for the bog spirits?

ANIMAL SACRIFICE IN IRON AGE EUROPE

Animals, and even humans, were not slaughtered in these rituals to be offered as a gift to the gods but rather to release the life-blood which had a unique and mysterious sacrificial efficacy.

IAN BRADLEY, *THE POWER OF SACRIFICE*[17]

This passage is a reminder that sacrifice was a more complex affair than simply the giving of presents to the gods. Archaeological evidence, from settlement sites, tombs and sanctuaries, suggests that ritual killing of animals was endemic within European Iron Age society. By far the most popular victims were domestic beasts: cattle, sheep and pigs. But horses, too, were sacrificed and, occasionally, wild species were chosen. Two sites exemplify the kind of activity that took place. Gournay-sur-Aronde was a Gallic 'war sanctuary', whose excavation revealed the deliberate burial in pits of thousands of weapons, some 'killed' by being wrenched out of shape. The shrine itself was surrounded by a ditched enclosure and it was here that a complex procedure of animal deposition took place, according to strictly organized ritual. Elderly oxen were killed with a precise axe-blow to the back of the neck, and then buried in a desiccation pit in the centre of the sanctuary. After about six months, the skeletal remains were disinterred and carefully repositioned in specific parts of the enclosure ditch. The skulls were removed and placed on either side of the entrance. The entire bodies of horses were buried in other parts of the ditch, and the remains of butchered pigs and sheep consumed in feasting ceremonies were placed elsewhere within it. So every species had its own interment location. Significantly, the remains of people were also present.[18]

Although the Iron Age hillfort of Danebury in southern England was a very different site from Gournay, in many ways the evidence for animal sacrifice has similar elements. Danebury was a fortified settlement that

Disembodied human skull from a grain silo at Danebury. Human heads were
important symbols of power and regeneration, and this head may have been
a thank-offering to the gods who guarded the seed-corn over the winter.

was probably home to up to 300 people at any one time. The identity of
this population can only be surmised: it may have comprised local chief-
tains, their extended families, entourages and slaves. The site is full of
roundhouses, corn-drying racks, granaries and storage pits dug deep into
the chalk. It is these pits that were the focus for ritual practice that involved
the deposition of both animals and people.[19] The pits were originally grain
silos, used for storing the corn produced not only by the inhabitants of
Danebury but also by farmers living in the villages and smallholdings in
the countryside surrounding the hillfort, and connected to it by a series of
droveways. Danebury appears to have been used as a central corn-storage
depot serving a large agricultural hinterland. The ritual function of the
silos began when they were empty of grain, when they were cleaned out
and used as a repository for the entire or partial carcasses of animals, or
just the skulls, sometimes alone but often in a mixed deposit containing
more than one species. The most common combination comprised horses
and dogs. As at Gournay, human remains were also present in the pits;
they were again treated in exactly the same manner as the animals: some
buried whole, some articulated pieces and several skulls. There is even a
shred of evidence for the butchery and therefore cannibalism of human
bodies (see p.139).[20]

THE SPECIAL NATURE OF HUMAN SACRIFICE?

The barbaric gods worshipped here had their altars heaped up with
hideous offerings, and every tree was sprinkled with human blood.

LUCAN, *PHARSALIA* III[21]

It was their religion to drench their altars in the blood of prisoners and
consult their gods by means of human entrails.

TACITUS, *ANNALS* 14.30[22]

Theologian Ian Bradley's comment (quoted on p.184) reminds us that the
spilling of blood was often central to sacrificial ritual. In ancient Greek
sacrifice, bloodletting was crucial to the efficacy of the ritual. The same
appears to be true of the Gaul and Britain referenced above by Lucan
and Tacitus, whose descriptions of human sacrifice in Gallic and British
sacred groves are virtually identical. Lucan's concerned a grove outside
Massilia (Marseille) encountered by Caesar's army on its way to meet that
of his political rival Pompey; Tacitus was setting the scene for the sack of a
shrine on Anglesey that was sacred to the Druids, just before the Boudican
rebellion in AD 60. In other ancient societies, such as those chronicled in
the Bible, it was the act of giving, of offering to God, that was the primary
purpose of animal sacrifice. In considering how special human sacrifice may have been to Iron Age communities, the exemplars of Gournay
and Danebury are crucial, for at both sites animals and people seem to
have been treated with little distinction, as if they were perceived to be of
similar value.

So how special were human beings and how special was human sacrifice? In answering this question, the nature of the societies involved
is a key consideration. Caesar describes Gallic society in the 1st century
BC as being strongly stratified, with everyone but the elite – the knights
and the Druids – virtually without status, having little more value than
slaves.[23] But Caesar was being somewhat simplistic, for archaeology provides rich evidence for the presence of free and landowning (or at least
tenant) farmers and metalworkers as well as slaves (the latter represented by the survival of shackles, manacles and gang-chains).[24] Strabo
commented that British slaves were highly prized exports,[25] and that
the Gauls valued Italian wine so much that they would happily barter
a slave for one amphora.[26] Tacitus's observations on slavery among the

Germanic tribes suggest that slaves held a curiously ambiguous place in society. He comments that they had autonomy over their own household but that their masters levied a charge on their possessions and produce. He also makes the interesting remark that, although it was unusual to flog slaves, they were often murdered at the ill-tempered whim of their owners.[27]

A crucial consideration is to what extent human beings were at the apex of worth in Iron Age European society. A glance at the spectrum of deliberate and arguably ritual deposition indicates that it included 'everyday' items such as quern stones and blacksmith's tools, precious and richly decorated objects, like swords, shields, cauldrons and jewelry (especially gold torcs),[28] and even great boats full of weapons[29]; it also included animals and, perhaps, people. The presence of slaves, probably regarded as no more than chattels, suggests that some humans were perceived as less human than others and, as Diodorus records, were of less value than precious objects, such as gold jewelry, finely wrought swords and shields, or jars of Mediterranean wine. So ritual murder was by no means certain to have been the ultimate sacrifice. A favourite horse or sword is likely to have had similar if not greater value. Having said all that, the archaeological evidence does still suggest that human sacrifice in the European Iron Age was comparatively rare.

THE EVIDENCE FOR RITUAL MURDER IN 'DRY' CONTEXTS: A FOCUS ON BRITAIN

CHILDREN

There was in their city a bronze image of Cronus, extending
its hands, palms up and sloping towards the ground, so that each
of the children when placed thereon rolled down and fell
into a sort of gaping pit filled with fire.

DIODORUS SICULUS [30]

Documentary sources and archaeological finds provide strong evidence for the practice of child sacrifice among the ancient Carthaginians of North Africa. The context for the passage quoted above was a war between Carthage and the Greek city of Syracuse in Sicily, over mastery of the Mediterranean trade routes. Having trounced the Carthaginian army, the Syracusan war-leader Agathocles laid siege to the walls of Carthage in 310 BC. In their desperate plight, the people of the city had recourse to the ritual murder of small children, offered to their god in a last-ditch hope for deliverance.[31]

Britain is a long way from Carthage. Yet here, too, there is recurrent evidence for the ritual slaughter of young children, although there is no indication that this was frequent practice. In all the three instances now to be considered, dismemberment appears to have been a key part of the procedure. Hornish Point is situated on the edge of the remote island of South Uist in the Western Isles. Before a house was erected there, four pits were dug, one at each corner of the planned building, and in each pit someone placed the carefully butchered and quartered remains of a 12-year-old boy[32] (first mentioned in Chapter 7 because of the violence of his treatment). The child's body appears to have been used as a foundation deposit, an offering to the local spirits in the hope that the house and its occupants would be blessed with good fortune. But the special nature of the burial suggests to me either that the 'house' was perhaps also (or instead) a shrine or that a calamity had either happened to the community or threatened it in some way. After all, even if the boy had been a slave, he must have been of value to such a small, isolated community, and he was about to reach puberty, with all the adult and reproductive capacity to contribute to his people that his age represented.

But the Hornish boy was not alone. The formidable earthworks that surrounded the hillfort at Wandlebury made a powerful statement in the flat landscape of Cambridgeshire. In one of a series of shallow pits that had been dug inside the defences lay the upper half of a six-year-old child, placed in a sack and interred face down; the legs had been severed with a sword or similar blade, probably at or just after the time of death.[33] Like the bog victims, and like the boy from South Uist, the grisly remains of this child were buried without grave goods.

The mutilation of children's bodies continued in Britain even into the Roman period: at Folly Lane, in the same ritual complex at Verulamium where the remains of a late Iron Age chieftain were interred with great ceremony and rich tomb-furniture (see p.155), a shrine was built. Outside it was a deep shaft containing the defleshed head of an adolescent boy, together with a puppy and a whetstone.[34] The boy had been killed by a savage blow that fractured his skull. More than 90 knife-cuts on the scalp indicated far more damage than necessary for defleshing, suggesting a similar kind of 'joint enterprise' as that exhibited by the multiply killed bog bodies, such as Lindow Man. The boy's head had been displayed on a pole for a time before its final interment. As at Hornish, it may have been the onset of puberty that triggered this child's religious killing.

ALL TRUSSED UP

No one may enter the sacred grove unless he is bound with a cord. By this he acknowledges his own inferiority and the power of the deity.

TACITUS, *GERMANIA* 39[35]

Tacitus's comment refers to a custom practised by the Germanic tribe of the Semnones, whom he describes as 'the oldest and noblest of the Suebi', a huge confederation of tribes to the east of the Rhine. The Roman chronicler had just before described human sacrificial practices that took place in a sacred wood at the beginning of religious ceremonies, and this passage refers to another ritual associated with the holy grove. The binding of celebrants was an important symbol of submission in the presence of the divine.

Some human bodies interred in British Iron Age contexts show signs that they went to their graves with bound hands and feet. The positions of some of the Danebury bodies, for example, indicate the presence of wrist restraints.[36] Their hands were pressed together and their lower limbs tightly flexed. In 1996, in advance of pipeline construction work, Northamptonshire Archaeology sent a team to investigate any archaeological features identified along the pipe's route in order to record them before they were disturbed or destroyed. One of these features, found at Great Houghton, was an Iron Age enclosure and associated with this was a single inhumation burial within a circular pit.[37] But this was no ordinary tomb, and the choice of whole burial rather than cremation – the 'norm' at the time – is itself significant. The body, too, was treated in a singular manner. The deceased was a mature woman, about 35 years old, who died in the early 4th century BC.[38] She had been placed face down in her pit-grave and the position of her hands and feet shows that they had been bound. The oddest thing about her was a lead torc placed *back to front* around her neck, with the terminals at the nape. Lead is a curious metal for an Iron Age torc – they were usually made of gold, silver, bronze and occasionally of iron.

One further feature about this woman was a slight but significant deformity: the excavator, Andy Chapman, described it as 'a hypoplastic hamulus, a reduced hook on the hamate wrist bone, a condition that occurs in only 1.4% of the modern population.'[39] The Great Houghton woman was not in the best of health: the worn condition of her knees indicates that she had spent a lot of her time kneeling, probably grinding corn or kneading bread. She had bad teeth and a large abscess on one molar that would have caused her excruciating pain and may even have led to septicaemia. She was almost certainly local and she may have been a distant ancestress of a man who died and was buried in an Anglo-Saxon cemetery here 1,000 years later, for he too had the same rare wrist deformity. But who was she? Why were her hands and feet tied? And what was the significance of her lead torc and her prone position? She may have been buried in this way because she was a malefactor. Lead was favoured in European antiquity as a base metal that symbolized the 'dark side' of things: witchcraft, sorcery and the making of inscribed curses or evil spells. The inversion of the torc from its normal way of wearing could also reflect maleficence. In addition, the pain from her arthritic knees and rotten teeth may well have made the woman bad-tempered and frightening, and so her burial may signify the need to neutralize her spirit at death. But it is always possible that she was a sacrificial victim, in a ritual designed to deflect evil from the settlement. The torc may even have been present as a symbolic ligature, all part of a binding ritual designed to emphasize the woman's submission to her community or to the gods.

AND SO TO THE BOG BODIES: VERY COLD CASES

The singular interment of the woman at Great Houghton has certain features in common with some of the bog bodies: the lack of grave goods, the inhumation, bodily deformity, and the indications of shaming, such as binding. But we do not know why she was bound and presumably deliberately killed, or how she met her death: she could even have been buried alive, like an Iron Age Irish woman from Curragh in County Kildare.[40] The binding of the Northamptonshire woman is reminiscent of the way the body of the adolescent boy from a bog at Kayhausen in North Germany was treated, only his fate was even worse in that he was hog-tied. It is interesting, too, that iconography occasionally depicts similar restraint:

Romano-British copper alloy amulet of a naked, bound
Briton (perhaps a sacrificial victim), from Brough-
under-Stainmore, Cumbria.

the tiny Romano-British bronze amulet, meant to be worn around the
neck, from Brough-under-Stainmore, depicts a naked British prisoner,
hog-tied very like the Kayhausen body.[41]

It is highly unlikely that all ancient bog bodies were victims of human
sacrifice. Some may have been murdered and deposited in bogs to conceal
the evidence of criminal behaviour. Certain victims of the IRA are thought
to have been buried 'in bog and dirt'[42] so that they would not ever be
found, in acts of humiliation and vengefulness that spilled over into the
suffering of their families. Some, especially those apparently uninjured,
may have died when they wandered heedlessly into the mire. In any case,
human sacrifice was itself complicated and multidimensional. According
to classical authors, it was tangled up with the punishment of criminals
and the execution of prisoners of war. But one thing very evident from
study of the bog bodies is the element of theatre in the rituals leading up
to and during the killings. The weight of evidence for religious involvement strongly indicates that sacrificial rites were the main reason for the
Iron Age European bog killings.

THE DRAMA OF BOG SACRIFICE

The images were stark, gloomy blocks of unworked timber, rotten with
age, whose ghastly pallor terrified their devotees...Superstitious natives
believed that the ground often shook, that groans rose from hidden
caverns below, that yews were uprooted and miraculously replanted, and
that sometimes serpents coiled about the oaks, which blazed with fire
but did not burn. Nobody dared enter this grove except the priest; and
even he kept out at midday, and between dawn and dusk – for fear that
the gods might be abroad at such hours.

LUCAN, *PHARSALIA*[43]

Lucan's description of the Gallic sacred grove near Marseille, encountered
by Julius Caesar's army in the mid-1st century BC, sets a distinctly theatrical scene for ritual acts and it is not difficult to imagine the occurrence of
human sacrifice in such an awesome, spiritually charged place. Even allowing for Lucan's love of purple passages, the central point is that certain
locations were, in a sense, fault-lines where the human and divine worlds
interacted, like tectonic plates rubbing against each other in earthquake
zones. The liminal, capricious and treacherous bogs are prime candidates
for the blurring and merging of the material and cosmic realms, and it was
therefore these places that attracted extreme rituals, perhaps in the hope
that the intrusion of the spirits into the real world could be contained and
controlled, and that the gods could be appeased to avert disasters and propitiated so that they worked for rather than against the local community.

The elaborate, multiple and often protracted ways in which bog victims
were killed, and the selection of visually special people (whether giants,
dwarves, those with lurching gait or physical abnormalities) all contributed
to the drama of the sacrificial ritual. The special final meal and the stripping
and sometimes head-shaving of the victim would have been accompanied
by prayers, chanting and lustration (purification) ceremonies. The religious
officials themselves dressed in special clothes, with headdresses, wands of
office and divination equipment (such as the pairs of spoons mentioned in
the previous chapter). Perhaps they shook noise-makers, such as the artificial branch with clattering metal leaves from Manching, or blew musical
instruments, like the one played by the stone statuette from Pauvreley.
In classical and Near Eastern antiquity, the sacrifice of living things was
enacted against a backdrop of noise deliberately made to drown out the

unlucky screams of the victims. Were the celebrants to have consumed alcohol in any quantity, as part of the 'festivities' (or mourning rites), the sounds of revelry and uninhibited shouting or singing would have contributed to a noisy, theatrical catharsis. We can imagine that those present experienced a sensory 'high' in which the sounds of killing and celebration, the smell of blood and the miasmic marsh, the sight of the naked victim and the regalia-clad priests engaged the witnesses and perhaps the victim, too, in spiritual transference.

Like the bogs themselves, the human victims deposited there were possibly marginal beings, on the edges of society, for whatever reason, whether by dint of physical deviance or their status as foreigners. Some were adolescents, neither children nor adult and thus temporarily suspended from normal society. So the victims and their place of interment were spiritually connected. We should not forget the way that the preservative properties of the bog 'freeze-framed' the bodies, holding them back from the natural processes of decay and incorporation into the world of the ancestors. This, too, was theatre, for the bodies might have been clearly visible in shallow marsh pools. It is possible that, just as some Iron Age graves became foci for persistent pilgrimage or 'revisitation' rituals,[44] bog bodies and the swamps in which they lay attracted pilgrims over many years. It is a grisly thought, but maybe the preserved bodies themselves were periodically exhumed, exhibited during such remembrance ceremonies and then re-interred.

A DEATH FOR ALL SEASONS

In the myths of early Ireland that are preserved in early medieval manuscripts, four major seasonal festivals were celebrated: in early February, Imbolc was associated with lambing and the lactation of ewes; Beltane on 1 May ushered in summer and the transhumance (movement to summer pasture) of cattle; Lughnasadh in August celebrated harvest-time. The most sinister festival was Samhain at the end of October, a dangerous and liminal event that marked the end of the old year and the beginning of the new. It was a period when time was in abeyance and the barriers between the spirits, the dead and living people were temporarily dissolved.[45] Many of the major Irish assemblies, a blend of political and religious gatherings, took place at Samhain and at Beltane. There is a glimmer of evidence that these Irish festivals existed back in the Gallo-Roman period. The bronze ritual calendar from Coligny in central France, written in the Gaulish language, mentions 'Samonios', a word surely cognate with Samhain.[46]

It is not easy to determine the time of year in which bog victims were killed because many of the seeds, nuts and cereal grains found in their intestines could have been dried and used much later than when harvested. But there are hints that some of the bog people, such as Grauballe Man and Tollund Man,[47] met their deaths in the wintertime. The condition of Lindow Man's body suggests a cold-weather death.[48] The absence of fruit and fresh berries in the last meals of all three victims makes this quite likely. By contrast Clonycavan Man died at a time of plenty, probably in late summer or very early autumn,[49] and perhaps during a harvest festival such as Lughnasadh.

The time of year may not have been the only factor in choosing when to sacrifice. In chronicling ancient Germanic customs, Tacitus emphasizes the importance attached to darkness by certain northern tribes:

> It is by nights that they fix dates or make appointments. Night is regarded as ushering in the day...The Harii black their shields and dye their bodies black and choose pitch dark nights for their battles.
>
> TACITUS, GERMANIA 11[50]

Caesar says almost exactly the same of the Gauls, although with more detail. He explains that because the Gauls considered that they were descended from the 'Father of the Underworld', they counted time by nights rather than by days, adding that it was the Druids who handed down this tradition to their people.[51] If we believe these two Roman writers, night had a particular religious significance for both Germans and Gauls. The Coligny calendar provides testimony that the lunar cycle played a key role in planning ritual events, and that the fortnight leading up to the full moon was a far more active time for festivals and ceremonies than the waning half of each month.

The picture Tacitus paints of the blackened Harii, creeping by stealth upon their enemies at night, is chilling enough. But what if the sacrifice of the bog people also took place in the darkness, the event perhaps lit only by torches and the light of the moon glinting coldly on the surface of the marsh? That would send an additional frisson of frightening anticipation through the assembled celebrants, it would have contributed to the theatre of the occasion, and it would have been all the more terrifying for the victim.

THE SPECIAL POWER OF BOG SACRIFICE

If at least some bog victims met their violent and untimely deaths as sacrifices, there must have been a strong motivation behind the decision. Divination – predicting events and the will of the gods – may have been one reason, but there are likely to have been others that were specifically associated with the victims' interment in swampy places. Tacitus tells us that the Semnones conducted human sacrifice to initiate religious ceremonies,[52] but there is no mention of bog deposition. Where he does refer to marshy graves, it is in the context of capital punishment for cowards, those deserting the field of battle and 'the unnaturally vicious' (see p.82).[53] I wonder whether the latter comment might not contain a clue. Given the preponderance of physical abnormalities in the bog body population, there is a possibility that at least part of the problem may have lain in the inbreeding resulting from a small genetic pool.

One way in which Tacitus's comment concerning unnatural acts might be relevant is in cases of incest. Although the connection between sexual relationships between close kin and the birth of damaged children may not have been made, incest would have been regarded with disgust. Tacitus refers to the emphasis on female chastity 'uncorrupted by the temptations of public shows or the excitements of banquets'.[54] According to this model, it might be that those who manifested physical (or indeed mental) deviances were sacrificed in a complex ritual involving a combination of aversion (avoidance) and reciprocity. So, in order to try to ensure that fresh births would produce perfect offspring, communities perhaps sacrificed someone they considered lacking in some way, in a kind of contractual exchange with the gods whom they hoped would provide them with new lives that were without blemish or imperfections. But one can turn this argument on its head, of course, and suggest instead that the afflicted were perceived as touched by the gods and sacrificed because of their high and spiritually charged value.

There might be many reasons for aversion sacrifices in swampy places. I have a theory concerning the Lindow men (PL. XII), who may each have died in the mid–late 1st century AD. In AD 60, the Roman governor of Britain, Suetonius Paulinus, led a large army to Anglesey in order to smash the Druidic stronghold there. Lindow Moss lies close to one of the most direct routes from southeast England, where Paulinus and his troops were stationed. The destruction of the Druids' holy of holies on the island was a cataclysmic event for native Britons. I wonder whether there might be an argument for linking the Lindow bog sacrifices to this threat, and whether they were killed in order to try to persuade the gods to prevent such a disaster. If so, this failed. Tacitus tells us that the sanctuary was burned to ashes, despite the Druids' curses and the imprecations of the shrine's wild, black-clad female guardians.[55]

Lindow II (Lindow Man) was young and able-bodied, and he is likely to have had experience in battle. His sacrifice would have represented a serious loss to his people and its ability to defend itself. A great deal had been invested in such a killing. Just as certain hunting communities performed rituals to ensure the return of the herds each year, so a fit young man, with the potential for battle prowess, might have been killed in the reciprocal hope that the spirits would multiply the supply of fighters against the coming Roman army. It is uncertain whether Lindow III died on the same occasion but, if he did, his two extra thumbs could have endowed him with magical powers that might have informed his selection. Opposing thumbs are a key feature of human dexterity and his possession of extra ones perhaps gave him particular spiritual currency as a sacrificial candidate.

There is a hint that people were sacrificed on the sacred island of Anglesey itself. The small boggy pool at Llyn Cerrig Bach, on the northwest of the island, contained a rich Iron Age ritual deposit of weapons and ironmongery, including two sturdy gang-chains, as we have seen. They may have been cast into the swampy place as valuable iron objects, but they may also have represented those who wore the collars. These may have been prisoners of war, criminals or slaves, shambling neck-to-neck to this remote place. There is a small amount of evidence for the discovery of human remains when the site was investigated in the early 1940s.[56] It is almost too terrible to contemplate but, just possibly, the two sets of captives met their deaths, still chained together, at Llyn Cerrig. They could have been killed with one of the swords found in the sacred lake, or they might have been ritually drowned, imprisoned in their collars and chains.

The choice of adolescents as sacrifices in marshes is likely to do with the particular properties of their age and stage of physical development. On the cusp of adulthood, they had all their reproductive capacity before them. They might also have been perceived as sexually pure, with the peculiar power with which virginal states can be imbued, a combination of asexuality and undissipated sexual potential. We have only to glance at the essential chastity of Roman Vestal Virgins to see how importantly sexual purity could be regarded in classical antiquity. Dressed in pure white robes, these women tended Rome's eternal fire, the heart of the city and its empire, which must always stay alight. An errant Vestal paid dearly for her lapse by the horrific punishment of live entombment.[57] In Welsh mythology, virginity was highly prized and gave its possessor enormous political force.[58] And Tacitus chronicles the presence of a virgin prophetess, Veleda, among the ancient Germanic tribes, whose power to read the will of the gods depended upon her celibacy.[59] It is possible that the pubescent children immersed in the bogs at Windeby, Kayhausen and Yde carried particular weight in terms of reciprocal sacrifices, if their deaths were connected with adverse fertility concerns such as ailing livestock or failing crops.

THE BOG GODS

The gift of sacrifice requires a recipient. In the case of the bog bodies, their mode of deposition suggests that the recipients were perceived to reside in the depths of boggy pools. Their presence may have been seen as manifest in the marsh gases arising as vapour from the surface, sometimes combusting in ephemeral bursts of flickering flame, a particularly disturbing sight in the dark. We have no names for the bog deities. Lucan gives us three divine names: Taranis, Teutates and Esus,[60] referring to them as 'merciless gods', all clamouring for human sacrificial victims. But Lucan was speaking of Gaul, not Britain, Ireland or the northern countries where bog bodies have been found. Could Tacitus's Nerthus have been a bog goddess?

Perhaps the wooden images from Braak and Oldenburg represented the marsh deities. Just as likely, though, is that the very potency and awesome nature of the bog spirits were enhanced by their invisibility. At Bath, the Roman spa-city of Aquae Sulis, the local goddess, Sulis, is known from the head of a gilded bronze statue and from numerous inscribed dedications. Some of the pewter curse tablets thrown into the sacred spring refer to Sulis not as the goddess of the spring but the personification of its healing waters. We can imagine that the bog spirits, too, were perceived as both divine entities and the numinous bogs themselves. Whatever they were, they held sufficient hold over the people living nearby (and perhaps further away, too) to incite them to commit human lives to their eternal service.

Listening to the Dead:
Bog Bodies Uncovered

> In arranging their ceremonies the Moïs pay particular
> attention to the type of death the defunct had suffered.
> There are specially complicated and expensive rites for those
> who have died from various kinds of violence....
>
> NORMAN LEWIS, *A DRAGON APPARENT*[1]

This description of death rituals relates to a Vietnamese people whom the writer Norman Lewis encountered during his travels in Indo-China in the early 1950s. His book *A Dragon Apparent* concerns societies that could hardly be further geographically removed from the bog bodies of ancient Europe. And Lewis was recording the funerary ceremonies of the Moïs in the mid-20th century, 2,000 years later than the Iron Age bog killings. Yet, despite the distance, his narrative strikes a chord, serving as a reminder that special deaths (and arguably special lives) could result in special burial rites. It can be a mistake for archaeologists to venture too far into the anthropological jungle but, just occasionally, a comment from a modern travel writer, like Lewis, goes straight to the heart of an ancient problem.

This book began with the wish to 'unveil the dead'. If it has succeeded, it is fitting to conclude it by reflecting on how far such unveiling enables modern scholars to hear the stories of the bog bodies as it were from their own lips. It is the job of archaeologists to discover, to interpret and to construct anew the lives of the dead.[2] Narratives are created from the monuments, buildings, objects and other detritus left behind by past lives. Ancient skeletons or cremated human remains provide the means to populate that constructed past. But the European bog bodies present a truly unique additional resource, for they permit us literally to gaze into the faces of Iron Age people: and sometimes they appear to be staring straight back at us. Scientists have the capacity to probe deep into their unprotesting bodies to find answers to questions about their chronology, health, diet and lifestyle. The preservation of skin and soft tissue allows for the identification of body paint and for taking fingerprints. Forensic teams can establish causes of death, and can frequently identify signs of abuse, torture and murderous intent. Bog bodies are able to tell us so much about their everyday lives and, of course, their deaths. The way the bogs have preserved them allows us the closest possible understanding of their world and of the beliefs and cosmologies that hedged that world about with ritual. These mummified bodies permit us to twitch aside the curtain between us and the people of the Iron Age, and to catch a glimpse of their hopes, fears, values and attitude to their gods.

RESPECT AND RESPONSIBILITY

Having an intense interest in ancient ritual practices and the beliefs that underpinned them, I have nonetheless always been uneasy about the disturbance and disinterment of the ancient dead by modern investigations. For the most part, Iron Age people whose remains survive were probably interred in tombs that were meant to be permanent.[3] So there is a sense in which the excavators of graves are interfering with and even desecrating the funerary intentions of past communities. But the bog bodies were not buried in 'real' graves, so the disposal of their remains might have had quite different purposes from the tombs of those who died naturally or as a result of accident or war. Even so, the individuals or groups who interred them with attendant ritual behaviour meant them to remain closely connected to the bogs into whose keeping they had been given and to whom they may have been offered as sacrificial gifts designed to be eternal.

Of course it is a pragmatic necessity to investigate the resting places of ancient individuals if we want to try to understand the thoughts and actions of the dead and those who buried them. But information gleaned

The serene face of Tollund Man. The stubble on his chin and the noose that throttled him are clearly visible. He looks as if he has just fallen asleep.

in this way carries with it a responsibility of respect. Whether the remains of the dead consist of charred bone fragments, skeletons or preserved bog mummies, they are not artifacts but people and, as such, they demand the dignity of sensitive engagement. In both scientific investigation and in the public dissemination of knowledge, the humanity of these individuals needs to remain at the forefront of their treatment. Ghoulishness and voyeurism can be natural responses to the sight of bog people, who present themselves as vulnerable, naked and violently killed. The bodies present a paradox, however, in that the action of the bog acids on human bodies can make them seem less like once-living, breathing beings and more like images. Seamus Heaney makes just this point in his poem *Punishment*, where he describes the shiny 'tar-black face' of what once had been a comely adolescent.[4] Wijnand van der Sanden referred to the female bog body from Huldremose as resembling an 'old smoked ham'.[5] In her book on bog bodies and imagination, Karin Sanders emphasizes the notion of bog bodies as art.[6] When excavated from the swamps, they may resemble tanned leather or even bronze, with artificially red hair or shining bald heads. Their faces may have been grotesquely flattened by the weight of bog vegetation, their bodies shrunken and their limbs distorted, so they appear like a parody or travesty of humanity. So their modern interpreters have a responsibility to them in terms of the manner in which their lives and deaths are presented in literature, in the texts accompanying museum displays and in the way the bodies are conserved and shown to the public. The respect due these fellow humans is vital for the maintenance of their dignity and, indeed, of our own.

The exhibition of Tollund Man at the Silkeborg Museum in Denmark, situated in a quiet village on an inland waterway, is an example of best practice. The visitor is directed to a small, windowless room, decorated to resemble a peat bog. The sole occupant is Tollund Man inside in a Perspex case, softly lit and resting on a bed of peat (PL. I). When I last went to see him in 2000, I was the only person in his room, and I could sit a few inches away in the stillness of his presence, able to look closely at his calm face, with the eyelashes framing closed eyelids and the stubble of a beard. Off the beaten track, Silkeborg has become a place of pilgrimage; it is impossible to visit the museum and its ancient guest and not come away touched with awe. The bog bodies of Iron Age Europe allow us to get as close up and personal to our ancient ancestors as it is possible to be.

APPENDIX: THE PRINCIPAL BOG BODIES

ENGLAND

LINDOW I & III

FINDSPOT:
Lindow Moss, Cheshire
DISCOVERED: 1983 and 1987
CONDITION: Severed head
(Lindow I) and fragmentary
body (Lindow III); naked;
body possibly painted
AGE: 35
CAUSE OF DEATH: Decapitation
DATE OF DEATH: 1st century BC/AD
CURRENT LOCATION
The British Museum

LINDOW MAN (LINDOW II)

FINDSPOT:
Lindow Moss, Cheshire
DISCOVERED: 1984
CONDITION: Head and large
portion of body; naked but
for a fox-fur armlet;
body possibly painted
AGE: Early 20s
CAUSE OF DEATH: Blunt force
trauma to the skull, garrotted,
throat cut
DATE OF DEATH:
1st century BC/AD
CURRENT LOCATION:
The British Museum

WORSLEY MAN

FINDSPOT: Worsley Moss,
Lancashire
DISCOVERED: 1958
CONDITION: Severed head
AGE: 24–40
CAUSE OF DEATH: Strangulation
DATE OF DEATH:
1st century BC/AD
CURRENT LOCATION: University
of Manchester Museum

IRELAND

CASHEL MAN

FINDSPOT: County Laois
DISCOVERED: 2011
CONDITION: Deliberately placed
on the bog-surface, perhaps
in a pool; body marked by
two hazel rods
AGE: Young adult
CAUSE OF DEATH:
Multiple wounds
DATE OF DEATH: 2000–1600 BC
CURRENT LOCATION: National
Museum of Ireland, Dublin

CLONYCAVAN MAN

FINDSPOT: County Meath
DISCOVERED: 2003
CONDITION: Upper half of body
including the head; naked;
hair elaborately dressed with
hair-gel
AGE: 20–30
CAUSE OF DEATH: Possible blunt
force trauma to the head,
disembowelling
DATE OF DEATH: 400–300 BC
CURRENT LOCATION: National
Museum of Ireland, Dublin

GALLAGH MAN

FINDSPOT:
County Galway
DISCOVERED: 1821
CONDITION: Complete body;
clothed; body marked
by hazel rods
AGE: 20s
CAUSE OF DEATH: Strangulation
DATE OF DEATH: 1st century BC
CURRENT LOCATION: National
Museum of Ireland, Dublin

OLDCROGHAN MAN

FINDSPOT: County Offaly
DISCOVERED: 2003
CONDITION: Upper half of body
minus the head; naked but
for a decorated leather armlet
AGE: 20s
CAUSE OF DEATH: Torture, stabbing
DATE OF DEATH: 400–300 BC
CURRENT LOCATION: National
Museum of Ireland, Dublin

DENMARK

BORREMOSE MAN

FINDSPOT: Himmerland
DISCOVERED: 1946
CONDITION: Fully-grown but only
155 cm (5 ft) tall; naked but a
bundle of two sheepskin cloaks
at his feet; heavy birch rod
laying over the body
AGE: Mature
CAUSE OF DEATH:
Strangulation/hanging
Date of death: 8th century BC
CURRENT LOCATION: National
Museum, Copenhagen

BORREMOSE WOMAN

FINDSPOT: Himmerland
DISCOVERED: 1948
CONDITION: Wrapped in a
woollen skirt; face badly
mutilated, probably
deliberately. (She is one of two
female bodies from this marsh:
the second, found in 1947, had
an infant with her)
AGE: 25–35
CAUSE OF DEATH: Uncertain;
perhaps mutilation
DATE OF DEATH: 8th/7th century BC
CURRENT LOCATION: National
Museum, Copenhagen

ELLING WOMAN

FINDSPOT: Bjaeldskovdal
Mose, Jutland
DISCOVERED: 1938
CONDITION: Complete body,
including a head with
plaited hair; covered with
two cloaks, one of sheepskin
and one of cowhide; legs lay
on a second cowhide
AGE: 25–30
CAUSE OF DEATH: Hanging
DATE OF DEATH:
Late 3rd century BC
CURRENT LOCATION: Silkeborg
Museum, Denmark

GRAUBALLE MAN

FINDSPOT: Nebelgårde Mose,
Jutland
DISCOVERED: 1952
CONDITION: Naked; nothing
found with body
AGE: 30
CAUSE OF DEATH: Massive throat-
wound; bled to death
DATE OF DEATH: c. 390 BC
CURRENT LOCATION: Moesgård
Museum

HARALDSKAER WOMAN, AKA 'QUEEN GUNHILD'

FINDSPOT: Gutskaer Mose,
Jutland
DISCOVERED: 1835
CONDITION: Naked but with
clothing near the body
together with a long lock of
hair; secured in the bog with
hurdles
AGE: 45–50
CAUSE OF DEATH:
Strangulation/hanging
DATE OF DEATH: c. 490 BC
CURRENT LOCATION: Saint Nicolai
Church, Vejle, Jutland

HULDREMOSE WOMAN

FINDSPOT: Djursland
DISCOVERED: 1879
CONDITION: Naked but with two
cloaks, a skirt, peplos and scarf
lying over body; severed right
arm lay nearby; left arm bound
to her side by a leather thong
AGE: Mature
CAUSE OF DEATH: Tortured, but
the actual cause of death
remains uncertain
DATE OF DEATH: AD 100
CURRENT LOCATION: National
Museum, Copenhagen

TOLLUND MAN

FINDSPOT: Bjaeldskovdal Mose,
Jutland
DISCOVERED: 1950
CONDITION: Head and most
of body; naked but for a
pointed sheepskin cap and
leather girdle
AGE 30–40
CAUSE OF DEATH Hanging
DATE OF DEATH 4th century BC
CURRENT LOCATION Silkeborg
Museum

NORTH GERMANY

DAMENDORF MAN

FINDSPOT: Rendsburg-
Eckernförde,
Schleswig-Holstein
DISCOVERED: 1900
CONDITION: Only the skin, nails
and hair preserved; several
garments nearby, including
openwork leather shoes, a
leather belt, breeches and
leg-wrappings
AGE: Adult
CAUSE OF DEATH: Impossible
to establish
DATE OF DEATH: c. AD 220
CURRENT LOCATION:
Schleswig-Holsteinische
Landesmuseen, Schloss
Gottorf, Schleswig

DÄTGEN MAN

FINDSPOT: Grosses Moor,
Schleswig
DISCOVERED: 1959
CONDITION: Naked, with hair
in Suebian Knot; body and
its severed head lay together,
staked down
AGE: 30
CAUSE OF DEATH: Stabbed three
times in the chest, decapitated
DATE OF DEATH: c. 150 BC
CURRENT LOCATION: Schleswig-
Holsteinische Landesmuseen,
Schloss Gottorf, Schleswig

HUNTEBURG COUPLE

FINDSPOT: North Osnabrück,
Lower Saxony
DISCOVERED: 1949
CONDITION: Pair of men,
wrapped in woollen blankets
AGES: 20 and 30
CAUSE OF DEATH: Uncertain
DATE OF DEATH: c. AD 250
CURRENT LOCATION:
Landesmuseum Hanover

KAYHAUSEN BOY

FINDSPOT: Bad Zwischenahn,
Lower Saxony
DISCOVERED: 1922
CONDITION: Naked but with a
cape; hog-tied with his own
clothes, possibly after death;
deformed hip
AGE: 12–14
CAUSE OF DEATH: Stabbing,
throat-cutting
DATE OF DEATH: 2nd/1st century BC
CURRENT LOCATION:
Landesmuseum für Natur und
Mensch, Oldenburg

OSTERBY MAN

FINDSPOT: Köhlmoor,
Schleswig-Holstein
DISCOVERED: 1948
CONDITION: Skull with a fine head
of hair, dressed in a complex
Suebian Knot; wrapped in a
deerskin; secured in the bog
with stakes
AGE: 55–60
CAUSE OF DEATH: Blunt force
trauma to the head,
decapitation
DATE OF DEATH: *c.* AD 100
CURRENT LOCATION: Schleswig-
Holsteinische Landesmuseen,
Schloss Gottorf, Schleswig

RED FRANZ

FINDSPOT: Neu-Versen, Lower
Saxony
DISCOVERED: 1900
CONDITION: Naked; long,
well-preserved hair and a
moustache and 'designer'
stubble; the striking red hair
that gave rise to his name was
likely to have been dyed that
colour by bog acids
AGE: Early 30s
CAUSE OF DEATH: Uncertain;
sustained several injuries,
perhaps in battle, throat
probably cut
DATE OF DEATH: Late 3rd/early 4th
century AD
CURRENT LOCATION:
Landesmuseum Hanover

WINDEBY CHILD

FINDSPOT: Schleswig-Holstein
DISCOVERED: 1952
CONDITION: Carefully laid, naked,
in a 'grave' within the bog, a
broken birch-staff lying across
the body; head shaved; woollen
hairband laying across her
nose; originally identified as
female, but latest investigations
indicate that the body is male;
the bones of the legs have
Harris Lines, indicative of
malnutrition

AGE: 12–14
CAUSE OF DEATH: Unknown;
possibly drowning
DATE OF DEATH: 1st century AD
CURRENT LOCATION: Schleswig-
Holsteinische Landesmuseen,
Schloss Gottorf, Schleswig

WINDEBY MAN

FINDSPOT: Schleswig-Holstein
DISCOVERED: 1952
CONDITION: Naked; body pinned
down into the bog with eight
wooden stakes; only a few
metres away from the
Windeby Child
AGE: Middle-aged
CAUSE OF DEATH: Strangulation
with a twisted rope of hazel,
found in position around
his neck
DATE OF DEATH: 1st century AD
CURRENT LOCATION: Schleswig-
Holsteinische Landesmuseen,
Schloss Gottorf, Schleswig

NETHERLANDS

WEERDINGE COUPLE

FINDSPOT: Bourtangermoor,
Drenthe
DISCOVERED: 1904
CONDITION: Two men interred
next to each other; one resting
on the right arm of the other,
as if embracing; both naked
AGE: Adult
CAUSE OF DEATH: One of them
stabbed in the chest and
disembowelled
DATE OF DEATH: 2nd century
BC–2nd century AD
CURRENT LOCATION: Drents
Museum, Assen

YDE GIRL

FINDSPOT: Drenthe.
DISCOVERED: 1897
CONDITION: Naked but covered
by an old woollen coat; right
side of head shaved, cut-off
hank next to body; suffered

from severe idiopathic
scoliosis that stunted her
growth and would have
caused her to walk with
a lurching gait and to suffer
constant pain
AGE: *c.* 16
CAUSE OF DEATH: Strangulation
with her woollen belt
DATE OF DEATH: *c.* 1st century AD
CURRENT LOCATION: Drents
Museum, Assen

ZWEELOO WOMAN

FINDSPOT: Drenthe
DISCOVERED: 1951
CONDITION: Only the skeleton
of this body survives; she
suffered from a form of
dwarfism, and had abnormally
short lower legs and forearms
and there is considerable
asymmetry between the bones
on the left and right sides of
the body – not only was she
very short, she would have
had a lurching, irregular gait
AGE: Mature
CAUSE OF DEATH: Unknown
DATE OF DEATH:
1st–3rd century AD
CURRENT LOCATION: Drents
Museum, Assen

NOTES

INTRODUCTION (pp. 8–13)

1   Coles 2001, 30
2   Glob 1969
3   Hvass 1998; Glob 1969, 70; Aldhouse-Green 2001, 117–18, fig. 49
4   Olivier Bruno pers. comm., 20 November 2014
5   See Appendix to Chapter One
6   See Van der Sanden 1996, 71–89 for a detailed discussion about the numbers of bog bodies and the problems in making accurate estimates
7   Information from Luke MacLaughlin of Bearkatt TV Productions, 2 December 2013

CHAPTER 1 (pp. 14–33)

1   Trans. Graves 1956, 78
2   Bergen *et al.* 2002, 18
3   Bergen *et al.* 2002, 20
4   Beuker 2002a, 107. This passage was taken from a local Drenthe newspaper article written a few days after the discovery of the Yde Girl's mummified body
5   Beuker 2002, 107–09
6   From the local daily newspaper *Jyllands-Posten* for 2 May 1952; quoted in Asingh 2007a, 21
7   Asingh 2007a, 15–22
8   Heinemeier and Asingh 2007, 197, 201
9   Glob 1969, 18
10   Fischer 1999, 96
11   Trans. Mattingly 1948, 132
12   Aldhouse-Green 2004b, 302, fig. 2
13   2002, 28–31
14   Gebühr 2002, 29
15   Glob 1969, 112
16   Van der Sanden 1996, 141
17   Van der Sanden 2013, 403, 410
18   Coles 2001, 30
19   Turner 1986, 10; 1995a, fig. 4
20   Gowlett *et al.* 1986, 22–23
21   Turner 1999, 228–29
22   *Geography* 4.5.4; trans. Jones 1923, 259
23   Raftery 1994, 188
24   Balguy 1734, 414, quoted in Turner 1995b, 200

25   Asingh 2007c, 312
26   Trans. Wright 1957, 2
27   Aldhouse-Green 2010, 73–74; Asingh 2007c, 314; Kelly 2006 (and pers. comm. 3 August 2007); Mulhall and Briggs 2007, and Mulhall pers. comm. 3 December 2007
28   5.28; trans. Tierney 1959–60, 249–50
29   *Op. cit.*; Aldhouse-Green 2004b
30   http://www.museum.ie/en/exhibition/ kingship-and-sacrifice.aspx; BBC 4 documentary *4,000 Year Old Cold Case: The Body in the Bog*, 28 November 2013
31   Aldhouse-Green 2001, 117

CHAPTER 2 (pp. 34–49)

1   Tacitus *Germania* 12; trans. Mattingly 1948, 112
2   Caesar *De Bello Gallico* 6.21; trans. Wiseman and Wiseman 1980, 124
3   Caesar *De Bello Gallico* 1.11 and onwards
4   Caesar *De Bello Gallico* 1.1; trans. Wiseman and Wiseman 1980, 17
5   For example Collis 2003; James 1999
6   Caesar *De Bello Gallico* 1.1
7   Tacitus *Germania* 7; trans. Mattingly 1948, 106
8   Savory 1976, pl. VI; Owen-Jones 2012, 10–11
9   Raftery 1994, 32–35
10   Bulleid and Gray 1911, 1917; Coles and Minnitt 1995
11   Bergen *et al.* eds. 2002, 92
12   Therkorn *et al.* 1984
13   Kaul 1991
14   Scarre 1998, 211–19
15   Zwicker 1935, 50
16   Gebühr 2002, 16–17; Aldhouse-Green 2004, 59–61, fig. 3.3
17   *Germania* 40
18   *Germania* 40; trans. Mattingly 1948, 134
19   Heaney 1998, 117
20   Asingh 2007, 281, fig. 5
21   Green 1993, 73; 1995, 44
22   Taylor 2002, 144–69
23   Raftery 1994, 98
24   Asingh 2007, 280
25   Savory 1976, 46–47, 80–81; Davies and Lynch 2000, 178–79; pl. 28
26   Cunliffe 1986, 155–71; 1993, 100–12

CHAPTER 3 (pp. 50–65)

1   Trans. Sherley-Price 1955, 260
2   Delap 1998, 14
3   Trans. Borca 2000, 76
4   Trans. Nash 1951, 63
5   Borca 2000, 76
6   Hope 2000, 112–20
7   Bodel 2000, 135–44. It is interesting that in modern Italy, by contrast, funeral directors are regarded as important and highly respected members of society. In his book *A Small Place in Italy*, the travel writer Eric Newby describes his encounter with the *impresario di pompe funebri* of Fivizzano in Tuscany: Newby 1994, 184
8   Asingh 2007b, 275
9   Beuker 2000b, 12
10 Van der Sanden 1996, 24
11 Tolkien 1968, 650
12 Beuker 2000b, 17; Asingh 2007b, 278
13 Strehle 2007, 45
14 http://en.wikipedia.org/wiki/Gristhorpe_ Man (accessed November 2013); Melton *et al.* eds, 2013
15 https://www.shef.ac.uk/archaeology/ research/cladh-hallan; Parker Pearson *et al.* 2007
16 Cummings 2003, 38
17 Jones 2002, 65; Green 1999
18 Sanders 2009, 25
19 Johnstone 1957, quoting Sir Mortimer Wheeler in 1954 in the BBC TV programme on the Danish bog body
20 Scaife 1986, 129
21 Beuker 2002c, 126; Van der Sanden 1996, 108
22 Harild *et al.* 2007, 158–59, 161
23 Aldhouse-Green 2010, 73; Kelly 2006
24 Hillman 1986, 110
25 Hillan 1986, 110–11; Holden 1995, 79
26 1986, 168
27 Pliny *Natural History* 16.95; Ross 1986, 167–68
28 Scaife 1986, 131
29 Scaife 1986, 133
30 The symptoms of ergot poisoning are graphically presented in Brian Callison's maritime novel *The Auriga Madness*, in which an entire ship's crew consumes food from ergot-infested grain and literally goes mad, driving the *Auriga* into the cantilevered Forth railway bridge, with appalling loss of life: Callison 1980
31 Van der Sanden 1996, 118
32 Harild *et al.* 2007, 175–76
33 Tolkien 1968, 653
34 Boyce 1979, 14–15, 44–45, 156, 222
35 Williams 2003, 2003, 91
36 Van der Sanden 1995, 156–57
37 Veil 2002, 104
38 Veil 2002, 105
39 Van der Sanden 1995, 154
40 Van der Sanden 1996, 101–02
41 Van der Sanden 1996, 179, fig. 245; Strabo *Geography* 7.2.3; Tacitus *Annales* 14, 30–31
42 Van der Sanden 1996, 18, fig. 14
43 Garland 1995, 106
44 Van der Sanden 1996, 154, fig. 200

CHAPTER 4 (pp. 66–81)

1   Gregersen *et al.*, 2007, 235
2   Readers wishing to get to grips with the details of radiocarbon dating are directed to Renfrew and Bahn 2008, 141–48. For an up-to-date survey of the problems associated with this technique see Papagianni and Morse 2013, 110–13
3   Heinemeier and Asingh, 2007, 201
4   For a discussion of the problems relating to the radiocarbon dating of the Lindow bodies see Otlet *et al.*, 1986, 28–30; Housley *et al.*, 1995, 40–45
5   Fischer, undated, 5
6   Story board for National Geographic Channel series *Tales of the Living Dead II. Bog Mummy*, filmed by Brighton TV, October 2004
7   Hvass 1998; Aldhouse-Green 2001, 202
8   Heinemeier and Asingh 2007, 196
9   Larsen and Poulsen 2007
10 Frederiksen 2007, 59–74
11 Gregersen *et al.* 2007
12 Boel and Dalstra 2007, 137, 139
13 Ahrenholt-Bindslev *et al.*, 2007, 145–46, 150, 152
14 Harild *et al.* 2007; Stødkilde-Jørgensen *et al.* 2007
15 Wilson *et al.*, 2007, 194–95
16 Raftery 1994, 188; http://archive. archaeology.org/online/features/bog/ violence3.html
17 Raftery 1994, 188
18 Mulhall 2010
19 Turner 1999, 228
20 Est 1986, 80
21 Taylor 1986, 41
22 Turner 1999, 229
23 Van der Sanden 1996, 63
24 Spindler 1995, 167–73
25 Spindler 1995, 170–71
26 Hingley and Unwin 2005, fig. 36
27 Caesar *De Bello Gallico* 5.14
28 A technique using radiographs impregnated with selenium, which

enhances imaging of ancient mummies: Bourke 1986, 46

29 West 1986, 77–78

30 In the Danish journal *Brage og Idun*; after Sanders 2009, 94–95; trans. Sanders

31 2009, 91–125

32 Quoted in Neave and Quinn 1986, 42. Galen of Pergamum was a Greek doctor working and writing in the 2nd century AD. He began his career as a physician to gladiators and he later became a court medical practitioner at Rome in the reign of Marcus Aurelius

33 Gerasimov 1971

34 Neave was not the only scientist to work on the facial reconstruction of bog bodies in the 1980s. Richard Helmer of Kiel University used similar methods to recreate the head of the Windeby Child: Van der Sanden 1996, 149

35 Stead *et al.* 1986

36 Neave and Quinn 1986, 42–43

37 Beuker 2002d, 128–29

38 Wilkinson 2007

39 Melton *et al.* 2013, 144; http://news.bbc.co.uk/local/york/hi/people_and_places/history/newsid_8877000/8877132.stm, 2 August 2010

CHAPTER 5 (pp. 82–113)

1 Trans. Mattingly 1948, 110

2 Taylor 2002, 128

3 Herodotus *Histories* 4.72–73

4 Conan Doyle 2007 (first published 1902), 68

5 *Beowulf. A New Translation*: Heaney 1999, 27

6 Virago Press 2003, 25 (the book was first published in 1936 by Victor Gollancz). *Jamaica Inn* was screened as a drama series for BBC One in April 2014

7 Briggs 1995, 168–82

8 Asingh 2007a, 17

9 Briggs 1995, 177–80

10 Van der Sanden 1996, 154–58; Stead 1986, 177

11 Ross 1986, 162–64

12 Briggs 1986, 179–80

13 Heaney 1998, 117–18

14 1948, 110

15 Glob 1969, 153

16 Chamberlain and Parker Pearson 2001, 79

17 Trans. Mattingly 1948, 115

18 Trans. Mattingly 1948, 116–17

19 Gebühr 2002, 32–47 and pers. comm. Schloss-Gottorf Museum, 2002

20 Beuker 2002a, 109

21 Thompson 2003, 217–18

22 Trans. Mattingly 1948, 132–33

23 Foucault 1977, 257–61

24 Aldhouse-Green 2004c

25 Plutarch *Life of Numa* 10

26 Bauman 1996, 18

27 BBC News, Saturday 12 April 2014; Boren 2014

28 1995, 13–14

29 Chapter 11; trans. Wright 1957, 43

30 Bauman 1996, 24

31 Caesar *De Bello Gallico* 6.13

32 Metzler 2002, 25

33 Van der Sanden 1996, 101

34 West 1986, 77

35 Newby 2011a, 255

36 Giles 2012, 1

37 *Ibid.*

38 Ogden 2001, 146, 162

39 Taylor 2002, 145–46

40 2009, 70–71, 127–68

41 Alberti 2012

CHAPTER 6 (pp. 114–29)

1 Mantel 2005, 44

2 Tope 2013, 199

3 *Jyllands-Posten* 2 May 1952; Asingh 2007a, 21

4 *Macbeth* Act 5, Scene 1; Harrison ed. 1937, 86

5 Aldhouse-Green 2004b, 316, fig. 13, after Filer 1997, 57, fig. 3; Spencer 1993, 52, fig. 32

6 Durand 1989, fig. 7

7 Aldhouse-Green 2004b, 317, fig. 14; Ferris 2003, figs. 5, 6; Settis *et al.* 1988, pls. 21, 57, 173

8 Gregersen, Jurik and Lynnerup 2007, 246–47 and fig. 6

9 Gregeren, Jurik and Lynneryp 2007, 252

10 Gregersen *et al.*, 254; Van der Sanden 1996, 161

11 7, 2–3, trans. Jones 1923–24

12 Gregersen *et al.* 2007, 254; Van der Sanden 1996, 101, 161

13 Asingh 2007c, 307; Tacitus *Germania* 38;

14 Strabo *Geography* 4.4.5; Aldhouse-Green 2001, 83

15 Giles 2008, 72–74; Giles 2012, 187; Aldhouse-Green 2010, 228

16 Gregersen *et al.* 2007, 242–46

17 Gregersen *et al.* 2007, 254–58; fig. 16

18 West 1986, 77; Bourke 1986, fig. 15

19 West 1986, 78–79

20 Gregersen *et al.* 2007, 246; Asingh 2007c, 297–99

21 23.24; trans. De Sélincourt 1965, 198

22 Diodorus Siculus *World History* 5.29, 4; trans. Tierney 1959–60, 250

23 For detailed discussion of the Saluvian evidence see Armit 2012
24 Turner 1999, 229
25 Armit 2012, 220–21
26 Pyatt *et al.* 1995, 69–73
27 Caesar *De Bello Gallico* 5.14; Pomponius Mela *Chorographia* 3.5.51; Pliny *Natural History* 22.2; Martial *Epigrams* 11, 52
28 Kelly 2006
29 Gebühr 2002, 28–29; Asingh 2007c, 309
30 *Germania* 38
31 Garland 1995; Turner 1999, 231
32 *Germania* 12; trans. Mattingly 1948, 110
33 Aldhouse-Green 2004c, 322; Foucault 1977, 259
34 Savory 1976, pl. VIb
35 Tacitus *Annals* 6.13
36 Aldhouse-Green 2006, 289, fig. 7; Van der Sanden 1996, pl. 117
37 Gebühr 2002, 32–47
38 *Germania* 40; trans. Mattingly 1948, 134
39 By a Berne commentator on Lucan's *Pharsalia* 1, 444–46; Zwicker 1934, 50; trans. Marilyn Raybould, for Aldhouse-Green 2001, 113
40 Van der Sanden 1996, 164
41 *History* 3.14.67; trans. Whittaker 1969, 359
42 Aldhouse-Green 2004a, 215
43 Pyatt *et al.* 1995
44 Van der Sanden 1996, 63
45 Scaife 1986, 131–33
46 Pliny *Natural History* 16.95
47 Ross 1986, 167–68
48 As an aside, but with relevance both to mistletoe and to body art, it is the *Valonia* oak that Pliny mentions as being sacred to the Druids and from which mistletoe must be harvested. In his book *On the Shores of the Mediterranean* (2011b, 164), Eric Newby comments that the term *valonia* refers to the 'acorn cups and unripe acorns of the Eurasian oak, *Quercus aegilops*, used in tanning, dyeing and making ink'
49 Van der Sanden 1996, 118

CHAPTER 7 (pp. 130–45)

1 From the Danish Journal *Brage og Idun* 1841, after Sanders 2009, 95
2 Hughes 1991, 139–65; Aldhouse-Green 2001, 144–45
3 1997, 24
4 Aldhouse-Green and Aldhouse-Green 2005, 12–13
5 West 1986, 77
6 West 1986, 79
7 Kelly 2006; Mulhall 2010
8 2006 and pers. comm.

9 Aldhouse-Green 2001, col. pl. 2; Van der Sanden 1996, 164
10 Lange 1997, 167
11 1977, 244–45
12 Girard 1977, 245
13 A term used by Hilary Mantel, *Beyond Black*
14 Girard 1977, 131
15 Ogden 2001, 146, 162
16 Taylor 2002, 147
17 Vine 1992, 81
18 Cunliffe 1983, 160
19 Walker 1984, 442–63; Hooper 1984, 463–74; Cunliffe 1993, 12–13
20 Aldhouse-Green 2001, 56–61. It is worth mentioning Strabo's comment that the people living in Ireland in the 1st century BC ate human flesh: *Geography* 4.5.4
21 Hartley 1957, 15, 27
22 Barber *et al.* 1989, 773–78
23 Meniel 1987, 25–31
24 Macdonald 1979, 415–24
25 Lejars 1994, 232–33; Aldhouse-Green 2001, 51, fig. 23
26 Aldhouse-Green 2010, 139; John Collis and Vincent Guichard, pers. comm.
27 Whitehead 1921, 59
28 Hutton 1991, 289–90
29 Baillot 2010; Baillot and Symmons 2012
30 Spindler 1982/3
31 Carman 1997, 228
32 Girard 1977, 4
33 Dio Cassius *Roman History* 62.7; trans. Ireland 1996, 67
34 Aldhouse-Green 2006, 189–90
35 Tacitus *Annals* 14.33; trans. Grant 1956, 319
36 Hughes 1991, 139–65

CHAPTER 8 (pp. 146–61)

1 4, 4.5–6; trans. Tierney 1959–60, 269–70
2 Armit 2006, 1
3 *Germania* 10; trans. Mattingly 1948, 108–09
4 From a poem by Steen Steensen Blicher, 'Queen Gunhild', published in the Danish journal *Brage og Idun* in 1841, quoted in Sanders 2009, 94–95
5 *Germania* 18
6 'The women often wear undergarments of linen, embroidered with purple, and, as the upper part does not extend to sleeves, forearms and upper arms are bare. Even the breast, where it comes nearest the shoulder, is exposed too': Tacitus *Germania* 17; trans. Mattingly 1948, 115
7 2012, 29–30, 38, 45, figs. 4 and 5

8   Van der Sanden 1995, 154–55;
    Aldhouse-Green 2004b, 302–03
9   Burkert 1985, 70
10 Lurker 1974, 67
11 Arnoldi 1995, 16–17
12 Gebühr 1979; Aldhouse-Green 2001, 119,
    fig. 50
13 Van der Sanden 1996, 164
14 *Germania* 19: 'Adultery in that populous
    nation is rare in the extreme and
    punishment is summary and left to the
    husband. He shaves off his wife's hair,
    strips her in the presence of his kinsmen,
    thrusts her from his house and flogs
    her through the whole village... Neither
    beauty, youth or wealth can find the sinner
    a husband'; trans. Mattingly 1948, 116–17
15 Nomberg-Przytyk 1985, 14
16 Heaney 1998, 118
17 *Roman Antiquities* 2.15.1–2; after Garland
    1995, 16
18 Garland 1995, 59
19 *Politics* 7.1335b 19–21
20 Plutarch *Life of Caesar*; trans. Warner 1958,
    231; Suetonius *Caesar* 45; trans.
    Graves 1962, 20
21 Suetonius *Claudius* 3; trans.
    Graves 1962, 163
22 Beuker 2002a, 108–09
23 Van der Sanden 1996, 141
24 Van der Sanden 1995, 156; 1996, 141
25 Garland 1995, 47 and see pls. 6–10, 13 for
    images of Greek and Roman dwarfs on
    painted vases and figurines of terracotta
    and bronze
26 Of course, these three people's inability to
    function fully in terms of physical fitness
    does not necessarily mean that they
    could not contribute to their community:
    sedentary occupations, such as making
    pots, spinning, weaving, cooking, grinding
    corn and minding small children were all
    open to them
27 Niblett 1999, 20–21
28 Garland (A), 1995, figs. 41–45
29 Brothwell and Bourke 1995, 56–57
30 Duval 1987, 42–46
31 Aldhouse-Green 2004a, 85, fig. 3.16
32 Aldhouse-Green 2015, 119; Davidson 1989;
    Mac Cana 1983, 107
33 Aldhouse-Green 2004, 180–81, fig. 7.1;
    Deyts 1992, 18
34 6.19; trans. Wiseman and Wiseman
    1980, 124
35 Parker Pearson 1999, 1–3; Jones 1968,
    425–30
36 Cochrane 2012, 143–44
37 Cochrane 2012, 143

38 Scullard 1981, 205–06
39 *Annals* 14.30
40 Plutarch *Life of Themistocles* 13.2
41 *De Bello Gallico* 6.16
42 Parker Pearson 1999, 1
43 As propounded in a television drama
    entitled 'Ghost Train', part of ITV's Lynda
    La Plante *Trial and Retribution* series
    screened on ITV 3 on Tuesday 10 June
    2014

CHAPTER 9 (pp. 162–79)

1   6.13; trans. Wiseman and Wiseman
    1980, 121
2   5.31, 2–5
3   *Germania* 7
4   Caesar *de Bello Gallico* 6.16
5   *De Bello Gallico* 6.21; trans. Wiseman and
    Wiseman 1980, 124
6   *Germania* 7; trans. Mattingly 1948, 106
7   Tacitus's treatise on Germany is shot
    through with copious references to honour,
    valour and the fear of disgrace: e.g.
    Germania 14
8   Coulon 2000, 52; Aldhouse-Green 2010, 53,
    fig. 16
9   Aldhouse-Green 2010, 52 (with references).
10 Book 8.38
11 Gordon *et al.*, 2010
12 'On a fixed date each year they assemble
    in a consecrated place in the territory of
    the Carnutes': Caesar *De Bello Gallico* 6.13;
    trans. Wiseman and Wiseman 1980, 121
13 This is discussed in detail in Aldhouse-
    Green 2010, 146–68
14 Parfitt 1995, 13, 155; Aldhouse-Green 2010,
    18, fig. 6, 154, 202
15 Savory 1976, 26–27 (where it had formerly
    been interpreted as part of a hanging
    bowl); Aldhouse-Green 2010, front cover;
    National Museum Wales pers. comm.
16 Perrin 2000, 22
17 Diodorus Siculus 5, 31. 3–4; Strabo
    Geography 4.4.5
18 Fitzpatrick 2000, 49; Aldhouse-Green 2010,
    162–63
19 Conducted by the author
20 *Germania* 10
21 4.4.5; trans. Tierney 1959–60, 269
22 Van der Sanden 1996, 110, 158; Aldhouse-
    Green 2010, 160; Gregersen *et al.* 2007, 254
23 Green 1991, 93, fig. 76. It is interesting, in
    this respect, that the handles of one pair
    of 'divination' spoons, from Ffynnogion,
    Llanarmon Dyffryn in Denbighshire,
    North Wales, are decorated with 'solar'
    circles: Savory 1976, 61, no. 25

24 Green 1989, 75–86
25 Green 1989, 78, fig. 32
26 Green 1989, 79, fig. 33
27 Lobel and Patel 2010
28 Adkins and Adkins 1985; de Vesly 1909,
 84–92; Horne and King 1980, 408;
 Green 1999, 51
29 Lejars and Perrin 2000, 39
30 Lejars and Perrin 2000, 37
31 14.95
32 Van der Sanden 1996, 106–19
33 Electron Spin Resonance (ESR) is a
 technique for measuring the highest
 temperature reached by particular tissue.
 It works by measuring the electrons
 trapped in the crystalline structure of
 minerals. For a detailed explanation as to
 how it works see Renfrew and Bahn 2008,
 158–59
34 Hillman 1986, 104; Holden 1995, 76–78
35 Holden 1995, 78
36 Harild et al. 2007, 156–57, 166–67
37 Silkeborg Museum undated, 5; van der
 Sanden 1996, 111
38 The Learned Banquet 4, 36; trans. Tierney
 1959–60, 247. Athenaeus was a gastrologue
 who came from Naucratis in Egypt. He was
 writing in c. AD 200
39 21; trans. Mattingly 1948, 118
40 5; 14
41 The Bellovaci, Ambiani and Viromandui:
 Brunaux 1986, 7
42 Brunaux 1986, 80; 2000, 27; Lambot
 2000, 35
43 Detienne 1989
44 2006
45 Raftery 1994, 83–84
46 39; trans. Mattingly 1948, 132
47 Among the Ngadju-Dyaks of Borneo,
 the ritual slaughter of slaves was done
 collectively, each participant being
 required to strike a blow in order to spread
 the burden of guilt: Girard 1977, 100–01
48 5.6; trans. Wiseman and Wiseman 1980, 90
49 De Divinatione 1.90
50 De Bello Gallico 6.13
51 Natural History 16.95
52 See Mees 2009 for a thorough and up-to-
 date survey of these objects
53 Gager 1992
54 Tomlin 1998; The Times Thursday 26 June
 2014, 22
55 Mees 2009, 53–72
56 Hayen 1987, 117–36; Aldhouse-Green
 2004a, 92, fig. 4.3
57 Van der Sanden and Capelle 2001, 16–17;
 Aldhouse-Green 2004a, 60, fig. 3.3
58 Coles 1998, 163–73

CHAPTER 10 (pp. 180–97)

1 6.16; trans. Wiseman and Wiseman
 1980, 123
2 For an in-depth discussion of literary
 and archaeological evidence for human
 sacrifice in Iron Age Europe see Aldhouse-
 Green 2001, passim
3 Germania 39, 40
4 Aldhouse-Green 2001, 144–45
5 Detienne 1989, 9
6 Van Straten 1995, 43
7 Devoto 1940; Aldhouse-Green 2001, 42
8 Durand 1989, fig. 7; Aldhouse-Green 2001,
 31, fig. 10; van Straten 1995, 113–14
9 Euripides Iphigeneia in Aulis lines 1547–
 97; Aechylus Agamemnon lines 198–248
10 Aldhouse-Green 2001, 19
11 Plutarch Life of Marcellus III
12 Bradley 1990
13 Stead 1985
14 Green and Howell 2000, 113
15 Kaul 1991
16 Raftery 1994, 124
17 Bradley 1995, 9–10
18 Brunaux 1986, 13; Meniel 1992, 47–68
19 Cunliffe 1993, 155–71
20 Cunliffe 1993, 163
21 From lines 372–417; trans. Graves 1956, 78
22· Trans. Grant 1956, 317
23 De Bello Gallico 6.13
24 Aldhouse-Green 2006b, 25–26, 135
25 Geography 4.5.2
26 Diodorus Siculus 5.26.3
27 Germania 25
28 The most spectacular British hoards of
 gold torcs, dating to c. 70 BC, are from
 Snettisham in Norfolk: Stead 1991. The
 adornment of several Iron Age stone
 images (themselves rare in any case)
 with torcs, and their presence on coin
 iconography, suggests their value as
 conferring status: see Aldhouse-Green
 2004a, 40–47, with references
29 Of which the most spectacular is the boat
 from a Danish peat bog at Hjörtspring:
 Randsborg 1995, 74–89
30 History 20, 14.6; trans. Geer 1954, 179, 181
31 For a discussion of Punic (Carthaginian)
 child-sacrifice see Brown 1991.
 For a summary of the literary and
 archaeological evidence see also Aldhouse-
 Green 2001, 75–77
32 Barber et al. 1989
33 Hartley 1957, 14–15, 26. The gender of the
 Wandlebury child is uncertain
34 Niblett 1999, 83–88. Several neighbouring
 shafts also contained ritual objects

35 *Germania* 39; trans. Mattingly 1948, 133
36 Cunliffe 1993, 161, fig. 90
37 Chapman 2000–2001, 9–11
38 Dated by radiocarbon
39 Chapman 2000–2001, 11; see also Anderson 2000–2001, 35–6 for detailed bone report on the wrist-anomaly. The hamate is a carpal bone on the lower outside edge of the hand where it joins the arm; the muscle attached to it works the little finger
40 Raftery 1994, 199. Raftery notes the unnaturally strained position of the neck and head
41 Aldhouse-Green 2006a, 291, fig. 8
42 BBC 1 6 p.m. News 1 May 2014
43 III, 413–17; trans. Graves 1956, 78–79
44 An example is the chariot burial found at Ferrybridge, East Yorkshire, discovered in 2003. Many years after the burial, people revisited the graves and engaged in feasting rituals that involved the consumption of vast amounts of meat: Boyle 2004
45 Ó hÓgáin, D., 1999, 97; Le Roux and Guyonvarc'h 1995
46 Duval and Pinault 1986, 262–75; Zavaroni 2007, 13
47 Harild *et al.* 2007, 176; Silkeborg undated, 5
48 Stead 1986, 177
49 Lobel and Patel 2010
50 11 and 43; trans. Mattingly 1948, 110, 136
51 *De Bello Gallico* 6.18
52 *Germania* 39
53 *Germania* 12; trans. Mattingly 1948, 110
54 *Germania* 19; trans. Mattingly 1948, 116
55 *Annals* 14.30–31 'Onward pressed their standards and they bore down their opponents, enveloping them in the flames of their own torches. Suetonius garrisoned the conquered island. The groves devoted to Mona's barbarous superstitions he demolished'; trans. Mattingly 1948, 317
56 Macdonald 2007, 173
57 Ferguson 1980, 57–58; Aldhouse-Green 2001a, 126–27
58 The fourth Branch of the *Mabinogion*, a medieval Welsh mythic prose tale, contains an account of a virgin called Goewin, who acted as 'footholder' to Math, King of Harlech. All his power was drawn from her, and he always had to sit with his feet in her lap unless he was going to war: Davies 2007, 47
59 Tacitus *Histories* 4.61
60 Lucan *Pharsalia* I, 444

EPILOGUE (pp. 198–201)

1 Lewis 1982, 97
2 The very first essay Professor Richard Atkinson set me as an undergraduate at Cardiff University had the title 'How far can archaeologists reconstruct the past?' He was setting a trap into which nearly all of us (including me) fell headlong because, of course, all that can be achieved is a construction based upon evidence, it is true, but evidence that has huge gaps and is inevitably heavily contaminated with our own modern context and mindset
3 This was by no means always the case in prehistory. For instance, the practice identified at many Neolithic long cairns was to make successive multiple interments, the bones of the earlier dead being systematically 'tidied away' in the recesses of the tombs to make way for newer burials. A good example of such funeral activity is Hazleton North, Gloucestershire: Saville 1990, 250–52
4 Heaney 1998, 118
5 Van der Sanden 1996, 160
6 Sanders 2009, 127–68

BIBLIOGRAPHY

Adkins, L. and Adkins, R., 'Neolithic axes from Roman sites in Britain', *Oxford Journal of Archaeology* 4 (1), 69–75.

Ahrenholt-Bindslev, D., Josephsen, K. and Jurik, A.G., 'Grauballe Man's Teeth and Jaws', in Asingh and Lynnerup eds., 2007, 140–53.

Alberti, B., 'Cut, pinch and pierce. Image as practice among the early formative La Candelaria, First Millennium AD, Northwest Argentina', in Danielsson *et al.* eds., 2012, 13–28.

Aldhouse-Green, M.J., *Dying for the Gods. Human Sacrifice in Iron Age and Roman Europe*, Stroud, 2001.

Aldhouse-Green, M.J., *An Archaeology of Images*, London, 2004a.

Aldhouse-Green, M.J., 'Crowning Glories. Languages of Hair in Later Prehistoric Europe', *Proceedings of the Prehistoric Society* 70, 2004b, 299–325.

Aldhouse-Green, M.J., 'Chaining and Shaming: images of defeat, from Llyn Cerrig Bach to Sarmitzegetusa', *Oxford Journal of Archaeology* 23 (3), August 2004c, 319–40.

Aldhouse-Green, M.J., 'Semiologies of Subjugation: The Ritualisation of War-Prisoners in Later European Antiquity', in Otto, T., Thrane, H. and Vandkilde, H. eds., *Warfare and Society. Archaeological and Social Anthropological Perspectives*, Århus, 2006a, 281–304.

Aldhouse-Green, M.J., *Boudica Britannia*, London, 2006b.

Aldhouse-Green, M.J., *Caesar's Druids. Story of an Ancient Priesthood*, New Haven & London, 2010.

Aldhouse-Green, M.J., *Celtic Myths. A Guide to the Ancient Gods and Legends*, London, 2015.

Aldhouse-Green, M.J. and Aldhouse-Green, S., *The Quest for the Shaman*, London, 2005.

Anderson, T., 'Appendix One: The Human Bone', in Chapman 2000–2001, 33–40.

Armit, I., *Inside Kurtz's Compound: Headhunting and the Human Body in Prehistoric Europe*, in Bonogofsky, M. ed., *Skull Collection, Modification and Decoration*, Oxford, 2006, 1–14.

Armit, I., *Headhunting and the Body in Iron Age Europe*, Cambridge, 2012.

Arnoldi, M.J., 'Introduction', in Arnoldi, M.J. and Kreamer, C.M. eds., *Crowning Achievements. African Arts of Dressing the Head*, Los Angeles, 1995, 9–25.

Asingh, P., 'The Man in the Bog', in Asingh and Lynnerup eds., 2007a, 15–32.

Asingh, P., 'The Magical Bog', in Asingh and Lynnerup eds., 2007b, 275–90.

Asingh, P., 'The Bog People', in Asingh and Lynnerup eds., 2007c, 291–315.

Asingh, P. and Lynnerup, N. eds., *Grauballe Man. An Iron Age Bog Body Revisited*, Århus, 2007.

Baillot, M., *Magie et sortilèges dans l'Antiquité romaine. Archéologie des rituels et des images*, Paris, 2010.

Baillot, M. and Symmons, R., 'Note from the Roman Palace at Fishbourne (Sussex): A Roman Magic Lead Figurine, *Britannia* 43, 2012, 249–60.

Balguy, C., 'An account of the dead bodies of a man and woman which were preserved 49 years on the moors in Derbyshire', *Philosophical Transactions of the Royal Society* 38 (434), 1733, 413–15.

Barber, J., Halstead, P., James, H. and Lee, F., 'An unusual Iron Age burial at Hornish Point, South Uist', *Antiquity* 63, 1989, 773–78.

Bauman, R.A., *Crime and Punishment in Ancient Rome*, London and New York, 1996.

Bergen, C., Niekus, M.J.L.Th. and van Vilsteren, V.T. eds., *The Mysterious Bog People*, Zwolle, 2002.

Beuker, J.R., 'The Girl and the Devil', in Bergen *et al.* eds., 2002a, 107–09.

Beuker, J.R., 'The Bog: A Lost Landscape', in Bergen *et al.* eds., 2002b, 12–17.

Beuker, J.R., 'The Last Supper', in Bergen *et al.* eds., 2002c, 126–27.

Beuker, J.R., 'Face to Face with Our Ancestors', in Bergen *et al.* eds., 2002d, 128–29.

Bodel, J., 'Dealing with the Dead in Ancient Rome', in Hope and Marshall eds., 2000, 128–51.

Borca, F., 'Towns and Marshes in the Ancient World', in Hope and Marshall eds., 2000, 74–84.

Boren, Z. Davies, 'Baby on trial for attempted murder has charges dismissed', 12 April 2014, http://www.telegraph.co.uk/news/worldnews/asia/pakistan/10762030/

baby-on-trial-for-attempted-murder-has-charges-dismissed.html

Bourke, J.B., 'The Medical Investigation of Lindow Man', in Stead *et al.* eds., 1986, 46–51.

Boyce, M., *Zoroastrians. Their Religious Beliefs and Practices*, London, 1979.

Boyle, A., 'Riding into History', *British Archaeology* 76, May 2004, 22–27.

Bradley, I., *The Power of Sacrifice*, London, 1995.

Bradley, R., *The Passage of Arms*, Cambridge, 1990.

Briggs, C.S., 'Did They Fall or Were They Pushed? Some Unresolved Questions about Bog Bodies', in Turner and Scaife eds., 1995, 163–82.

Brothwell, D. and Bourke, J.B., 'The Human Remains from Lindow Moss', in Turner and Scaife eds., 1995, 52–61.

Brown, S., *Late Carthaginian Child Sacrifice and Sacrificial Monuments in their Mediterranean Context*, Sheffield, 1991.

Brunaux, J.-L., *Les Gaulois. Sanctuaires et Rites*, Paris, 1986.

Brunaux, J.-L., 'Être Prêtre en Gaule', in *L'Archéologue Hors Série* No. 2, 26–29.

Bulleid, A., and Gray, H. St George, *The Glastonbury Lake Village. Vols 1 & 2*, Glastonbury, 1911 & 1917.

Burkert, W., *Greek Religion*, Oxford, 1985.

Callison, B., *The Auriga Madness*, Glasgow, 1980.

Caplan, J. ed., *Written on the Body. The Tattoo in European and American History*, London, 2000.

Carman, J., 'Giving Archaeology a Moral Voice', in Carman ed., 1997a, 220–39.

Carman, J. ed., *Material Harm. Archaeological Studies of War and Violence*, Glasgow, 1997b.

Chamberlain, A. and Parker Pearson, M., *Earthly Remains. The History and Science of Preserved Human Bodies*, Oxford, 2001.

Chapman, A., 'Excavation of an Iron Age Settlement and a Middle Saxon Cemetery at Great Houghton, Northampton, 1996', *Northamptonshire Archaeology* 29, 2000–2001, 1–42.

Cochrane, A., 'The Immanency of the Intangible Image. Thoughts with Neolithic Expression at Loughcrew', in Danielsson *et al.* eds., 2012, 133–60.

Coles, B., 'Wood Species for Wooden Figures: A Glimpse of a Pattern', in Gibson, A. and Simpson, D.D.A. eds., *Prehistoric Ritual and Religion*, Stroud, 1998, 163–73.

Coles, B., Coles, C. and Jørgensen, M.S. eds., *Bog Bodies, Sacred Sites and Wetland Archaeology*, Exeter, 1999.

Coles, G.M., *The Echoing Green*, London, 2001.

Coles, J. and Minnitt, S., *Industrious and Fairly Civilized. The Glastonbury Lake Village*, Somerset County Council, 1995.

Collis, J., *The Celts. Origins, Myths, Inventions*, Stroud, 2003.

Conan Doyle, A., *The Hound of the Baskervilles*, published as a Penguin Red Classic, London, 2007.

Coulon, G., 'La Survivance du Druidisme à l'époque gallo-romaine', *L'Archéologue Hors Série* No. 2, 52–55.

Cunliffe, B., *Danebury. Anatomy of an Iron Age Hillfort*, London, 1983.

Cunliffe, B., *Danebury. An Iron Age Hillfort in Hampshire*, York, 1984.

Cunliffe, B., *The English Heritage Book of Danebury*, London, 1993.

Danielsson, I.-M. Back, 'The Rape of the Lock. Or a Comparison between Miniature Images of the Eighth and Eighteenth Centuries', in Danielsson *et al.* eds., 2012, 29–49.

Danielsson, I.-M. Back, Fahlander, F. and Sjöstrand, Y. eds., *Encountering Imagery. Materialities, Perceptions, Relations*, Stockholm, 2012.

Davidson, H.E., 'The Seer's Thumb', in Davidson, H.E. ed., *The Seer in Celtic and Other Traditions*, Edinburgh, 1989, 66–75.

Davies, J.L. and Lynch, F., 'The Late Bronze Age and Iron Age', in Lynch, F., Aldhouse-Green, S., and Davies, J.L. eds., *Prehistoric Wales*, Stroud, 2000, 139–219.

Davies, S., *The Mabinogion*, Oxford, 2007.

De Vesly, L., *Les Fana ou petits Temples Gallo-Romains de la Région Normande*, Rouen, 1909.

Delap, D., *Pitkin Guide to Celtic Saints*, Alnwick, 1998.

Detienne, M., 'Culinary Practice and the Spirit of Sacrifice', in Detienne, M. and Vernant, J.-P. eds., *The Cuisine of Sacrifice among the Greeks*, Chicago, 1989, 1–20.

Devoto, G., *Tabulae Iguvinae*, Rome, 1940.

Deyts, S., *Images de Dieux de la Gaule*, Paris, 1992.

Du Maurier, D., *Jamaica Inn*, London (Virago Press edition), 2003.

Durand, J.-L., 'Ritual as Instrumentality', in Detienne, M. and Vernant, J.-P. eds., *The Cuisine of Sacrifice among the Greeks*, Chicago, 1989, 119–28.

Duval, P.-M., *Monnaies Gauloises et Mythes Celtiques*, Paris, 1987.

Duval, P.-M. and Pinault, G., *Recueil des Inscriptions Gauloises (RIG) Vol. III. Les Calendriers (Coligny, Villards d'Héria)*, Paris, 1986.

Ferguson, J., *Greek and Roman Religion*, Park Ridge (New Jersey), 1980.

Filer, J.M., 'Ancient Egypt and Nubia as a source of information for violent cranial injuries', in J. Carman ed., 1997, 53–68.

Finn, C., 'Words from kept bodies. The bog body as literary inspiration', in Coles *et al.* eds., 1999, 79–83.

Fischer, C., 'The Tollund Man and the Elling Woman', in Coles *et al.* eds., 1999, 93–97.

Fischer, C., *The Tollund Man and the Elling Woman*, Silkeborg, undated.

Fitzpatrick, A.P., 'Les Druides en Grande-Bretagne', in *L'Archéologue Hors Série* No. 2, 47–49.

Foucault, M., *Discipline and Punish. The Birth of the Prison*, New York, 1995 (trans. Alan Sheridan).

Frederiksen, J. (with a contribution from Jens Glastrup), 'Conservation and Analysis of Grauballe Man 2001–2002', in Asingh and Lynnerup eds., 2007, 58–77.

Gager, J.G., *Curse Tablets and Binding Spells from the Ancient World*, Oxford, 1992.

Garland, A.N., 'Worsley Man, England', in Turner and Scaife eds., 1995, 104–07.

Garland, R., *The Eye of the Beholder. Deformity and Disability in the Graeco-Roman World*, Ithaca NY, 1995.

Gebühr, M., 'Das Kindergrab von Windesby. Versuch einer 'Rehabilitation', *Offa. Berichte und Mittelungen zur Urgeschichte, Frühgesichte und Mittelalterarchäologie* 36, 75–107.

Gebühr, M., *Moorleichen in Schleswig-Holstein*, Schleswig, 2002.

Geer, R.M., trans., *Diodorus of Sicily. The Library of History*, Cambridge MA, 1954.

Gerasimov, M., *The Face Finder*, English language edition, Hutchinson, 1971.

Giles, M. 'Seeing red: the aesthetics of martial objects in the British and Irish Iron Age', in Garrow, D., Gosden, C. and Hill, J.D eds., *Rethinking Celtic Art*, Oxford, 2008, 59–77.

Giles, M., *A Forged Glamour. Landscape, Identity and Material Culture In the Iron Age*, Oxford, 2012.

Girard, R., *Violence and the Sacred*, Baltimore and London, 1977.

Glob, P.V., *The Bog People. Iron Age Man Preserved*, London, 1969.

Gordon, R., Joly, D. and Van Andringa, W., 'A prayer for blessings on three ritual objects discovered at Chartres-*Autricum* (France, Eure-et-Loir), in Gordon, R. and Marco Simón, F. eds., *Magical Practice in the Latin West. Papers from the International Conference held at the University of Zaragoza 2005*, Leiden, 2010, 487–518.

Gowlett, J.A.J., Gillespie, R., Hall, E.T. and Hedges, R.E.M., 'Accelerator Radiocarbon Dating of Ancient Human Remains from Lindow Moss', in Stead *et al.* eds., 1986, 22–26.

Grant, M., *Tacitus. The Annals of Imperial Rome*, Harmondsworth, 1956.

Graves, R., trans., *Lucan Pharsalia. Dramatic Episodes of the Civil Wars*, Harmondsworth, 1956.

Graves, R., trans., *Suetonius. The Twelve Caesars*, London, 1962.

Green, M.J., *Sun Gods and Symbols of Ancient Europe*, London, 1991.

Green, M.J., *Celtic Myths*. London, 1993.

Green, M.J., *Celtic Goddesses. Warriors, Virgins and Mothers*, London, 1995.

Green, M.J., 'Back to the Future. Resonances of the Past in Myth and Material Culture', in Gazin-Schwarz, A. and Holtorf, C.J. eds., *Archaeology and Folklore*, London and New York, 1999, 48–66.

Gregersen, M., Jurik, A.G. and Lynnerup, N., 'Forensic Evidence, Injuries and Cause of Death', in Asingh and Lynnerup eds., 2007, 235–60.

Harild, J.A., Robinson, D.A. and Hudlebusch, J., 'New Analysis of Grauballe Man's Gut Contents', in Asingh and Lynnerup eds., 2007, 155–87.

Harrison, G.B. ed., *Macbeth*, The Penguin Shakespeare, Paulton and London, 1937.

Hartley, 'The Wandlebury Iron Age Hill-Fort, Excavations of 1955–6', *Proceedings of the Cambridge Antiquarian Society* 50, 1–27.

Hayen, H., 'Peatbog Archaeology in Lower Saxony, West Germany', in Coles, J. and Lawson, A. eds., *European Wetlands in Prehistory*, Oxford, 1987, 117–36.

Heaney, S., *Opened Ground. Poems 1966–1996*, London, 1998.

Heaney, S., *Beowulf. A New Translation*, London, 1999.

Heinemeier, J. and Asingh, P., 'Dating of Grauballe Man', in Asingh and Lynnerup eds., 2007, 197–201.

Hillman, G., 'Plant Foods in Ancient Diet: The Archaeological Role of Palaeofaeces in General and Lindow Man's Gut Contents in Particular', in Stead *et al.* eds., 1986, 99–115.

Hingley, R. and Unwin, C., *Boudica. Iron Age Warrior Queen*, London, 2005.

Holden, T.G., 'The Last Meals of the Lindow Bog Men', in Turner and Scaife eds., 1995, 76–82.

Hooper, B., 'Anatomical Considerations', in Cunliffe, 1984.

Hope, V., 'Contempt and Respect: the Treatment of the Corpse in Ancient Rome', in Hope and Marshall eds., 2000, 104–27.

Hope, V.M. and Marshall, E. eds., *Death and Disease in the Ancient City*, London, 2000.

Horne, P.D. and King, A.C., 'Gazetteer of Romano-Celtic Temples in Continental Europe', in Rodwell, W. ed., *Temples, Churches and Religion: Recent Research in Roman Britain*, Oxford, 1980, 399–555.

Hostrup, J.C., *A Sparrow Amongst Hawks (En Spurv I Tranedans)*, Copenhagen, 1846.

Housley, R., Walker, A.J., Otlet, R.L. and Hedges, R.E.M., 'Radiocarbon Dating of the Lindow III Bog Body', in Stead *et al.* eds., 1986, 39–46.

Hughes, D., *Human Sacrifice in Ancient Greece*, London, 1991.

Hutton, R., *The Pagan Religions of the Ancient British Isles*, Oxford, 1991.

Hvass, L., *Dronning Gunhild – et moselig fra jernalderen*, Vejle, 1998.

Ireland, S., *Roman Britain. A Source Book*, London, 1996.

James, S., *The Atlantic Celts: Ancient People or Modern Invention?*, London, 1999.

Johnstone, P., *Buried Treasure*, London, 1957.

Jones, G., *A History of the Vikings*, Oxford, 1968.

Jones, H.L., trans., *The Geography of Strabo*, London, 1923–24.

Kaul, F., *Gundestrupkedlen*, Copenhagen, 1991.

Kelly, E., *Sacrifice and Kingship. Iron Age Bodies and Boundaries*, Dublin, 2006.

Lambot, B., 'Victimes, Sacrificateurs et Dieux', in *L'Archéologue Hors Série* No. 2, 30–36.

Lange, C., 'Violence and the Face', in Carman ed., 1997, 166–73.

Larsen, R. and Poulsen, D.V., 'Infrared Reflectography (IRr) Surface Analysis', in Asingh and Lynnerup eds., 2007, 84–91.

Le Roux, F. and Guyonvarc'h, C.J., *Les Fêtes Celtiques*, Rennes, 1995.

Lejars, T., *Gournay III. Les Fourreaux d'épee: Le Sanctuaire de Gournay-sur-Aronde et l'armament des Celtes de la Tène moyenne*, Paris, 1994.

Lejars, T, and Perrin, F., 'Des Tombes des Druides?', in *L'Archéologue Hors Série* No. 2, 2000, 37–40.

Lewis, N., *A Dragon Apparent. Travels in Cambodia, Laos and Vietnam*, London, 1982 (first published 1951).

Lobel, J.A. and Patel, S., 'Clonycavan and Oldcroghan Man', *Archaeology Magazine* 63 (3), May/June 2010. http://archive.archaeology.org/1005/bogbodies/clonycavan_croghan.html

Lurker, M., *The Gods and Symbols of Ancient Egypt*, London, 1974.

Mac Cana, P., *Celtic Mythology*, London, 1983.

Macdonald, J.L., 'Religion', in Clarke, G., *The Roman Cemetery at Lankhills*, Oxford: Winchester Studies 3, 1979, 403–33.

Macdonald, P., *Llyn Cerrig Bach*, Cardiff, 2007.

Mantel, H., *Beyond Black*, London, 2005.

Mattingly, H., trans., *Tacitus on Britain and Germany*, Harmondsworth, 1948.

Mees, B., *Celtic Curses*, Cambridge, 2009.

Melton, N.D., Montgomery, J. and Knüsel, C. eds., *Gristhorpe Man. A Life and Death in the Bronze Age*, Oxford, 2013.

Meniel, P., *Chasse et élevage chez les Gaulois*, Paris, 1987.

Meniel, P., *Les Sacrifices d'Animaux chez les Gaulois*, Paris, 1992.

Metzler, A., 'Trackways through the Bogs', in Bergen *et al.* eds., 2002, 24–25.

Mulhall, I., 'The Peat Men from Clonycavan and Oldcroghan', *British Archaeology* 110, January/February 2010, 34–41.

Mulhall, E. and Briggs, E.K., 'Presenting a Past Society to a Present Day Audience. Bog Bodies in Iron Age Ireland', *Museum Ireland* 17, 2007, 71–81.

Nash, H.B., *Columella. Res Rustica*, London, 1951.

Neave, R.A.H. and Quinn, R., 'Reconstruction of the Skull and the Soft Tissues of the Head and Face of Lindow Man', in Stead *et al.* eds., 1986, 42–44.

Newby, E., *A Small Place in Italy*, London, 1994.

Newby, E., *Slowly Down the Ganges*, London, 2011a (first published 1966).

Newby, E., *On the Shores of the Mediterranean*, London, 2011b.

Newby, E., *Round Ireland in Low Gear*, London 2011c (first published 1987).

Niblett, R., *The Excavation of a Ceremonial Site at Folly Lane, Verulamium*, Exeter: *Britannia* Monograph Series No. 14, 1999.

Nomberg-Przytyk, S., *Auschwitz. True Tales from a Grotesque Land* (trans. Roslyn Hirsch), Chapel Hill NC, 1985.

Ogden, D., *Greek and Roman Necromancy*, Princeton, 2001.

Ó hÓgain, D., *The Sacred Isle. Belief and Religion in pre-Christian Ireland*, Woodbridge, 1999.

Otlet, R.L., Walker, A.J. and Dadson, S.M., 'Report on Radiocarbon Dating of the Lindow Man by AERE Harwell', in Stead *et al.* eds., 1986, 27–30.

Owen-Jones, E., 'A remarkable find at Valley', in Steele, P. ed., *Llyn Cerrig Bach. Treasure from the Iron Age*, Llangefni, 2012, 10–11.

Papagianni, D. and Morse, M., *The Neanderthals Rediscovered. How Modern Science is Rewriting their Story*, London, 2013.

Parfitt, K., *Iron Age Burials from Mill Hill, Deal*, London, 1995.

Parker Pearson, M., *The Archaeology of Death and Burial*, Stroud, 1999.

Parker Pearson, M., Chamberlain, A., Collins, N., Cox, C., Gray, G., Hiller, J., Marshall, P.,

Mulville, J. and Smith, H., 'Further Evidence for Mummification in Bronze Age Britain', *Antiquity* 81 (313), September 2007, http://http://www.antiquity.ac.uk/projgall/parker/

Perrin, F., 'Le Gui', in *L'Archéologue Hors Série* No. 2, 21–22.

Pyatt, F.B., Beaumont, E.H., Buckland, P.C., Lacy, D., Magilton, J.R. and Storey, D.M., 'Mobilisation of Elements from the Bog Bodies Lindow II and III and some Observations on Body Painting', in Turner and Scaife eds., 1995, 62–73.

Raftery, B., *Pagan Celtic Ireland*, London, 1994.

Randsborg, K., *Hjörtspring. Warfare and Sacrifice in Early Europe*, Århus, 1995.

Renfrew C. and Bahn, P. eds., *Archaeology: Theories, Methods and Practice* (5th Edition), London, 2008.

Ross, A., 'Lindow Man and the Celtic Tradition', in Stead *et al.* eds., 1986, 162–69.

Sanders, K., *Bodies in the Bog and the Archaeological Imagination*, Chicago, 2009.

Saville, A., *Hazleton North / The excavation of a Neolithic long cairn of the Cotswold-Severn group*, London, 1990.

Savory, H.N., *Guide Catalogue of the Early Iron Age Collections*, Cardiff, 1976.

Scaife, R.G., 'Pollen in Human Palaeofaeces; and a Preliminary Investigation of the Stomach and Gut Contents of Lindow Man', in Stead *et al.* eds., 1986, 126–35.

Scarre, C., *Exploring Prehistoric Europe*, Oxford, 1998.

Scullard, H.H., *Festivals and Ceremonies of the Roman Republic*, London, 1981.

Sherley-Price, L., trans., *Bede. A History of the English Church and People*, Harmondsworth, 1955.

Spencer, A.J., *Early Egypt. The Rise of Civilization in the Nile Valley*, London, 1993.

Spindler, K., 'Anthropomorphe Terrakotten aus den römischen Lagerdörfern von Eining und Straubing', *Das archäologische Jahr in Bayern*, 113–15.

Spindler, K., *The Man in the Ice*, London, 1995.

Stead, I.M., *The Battersea Shield*, London, 1985.

Stead, I.M., 'Summary and Conclusions', in Stead *et al.* eds. 1986, 177–80.

Stead, I.M., 'The Snettisham Treasure: excavations in 1990', *Antiquity* 65, 1991, 447–65.

Stead, I.M., Bourke, J.B. and Brothwell, D. eds., *Lindow Man. The Body in the Bog*. London, 1986.

Stødkilde-Jørgensen, H., Jacobsen, H.J., Jacobsen, N.O., Jensen, F.T., Pedersen, M. and Warncke, E., 'Microscopy, Magnetic Resonance Imaging and Spectroscopy of the Intestines of a 2000-Year Old Human Bog Body', in Asingh and Lynnerup eds., 2007, 202–15.

Strehle, H., 'The Conservation of Grauballe Man', in Asingh and Lynnerup eds., 2007, 33–50.

Taylor, G.W., 'Tests for Dyes', in Stead *et al.* eds., 1986, 41.

Taylor, T., *The Buried Soul. How Humans Invented Death*, London, 2002.

Therkorn, L.L., Brandt, R.W., Pals, J.P. and Taylor, M., 'An Early Iron Age Farmstead: Site Q of the Assendelver Polders Project', *Proceedings of the Prehistoric Society* 50, 1984, 351–73.

Thompson, F. H., *The Archaeology of Greek and Roman Slavery*, London, 2003.

Tierney, J.J., 'The Celtic Ethnography of Posidonius', *Proceedings of the Royal Irish Academy* 60, 1959–60, 189–275.

Tolkien, J.R.R., *The Lord of the Rings. Vol. 2: The Two Towers*, London, 1968 (first published 1955).

Tomlin, R.S.O., 'The Curse Tablets;, in Cunliffe, B., *The Temple of Sulis Minerva at Bath. Vol. 2. The Finds from the Sacred Spring*, Oxford, 1988, 58–277.

Tope, R., *Shadows in the Cotswolds*, London, 2013.

Turner, R.C., 'Discovery and Excavation of the Lindow Bodies', in Stead *et al.* eds., London, 1986, 10–13.

Turner, R.C., 'Discoveries and Excavations at Lindow Moss 1983–8', in Turner and Scaife eds., 1995a, 10–18.

Turner, R.C., 'The Lindow Mam Phenomenon: Ancient and Modern', in Turner and Scaife eds., 1995b, 188–204.

Turner, R.C., 'Dating the Lindow Moss and other British bog bodies', in Coles *et al.* eds., 1999, 227–34.

Turner, R.C. and Scaife, R.G. eds., *Bog Bodies. New Discoveries and New Perspectives*, London, 1995.

Van der Sanden, W., 'Bog Bodies on the Continent: Developments since 1965, with Special Reference to the Netherlands', in Turner and Scaife eds., 1995, 146–65.

Van der Sanden, W., *Through Nature to Eternity. The bog bodies of northwest Europe*, Amsterdam, 1996.

Van der Sanden, W., 'Bog Bodies: Underwater Burials, Sacrifices and Executions', in Menotti, F. and O'Sullivan, A., *The Oxford Handbook of Wetland Archaeology*, Oxford, 2013, 401–16.

Van der Sanden, W. and Capelle, T., *Mosens Guder: Antropomorfe Traefurer fra Nord- og Nordvesteuropas Fortid/ Immortal Images: Ancient Anthropomorphic Wood Carvings*

from Northern and Northwest Europe,
Silkeborg, 2001.

Van Straten, F.T., *Hierà Kalá. Images of Animal Sacrifice in Archaic and Classical Greece,* Leiden, 1995.

Veil, S., 'Two Bodies in Woollen Coats', in Bergen *et al.* eds., 2002, 104–06.

Vine, B., *King Solomon's Carpet,* London, 1992.

Wakely, J., 'Identification and analysis of violent and non-violent head injuries in osteo-archaeological material', in Carman ed., 1997, 24–46.

Walker, L., 'The deposition of the human remains', in Cunliffe, 1984.

Warner, R. trans., *Plutarch. Life of Caesar,* Harmondsworth, 1958.

West, I.E., 'Forensic Aspects of Lindow Man', in Stead *et al.* eds., 1986, 77–80.

Whitehead, H., *The Village Gods of South India,* New Delhi, 1921 (1983 reprint of original edition).

Whittaker, C.R. trans., *Herodian,* London (Loeb Edition), 1969.

Wilkinson, C., 'Facial Reconstruction of Grauballe Man', in Asingh and Lynnerup eds., 2007, 261–71.

Williams, M., 'Tales from the Dead. Remembering the Bog Bodies in the Iron Age of North-Western Europe', in Williams, H., ed., *Archaeologies of Remembrance. Death and Memory in Past Societies,* New York and London, 2003, 89–112.

Wilson, A.S., Richards, M.P., Stern, B., Janaway, R.C., Pollard, A.M. and Tobin, D.J., 'Information on Grauballe Man from his Hair', in Asingh and Lynnerup eds., 2007, 188–95.

Wiseman, A. and Wiseman, P., trans., *Julius Caesar. The Battle for Gaul,* London, 1980.

Wright, D. trans., *Beowulf,* Harmondsworth, 1957.

Zavaroni, A., *On the structure and terminology of the Gaulish calendar,* Oxford, 2007.

Zwicker, J., *Fontes Historiae Religionis Celticae,* Berlin, 1934.

ACKNOWLEDGMENTS

My thanks go to the following for their help and support. First, I am very grateful to the staff of Thames & Hudson, especially Colin Ridler, Ben Plumridge, Jen Moore, Alex Wright, Celia Falconer and Louise Thomas for all their help in seeing *Bog Bodies Uncovered* to press. Lone Hvass and Michael Gebühr provided me with invaluable information on bog bodies from Denmark and Schleswig-Holstein. On a personal level, thank you to Stephen, Elisabeth, Lily, Marlies, Alison, James, Francis, Jan, Diane and Edward. Merleen, Paul and Grace, this book is for you, with gratitude.

SOURCES OF ILLUSTRATIONS